# WILLIAM *and* CATHERINE

*The love story of the founders of*
*The Salvation Army, told through their letters*

## Cathy Le Feuvre

MONARCH
BOOKS

Oxford, UK & Grand Rapids, Michigan, USA

Published by Monarch Books

an imprint of

**Lion Hudson plc**

Wilkinson House, Jordan Hill Road,

Oxford OX2 8DR, England

Email: monarch@lionhudson.com

www.lionhudson.com/monarch

ISBN 978 0 85721 312 9

e-ISBN 978 0 85721 516 1

First edition 2013

A catalogue record for this book is available from the British Library

Printed and bound in the UK, August 2013, LH26

*For Dad and Mum, with enduring thanks*
*for their love, support,*
*and Christian example*
*of lives spent in the service*
*of Jesus Christ.*

# CONTENTS

Introduction: A picture of the past      9

*Chapter*

One      13
Two      33
Three      45
Four      59
Five      75
Six      99
Seven      121
Eight      145
Nine      165
Ten      177
Eleven      195
Twelve      211
Thirteen      221
Fourteen      229
Fifteen      243
Sixteen      249
Seventeen      265
Eighteen      283
Nineteen      297
Twenty – Epilogue      307

Notes      317
Bibliography      329

# Introduction:
# A picture of the past

There is a photograph of William Booth, the Founder and first General of The Salvation Army, which is quite familiar to members of The Salvation Army Church. The black and white image shows William as an old man. He still has a mop of thick white hair, although the hairline is receding to reveal a high brow. His matching long, thick, bushy white beard covers the front of his uniform "tunic", on the front of which you can just about spy the Salvation Army crest. William is resting his right elbow on a table and his head is cradled in his right hand, so to look at his face properly you have to incline your head slightly to the left. He appears tired and his eyes under those thick white eyebrows have the look of someone staring into space.

I remember being intrigued by this as a child, and wondering about this old man who looked a bit grumpy and seemed so far from my own life and experience.

The photo was taken in 1907, when William was around seventy-eight years of age – fairly ancient for that time, when reaching the biblical promise of "three score years and ten" was quite a feat – and he still had five more years to live. Today, looking at the picture, I realize that it indicates a man who is at the end, or nearing the end, of his great mission in life and if he was tired then he deserved to be. He had also already spent fifteen years without his beloved wife, Catherine, with whom he had created The Salvation Army and shared not just great spiritual ambition but also a great love. Catherine was only sixty-one when she died in 1890 so there are fewer pictures available of her, yet in the ones we have her personality also seems stuck in time, unsmiling and rather severe.

For most of the time they were together, from their first meeting in 1852 until Catherine's death in 1890, they wrote to each other, and it was through their letters that William and Catherine Booth came alive for me. As I listened to the few available recordings of William Booth, again made very late in his life, I picked up the traces of his Midlands accent. As I read some of the accounts and memories of those who actually met the Founders, the more real they became to me.

I realized they were inspired, fallible, quirky, loving, complicated: yet so much more. I realized, of course, that they were people of their time – Victorians, living through a period of great religious revival, phenomenal industrial change, and political and social upheaval, which particularly affected the urban poor. Attitudes to life, cultural morals, and family dynamics were vastly different from the twenty-first century, and personal matters were not easily shared. So it was refreshing to find that William and Catherine's correspondence gave me a glimpse not just into the spiritual lives of this couple who created a worldwide church and charity organization, but also of their day-to-day existence as middle-class Victorians and parents of a large family.

Poring over their letters in the British Library, where the family collection known as *The Booth Papers* includes letters donated by their granddaughter Commissioner Catherine Bramwell Booth, I learned more about these rather distant historical characters. The papers, and other documents gleaned from various research works and sources, told me a good deal about the Booths, as did their handwriting. The letters are not just love letters, they are also contain deeply spiritual matters, and, for some modern readers with notions of how "romantic love" works, this might appear peculiar. But the truth is that God came first for Catherine and William, even above the other partner.

There are more letters from the start of their relationship, before and during their engagement and in the early years of their marriage, when they struggled to find a spiritual home before The Salvation Army emerged. Obviously in later years they wrote to each other less, unless they were apart, so this narrative does detail more of their early days than of the later times, when to fill in the story I have supplemented their words to each other with notes they wrote to other family members and other materials found during my research.

This book is my attempt to bring William and Catherine Booth to life for a new generation – and my hope is that readers will begin, as I did, to see them as young, vibrant Christians making their way in a challenging world, struggling to find a spiritual home and raising a family. To add some context, I provide a little background to the times in which they were writing and the realities through which they were living. I am indebted to authors past and present who have already written extensively about the Booths and I commend to you many of their excellent works if you wish to read more about the life and times of William and Catherine. I am particularly thankful to David Malcolm Bennett, whose transcripts of the Letters of

William and Catherine Booth, meticulously researched over many years, were the first inspiration for this book. I also thank the Booth family and The Salvation Army for use of the material and photographs, and the British Library, where many of William and Catherine's original letters are held in trust.

If this book does nothing else, I hope it will encourage readers to be inspired to look at, again or for the first time, the ongoing work of The Salvation Army across the world. As the Christian movement which is the heart and brain child of a mid-Victorian, middle-class couple approaches its 150th anniversary in 2015, it is still vital and vibrant and at work and witness in more than 120 countries around the world. Every week millions of people across the world attend its churches to learn about the love of God, and through its caring mission it reaches out to many millions more people in need – homeless people, families, people with addictions and in debt, prisoners, victims of human trafficking, and people who just need a little extra support to help them on their way.

It all started with a lad from Nottingham who didn't want to be part of the "commonalty" and the quiet but single-minded Derbyshire-born girl with whom he fell in love in 1852, more than half a century before he became that old man with his head in his hand, staring at a camera.

# CHAPTER

## 1

The young man picked up his quill pen and smoothed the nib between his thumb and index finger, stretched across the desk to dip it into the inkpot, took a moment to collect his thoughts, and stared intently at the clean crisp sheet of writing paper in front of him. Taking a deep breath, he closed his eyes for a second or two as if to pray, and then began to write, at first as neatly as he was able but then, within seconds, growing more animated, his cheeks beginning to burn. Stopping briefly, he ran his fingers through his thick unruly mop of hair, drawing it away from his forehead. William was a man in love. As he wrote, the image of the object of his affection came clearly to mind. Her pale face framed with brown curls, her quiet smile and her lively, sparkling eyes shining with a sharp intelligence. It was but a few weeks since they had met, yet already Catherine's personality and beauty were imprinted on William's heart. When he thought about her, his heart pounded, his mouth grew a little dry, and his hand shook ever so slightly as he wrote.

"I honour you, I worship, I adore, I have loved you…but I forbear: I would not write about myself. I want you to be happy and in the future to…but again I am rambling onto forbidden ground. …I will work harder, study more closely…and seek to gain equilibrium for my spirits and employment for my thoughts. Fear not for me. If

*I love you at all, if you wish to know how much I love, measure it by my calmness and my willingness in any way to do as you wish. I will. If you wish to see me, name the time and then nothing positively presenting, I will come, though it be every night or only every year..."*

Like every young man who finds himself suddenly, desperately and deeply in love, William Booth was overwhelmed by his feelings, and, most importantly for him, his Catherine – Miss Mumford of nearby Russell Street – appeared to feel the same.

It had been but a few weeks since they had met, yet already they were speaking about long-term commitment and marriage. Several letters had passed between them, in which they were able to pour out their new feelings of love in a way they were unable to do when they actually met, since that was often in the company of others. But it was clear to them both that this was not just a passing fancy or an infatuation; it was much more than a developing friendship or mutual admiration, and it surpassed a growing love affair.

In 1852 love was usually less than "romantic", with couples at all levels of society often finding themselves together for practical, family, and economic reasons. But, although many marriages were largely "of convenience", that did not mean that "love" was entirely excluded. As arranged by their families just a few years earlier, the young Queen Victoria had married her cousin Albert in 1840, but theirs had also turned out to be a true love match.

Catherine Mumford had first caught sight of William Booth from a distance when he stood to preach at the church she attended, Binfield House Methodist Chapel in Clapham, South London.

Was she immediately struck by the sight of the young man standing more than six feet tall in the pulpit? Did she find him imposing and attractive with his dark hair and the short trimmed beard that framed his chin? Or was it the power of his voice, his energetic preaching style, his intensity of spirit, and his religious zeal that made the greatest impact as he urged people not just to live a Christian life but to give their lives to Christ and to strive for a holy life? Whatever the case, she was sufficiently impressed by the young visiting preacher to express her admiration to a church friend, a prosperous Walworth bootmaker and businessman, Mr Edward Harris Rabbits, who was also William's sponsor and supporter.

Within a fortnight Mr Rabbits, an unlikely matchmaker, had arranged afternoon tea at his house and Catherine, her mother, Sarah, and William were among the invitees.

This first personal contact may have confirmed Catherine's opinion. William was sincere, deeply religious, and driven by the same ambition – to see the world and individual people transformed by Christian faith. In William, Catherine recognized a kindred spirit.

William may have noted with admiration the outspoken young woman whom he met that day, but he later reported that it was on his twenty-third birthday, 10 April 1852, a Good Friday and some weeks after the Rabbits party, that he fell in love with his future wife.[1]

After just a couple of meetings and one carriage ride, their future was sealed. But neither could have foreseen the consequence of their meeting: the eventual creation not just of a Christian ministry based on that "personal salvation" that William had preached about from the Binfield chapel pulpit, but of an entirely new "church", a Christian organization that would change society, and which would extend across the globe. A "movement" of Christian people that would eventually become The Salvation Army.

Just now, though, William and Catherine were two young people getting acquainted at the start of a great, lifelong love affair, with William, at least, expressing himself as lovers have done down the centuries.

PRINCE'S ROW
WALWORTH ROAD

*My own dear Catherine*

*I know you will, at least I presume you will, forgive the liberty I take in writing you a line, altho' it is not so long since we met, but for some reason or other I am happier than I have been for some time back, and when there is a ray of sunshine in my heart I conceive you have a right to know it, especially seeing you have been so minutely acquainted with every dark cloud that hath flitted across the horizon of my soul of late. I have been thinking of you very much yesterday and this morning. I feel that the affection I entertain for you is a growing, deepening, expanding and extending feeling; I trust that on both sides it shall be ever & ever thus. To love as one, live as one, with one, only one, class of cares and anxieties and sorrows. What is thine in this respect shall be mine, and what is mine shall be thine.*

*… Farewell for a season, I shall soon hold you in my arms again, by the blessings of heaven…*

*Until we meet be assured that I am for ever, your dearest and most sacred friend and lover.*

*William*

Although a respectable and once quite affluent Nottingham family, the Booths were certainly not prosperous. William had few economic prospects to offer any potential wife, and it worried him.

He had hated his job as a pawnbroker and, just a few weeks after meeting Catherine, on that same Good Friday on which he took a carriage ride with her and reported falling in love, he had resigned his post and was chasing his dream of becoming a Christian preacher. William knew that the life of a travelling evangelist presented little in the way of security and stability, economic or otherwise, so he was certainly not marriageable material. Society in general and most young women and their parents or guardians at the time would insist upon certain securities before entering into an "understanding", an engagement, and marriage. Furthermore, while the young and sincerely devout William Booth might not have articulated the thought, any woman whom he would eventually marry had to share his deep spiritual sense of purpose, ambition, and Christian vocation.

But Catherine Mumford was no "ordinary girl" yearning for a grand love affair. She was far more practical than that. More than two decades later she would write:

> *Every courtship ought to be based on certain definite principles. A fruitful cause of mistake and misery is that very few have a definite idea as to what they want in a partner, and hence do not look for it. They simply go about the matter in a haphazard fashion, and jump into an alliance upon the first drawings of mere natural feeling regardless of the laws which govern such relationships.*

*In the first place, each of the parties ought to
be satisfied that there are to be found in the other
such qualities as would make them friends if they
were of the same sex. In other words, there should be
a congeniality and compatibility of temperament.
And yet how many seek for a mere bread-winner, or
a housekeeper, rather than for a friend, counsellor
and companion. Unhappy marriages are usually the
consequences of a too great disparity of mind, age,
temperament, training or antecedents.*[2]

Catherine, just a few months older than the sincere young man
on whom she had set her heart, was as determined as he that any
attachment would not just be about romantic love and physical
attraction. Although the guidance she delivered in later life draws
up strict criteria for finding a suitable mate, there is no indication
that she thought otherwise as a young woman. When other young
girls were dreaming about a tall, dark, handsome stranger and
were already drawing up lists of requirements for their longed-for
wedding day, by the age of sixteen Katie Mumford was already
determining the sort of man she eventually wanted to marry.

First, she had decided, he must be truly "converted". She had
made this decision very soon after she was, in the language of
the future Salvation Army, "saved" – when she gave her whole
life to God to be used by Him in whatever way He saw fit – and
she would settle for nothing less in the man she hoped to marry.
A cousin had once declared love for her but she had turned him
down on the basis that he was *not* "truly converted".

Second, the man Catherine hoped to marry would be a
Total Abstainer. Drinking alcohol was not something she would
tolerate. She had been a member of the Temperance Movement

since she was a young girl, and by eighteen would be writing articles on the dangers of alcohol.

Third, her future husband must be "a man of sense". She wanted to be able to respect any potential spouse.

Finally, she determined that, if they were to be happy, they would have to think alike on all important matters.

However, this list of requirements for a future spouse wasn't apparently without a touch of romanticism. Catherine also secretly prayed that her husband would be a minister in the church, she rather liked the name "William", and she yearned for him to be "tall and dark".[3]

So did Catherine's heart skip a beat when William Booth got up to preach at Binfield House that day in March 1852? Did she immediately recognize in him all that she was looking for in a husband, partner, lover, and friend? Tall and dark he certainly was, already a budding minister and powerful preacher, and, judging from his words from the pulpit, not only "truly converted" himself but also desperately wanting the whole world to be similarly transformed by Jesus Christ.

If not on that first evening at Binfield House, then certainly by the time they had taken that Good Friday carriage ride, it is likely that Catherine had determined that William was the man for her. However, she was acutely aware that he felt insecure about his future. Right and proper behaviour was paramount and he wavered, one moment expressing deep, undying love, the next acknowledging the practicality and the reality of his situation.

Catherine backed off, not wanting to put pressure on the man she had very quickly learned to love and respect, recognizing that he had a spiritual destiny and not wishing to put any obstacles in his way. If William was to be a great evangelist, would a wife, and the inevitable family which, please God, would soon follow marriage, be a hindrance? Unless they were both convinced that God wanted them to spend their lives together, neither would commit to the future.

*My Dear Friend,*

*I promised you a line. I write. I know no more than I knew yesterday.*

*I offered as you know full well then and there to make the/an engagement. You declined on what without doubt are good grounds, but still I cannot do more… You know the inmost feelings of my heart, and I can say no more than that I have not, as I could have wished, seen anything striking to intimate the will of God. If my circumstances had not been so benighted I might not have desired this, but feel the importance of the affair, if I feel nothing else.*

*Now understand me. As I said yesterday, I offer now <u>a step in the dark</u>. I will promise you anything you wish <u>for your own dear sake</u>, but mind, my feelings are still the same. But the tie shall be as sacred as though made under the influence of sunnier feelings and in prospect of brighter days. You can write me your mind. I do not wish to trouble you for a long letter. Put down in a line what you think.*

*If you decline as yesterday, I ask the favour of being allowed to keep as sacred as my Bible and as full to me of inspiration, and as sacred as my soul's inmost feelings, the notes I already have in your writing. As you wish you can keep or burn mine. I could almost* trust you with the keeping of the Title Deeds of my soul's salvation, so highly do I esteem your character. Perhaps I write wildly. Excuse me. I began calm.

After this is ended, this awful controversy, I shall call on you again. If you accept what I have stated, I will come Saturday. If not, I shall call as a friend in the course of a few days and show you how I bear the matter. If it be of man, if it be wrong, it will pass forgotten away. If it be of God He will still bring it to pass.

All I fear is your suffering and your mother's condemnation. But I cannot help it. Believe every word I have here said. If you accept, we are henceforth and for ever one. If you decline, the matter must be forgotten. I leave you in the hands of my God.

*I am, Yours, etc., William Booth.*

RUSSELL ST
(THURSDAY) MAY 13 1852

*My Dear Friend,*

*I have read and re-read your note & I fear you did not fully understand my difficulty. It was not circumstances, I thought I had fully satisfied you on that point. I thought you felt sure that a bright prospect could not allure me, nor a dark one affright me, if we are only one in heart. My difficulty, my only reason for wishing to defer the engagement was that you might feel satisfied in your own mind that the step is right. To cause you to err would cost me far more suffering than anything else.*

*I have deeply pondered over all your words at our last interview, especially the objections which you so honourably confessed had influenced your mind, & I <u>dare</u> not enter into so solemn an engagement till you can assure me that you feel I am in every way suited to make you happy & that you are satisfied that the step is not opposed to the will of God.*

*You say if your circumstances were not so blighted, you could not desire so striking an indication of God's will. I answer if you are satisfied of <u>His will</u> irrespective of circumstances, let circumstances go & let us be one come what will, but if there is an thing in me which you fear, anything which you think would mar your <u>completest happiness</u>, banish the thought of an union <u>forever</u>, & let us regard each other as true & tried friends.*

*But if you feel satisfied on these two points, first, that the step is not opposed to the will of God & secondly, that I am calculated to make you happy, come on Saturday evening and on our knees before God let us give ourselves afresh to Him & to each other; for His sake consecrate our whole selves to His service for <u>Him to live & die</u>. When this is done what have we to do with future? We and all our concerns are in His hands, under His all wise & gracious providence.*

*I wish you could see into my heart for a moment. I cannot transfer to paper my <u>absorbing</u> desire that the <u>will of God may be done in this matter</u>. I dare* *no more say I decline or accept (except on the before mentioned grounds) than I dare take my destiny into my own hands. The cry of my <u>inmost soul</u> is, "Thy will be done". If you come on Saturday, I shall presume that you are satisfied on those two points & that henceforth we are one. In the mean time I shall not cease to pray that God may guide you <u>right</u>. May He bless you & if He sees that I am not such an one as you need to be an help mate for you, may He enable you to <u>forget me</u>. I know you will rightly appreciate what I have said; you will not attribute anything to hardness of heart or indifference. I think I know you too well to suppose it.*

*What you said about my health is not forgotten. I have arranged to see Mr F[ranks] tomorrow in order to get his candid opinion of my present state of health & my future prospects, on which point I will not fail to satisfy you. God knows my sincere desire to act towards you, as I would wish you to act towards me. Again I commend you to Him. It cannot, shall not be that you shall get wrong.*

*Let us besiege His Throne with all the powers of prayer, and believe me yours affectionately, Catherine.*

The sincere young woman with bright eyes could not say it more clearly. Her heart thumped as she put the final full stop alongside her name.

"Catherine."

She looked back at the letter, in her usual efficient manner. The handwriting was small, compact, and controlled.

"Yours affectionately". Was that too formal a sign-off? It was certainly "proper", but how would William interpret this? Would it be the word he wanted, an open door to her heart, or would he read into it a way out of their new attachment? Would he come to the Mumford home in Russell Street on Saturday? Would he make the decision to give his life in service to God at least for the time being, without the encumbrance of a wife, no matter how devout?

She took up the writing sheet, blew on it ever so slightly to ensure the ink was entirely dry, then carefully folded the paper and reached for an envelope.

Catherine grasped her pen once again to write – William Booth, Walworth Road.

Just a short distance from her home in Russell Street in Brixton, her letter would soon be in his hands, those hands which had already clasped her own. She remembered the first time they had touched. A simple, polite handshake and yet in that touch she had felt an immediate attraction to this rather dishevelled-looking young man with the strong voice and straightforward attitude.

Catherine shook her head at her sentimentality. She wasn't one for romantic novels, having always preferred spiritual texts. Yet she could not help but feel excited by the thought of William. She took a long, deep breath, rose from the desk and made for the door, to arrange for the delivery of the letter.

For both William Booth and Catherine Mumford, it was obvious from the start that they shared the same desire not just for each other but for a world they saw as needing a new beginning, a new influx of faith, a new Christian revival.

William, a thin, gangling young man, was not classically handsome, with his large hooked nose that many suggested gave him the look of a Jew, though he had no eastern blood in his heritage. His mass of thick dark hair often remained uncontrollable, no matter how slicked down, and a thick moustache-less beard framed his rather prominent chin. His heavy workload left him physically exhausted. For months he had juggled his work in a pawnbroker's in Kennington with volunteering as a lay preacher in the church and pursuing his own preaching ministry on the streets of South London. But he hadn't allowed the physical challenges, no matter how much he found himself dwelling on them, to affect his intensity of spirit, personality, and drive. And he suited Catherine.

Quiet and thoughtful, frail and sickly, having suffered ill health for a good deal of her life to date, Catherine was earnest and somewhat severe in appearance, with a high forehead, curls framing a pale face, and sparkling eyes that hinted of a deep intelligence and spirituality. Catherine captivated William.

On their first meeting at the home of Mr Rabbits, William could not have failed to notice Catherine's ability to argue her point of view. He would soon discover her depth of spiritual experience and her scrupulous, exacting, and rather pious opinions on many matters of importance to her. But William loved the way Catherine could argue with him, standing up for herself in a way that women were not expected to do and which he may well not have encountered before. He loved the fact that her Christian faith was already well developed and yet she was still seeking a deeper spirituality. It thrilled him that they could already share their innermost thoughts on so many matters, both corporal and spiritual, and that they did not just speak about love and trivial matters but also quickly found themselves able to discuss deep spiritual concerns important to them both – God, Jesus Christ, the Holy Spirit.

The couple were well suited. Both were already, in their early twenties, deeply religious, sincere, even austere, and somewhat judgmental with regard to issues and circumstances that did not square with their highly principled views on life.

When William Booth stood up to preach in Binfield House he knew it was what he was destined to do. He already had experience as a Methodist local preacher but he wanted more. He desired to reach more people, not just those who went to church. His heart was for the "lost". He was a young man on a mission.

He also felt he was destined for great things. Aged just twenty, while walking with his friend Walter James in his home area of Sneinton in Nottingham, he had discussed the future.

"Have you no ambition?" he had asked Walter.

"What do you mean?"

"Because I have," William had continued. "I intend to be something great; I do not mean to belong to the commonalty."[4]

Was he arrogant? Possibly. Ambitious? Certainly. But William Booth's confidence was not based on selfish ambition, and in Catherine Mumford he would find a partner who would not just support him in his Christian ministry, but would also admonish him on his propensity to let his ego run amok and remind him of the need for focus on spiritual matters, and that he should continually consider how his actions would affect his mission in life.

It was important that Catherine shared his enthusiasm for the Reform Movement within the Methodist Church, to which William had quite recently formally attached himself. It was not coincidental that they had met at Mr Rabbits' home, for the sponsor and friend was deeply committed to the movement that had been causing ructions among Methodists.

Although raised in a Wesleyan tradition, the serious-minded and devout Catherine had become entranced by the Reform Movement, which promised a revival of old-style Methodism.

She had embraced Reform thinking and as a result had been expelled from the Wesleyan congregation of which she had been a part since her family had moved to London. Although quiet on the surface, Catherine could be outspoken and opinionated and was already displaying a spiritual zeal and determination very similar to that of her future husband.

William had been born into the Church of England. His family had not been particularly devout, and from the age of thirteen he had sought a different spirituality after a friend had encouraged him to attend the Methodist chapel in Nottingham named after the "founders" of Methodism – the Wesley Chapel. In 1844, about the time Catherine was moving with her family from her birthplace in Derbyshire, a sincere fifteen-year-old William Booth was becoming more aware that he needed to be truly "converted" and one night, while walking home from a church meeting, he gave in to these innermost feelings of religious conviction and, standing in the street, offered himself to God.

In 1846 William heard the renowned American evangelist James Caughey preach with the passion he had been seeking. After this, with a small group of friends including his closest acquaintance, Will Sansom, the young Booth started speaking out and "spreading the gospel". The lads organized street and cottage meetings and other activities and, aged just seventeen, William had been appointed as a Methodist local preacher, which allowed him to travel to different preaching appointments across the city. All this despite a lack of physical strength and a rather nervous disposition.

He balanced his busy schedule with a working life in pawnbroking, the business he had been entered into in Nottingham at the age of thirteen when his father, Samuel, a speculator and failed businessman, could no longer afford to keep him at school. Soon after he was taken out of school and sent to work, his father died, and William's meagre wages helped to support his mother, Mary, and his three sisters.

William loathed and detested pawnbroking, which preyed on the poverty and insecurities of the poor working class who could not make ends meet, but by the late 1840s he had completed his apprenticeship, was beholden no longer to his taskmaster, and was determined to move on. However, when he relocated to London in November 1849, pawnbroking was the only experience he could rely on for employment and once again he was forced to take up work in a shop adorned with the infamous cluster of three balls.

He yearned to be a Christian evangelist and gave up all his spare time and his Sundays to work in his church as a local preacher, but he wasn't the only young man with such an ambition and he grew increasingly frustrated at the lack of opportunities to step into the pulpit as he vied with around twenty others who were also part of the local Methodist "preaching plan".

William wasn't about to stand around and wait for the opportunities to drop into his lap. Instead, he resigned from his honorary position as a Methodist lay preacher and took to the streets around Kennington, just south of the River Thames, to preach to whomever would listen.

About this time the Reform Movement was growing in popularity, and, although William was not aligned with them, his minister assumed rebellion. He struck the young man's name from the membership list of the church, despite William's protestations. He had resigned his official lay ministry in the Methodist Church so that he could pursue his own ministry, but he still wished to remain a Methodist. William felt hurt and discarded, but no sooner had he been formally removed from the "roll" of his church than the Reformers invited the fervent young preacher to join their ranks.

Edward Rabbits, a leading Reformer, had been greatly impressed when he heard William speak at the Walworth Road Chapel: the young man had tremendous vigour and sincerity and was as devoted to revivalism as Mr Rabbits himself. Only through revival – people again seeking true Christian faith and holy living rather than just the "religion" of churchgoing – would God's world be set straight. Mr Rabbits agreed to sponsor William in his ministry at least for the first three months, and, not a man to turn down an opportunity, however small, on 10 April 1852, his twenty-third birthday, William left the hated pawnbroking trade for the final time. He was taken on as a minister of Binfield House, the Methodist Reform chapel attended by Sarah Mumford and her daughter Catherine, who had also recently been thrown out by the Wesleyans.

On that Good Friday, at the end of a "tea" meeting at the Cooper House School off the City Road during which Catherine had felt unwell, William had agreed to take her home and on that "little carriage ride," paid for by one Edward Rabbits, they had fallen in love.

Barely one month after this ride and having known Catherine for only a little longer, William Booth put aside any doubts he might have had about marriage, and on Saturday 15 May 1852 he and Catherine Mumford announced their engagement, committing themselves not just to each other but, together, to God, for whatever purposes He intended for them.

*My dearest William,*

*The evening is beautifully serene and tranquil, according sweetly with the feelings of my soul. The whirlwind is past and the succeeding calm is in proportion to its violence. Your letter – your visit – have hushed its last murmurs and stilled every vibration of my throbbing heartstrings. All is well. I feel it is right, and I praise God for the satisfying conviction.*

*Most gladly does my soul respond to your invitation to give myself afresh to Him, and to strive to link myself closer to you, by rising more into the image of my Lord. The nearer our assimilation to Jesus, the more perfect and heavenly our union. Our hearts are indeed one, so one that division would be more bitter than death. But I am satisfied that our union may become, if not more complete, more divine, and, consequently, capable of yielding a larger amount of pure unmingled bliss.*

*The thought of walking through life <u>perfectly united</u>, together enjoying its sunshine and battling its storms, by softest sympathy sharing every smile and every tear, and with thorough unanimity performing all its momentous duties, is to me exquisite happiness; the highest earthly bliss I desire. And who can estimate the glory to God, and the benefit to man, accruing from a life spent in such harmonious effort to do <u>His will</u>? Such unions, alas, are so rare that we seldom see an exemplification of the divine idea of marriage.*

If, indeed, we are the disciples of Christ, "in the world we shall have tribulation"; but in Him and in <u>each other</u> we may have peace. If God chastises us by affliction, in either mind, body, or circumstances, it will only be a mark of our discipleship; and if borne equally by us both, the blow shall not only be softened, but sanctified, and we shall be able to rejoice that we are permitted to drain the bitter cup <u>together</u>. Satisfied that in our souls there flows a deep undercurrent of pure affection, we will seek grace to bear with the bubbles which may rise on the surface, or wisdom so to burst them as to increase the depth, and accelerate the onward flow of the pure stream of love, till it reaches the river which proceeds out of the Throne of God and of the Lamb, and mingles in glorious harmony with the love of Heaven.

The more you lead me up to Christ in all things, the more highly shall I esteem you; and, if it be possible to love you more than I do now, the more shall I love you. You are always present in my thoughts.

Believe me, dear William, as ever,

Your own loving, Kate.

# CHAPTER

2

Catherine's hand trembled as she reread the words that William had penned.

> "I have been thinking of you very much yesterday and this morning.
>
> "I feel that the affection I entertain for you is a growing, deepening, expanding and extending feeling.
>
> "What is thine in this respect shall be mine, and what is mine shall be thine. We henceforth & for ever will live, not to ourselves, but to each other & to Him supreme who bought us not with corruptible things but with blood. In the waves of sorrow, in the hour of gladness, in darkness, & in the bright summer's light, with hands clasped & with hearts knit to Him 'who all our sins hath borne,' we will stand the test and live for the pure inheritance which passeth not away."

She could hardly believe the words were intended for her, or that someone so wonderful would think her worthy of such fine accolades.

In the few days since their engagement William had, of course, been often in her home. Mother and Father, although at first rather shocked by the speed at which the young couple appeared to have attached themselves to each other, were learning to know William and, Catherine prayed, would soon love him as she did. Well, not exactly as she did, of course, but as a son. William, so polite yet still willing to stand his ground in a discussion, felt like the other half of herself, a piece that up to now had been missing.

It was highly unfortunate that William had got off onto a wrong foot with Mother at that first meeting at Mr Rabbits' house. Why on earth he had been persuaded to recite that ridiculous poem – what was it? "The Grog-seller's Dream" – she would never know. It had created such strong debate, even argument, about the value of teetotalism that only the call to supper had saved the day.[1]

But, despite their misgivings, when discussing the swiftness of the engagement to William, both Mother and Father Mumford had concluded that there was little point in denying their daughter.

"Mother, you know that once Catherine puts her mind to something, there is little point in argument. Our daughter wants William Booth and William Booth she shall have!"

When Catherine met William she undoubtedly saw in him a character with determination and potential for greater things. But during their early meetings and even into their engagement and beyond, although they were of like mind in their devotion to God and His work, they disagreed on a number of matters and it is likely there were some heated, if ever so polite, "debates" between the two.

Catherine was a teetotaller, a devoted abstainer from any forms of alcohol. William was not. He had admitted to occasionally imbibing "for medicinal purposes", and this, in Catherine's mind, would have to stop if they were to be wed. On this she was quite clear.

Although she had been brought up and still lived with her parents in the confines of a strict Victorian home, and while she might have given the impression of a quiet individual, she was certainly not shy. Opinionated and strong-willed, at the age of twelve Catherine Mumford had seen a collier beating his donkey in the street with a hammer and had run after him to snatch it away. Later she gave up taking sugar, as her personal protest against the oppressed "natives" in distant lands who worked the fields and harvested the sugar. At an early age she was a pillar of her local Temperance Movement, which preached against the excessive use, and misuse, of alcohol and promoted total abstinence. It was a cause to which her father John Mumford had once been dedicated.[2]

However, by the time his daughter became engaged to the young preacher William Booth, John Mumford was a rather different character from the man who had married Catherine's mother, Sarah Milward. Then he was a Methodist lay preacher, an upstanding member of society, and a carriage maker whose profession had taken him from Ashbourne in Derbyshire, where Catherine had been born the only daughter of five children, first to Boston in Lincolnshire and then to Brixton in London.

In common with many families in early nineteenth-century England, the Mumfords had unfortunately not raised all five of their children. Indeed, of the four boys born to them only one – John – had survived into adulthood, and Catherine was the only daughter. Although infant and child mortality was declining at that time, certainly within the middle classes, the death of children was far from uncommon. However, it would not be until 1837 with the establishment of the General Register Office that there was a legal requirement to register all births, deaths, and marriages in England and a clearer picture of the state of the population would begin to emerge, helped by the ten-yearly population census or "head count" which had been initiated in 1801.

Suffice to say, the experience of losing three of her children had undoubtedly had an effect on Sarah Mumford because she kept Catherine, in particular, very close. Although brother John was sent away to school it was only on one occasion – while the Mumfords were living in Boston – that Sarah allowed Catherine briefly to attend a school. Otherwise, she was educated at home, coming under her strict and devout mother's instruction and being schooled not just in basic reading, writing, and arithmetic but also in history and culture. Most importantly, she was trained in spiritual matters and encouraged to read theology and delve deeply into the Bible. It's said that by the time she was twelve Catherine had read the Bible eight times.

Catherine had been a rather isolated, even lonely, girl, suffering ill health, fainting, and "palpitations". She was often confined to home, did not mix much with other children, and spent a good deal of her early days reading, studying, and formulating ideas that would not only frame her own thinking and character but would ultimately enter her and William's joint decision making and theology.

And on the subject of alcohol she would not be moved. Her father, who had started out with seemingly good prospects, had proved to be rather "unstable and unreliable".[3] When she was eighteen Catherine would anguish about the state of her father's spiritual health in her diary, imploring the Lord to "…answer prayer and bring him back to Thyself!"[4] When Catherine was still a girl Mr Mumford had stopped his lay preaching, taken to being melancholy, become disappointed with his lot in life and even lost his enthusiasm for politics, another of his early interests. Although there is no evidence that John Mumford Snr became an alcoholic, he certainly shifted from his teetotal lifestyle, which was a great disappointment to his intensely religious wife and daughter.

What Catherine wanted in a husband was more than a lover. She desired, above anything else, a partner who would be as committed as she was to the cause of Jesus Christ.

From the outset theirs was a remarkably open and honest relationship at a time when it was more common for husband and wife, and certainly betrothed individuals, to keep a certain distance.

PRINCES ROW, WALWORTH ROAD,
SECOND HALF OF MAY 1852 (CONT)

*The Quarterly meeting last night was rather a stormy one. Your dearly beloved had a little skirmishing with your dear friend & minister Brother Gaze, who had the impudence to ask if paid agents would be admitted into the Delegate meeting. This roused all my soul and I should have given him the knowledge of a few ideas that have flitted through my brain at different times, if I had not been almost forcibly restrained by my friends Messrs. Rabbits, Bolton, & Barron.*

*Who do you think were elected? Messrs. Gaze & Rabbits! The first friend had a lot of his own members there; I do not say that he invited them, but so it was. He holds just my views of Church Politics and so it will be perhaps as well after all, only that I had rather the choice had been more respectable.*

*A letter has just come to hand enclosing 4/6 in postage stamps, money lent some 12 months back and almost forgotten so I can write away now.*

*Dr Campbell was out yesterday. I see him tomorrow morning: ½ past 8 o'clock.*

*You will write a line to my dear mother before I come to see you. I should like to see it before you send it; do not call that selfish, but you may!*

*Pray for me, Kate, earnestly pray that I may be kept. Been much tempted since I began this letter. God knows my heart, that the ruling of my soul is to serve him.*

*Farewell for a season. I shall soon fold you in my arms again, by the blessing of Heaven. May we be guided in all things. I go to Sydenham on Thursday afternoon. My love to your dear mother; her kindness is indelibly graven on my heart, a heart, Catherine, which is all yours now. May your influence & companionship hallow, soften, and imbue it with more of your own gentleness & sweet meekness. Until we meet be assured that I am for ever, your dearest and most sacred friend & lover.*

*William.*

Since the moment when he and his friend Will Sansom had stepped onto the streets of Nottingham and begun their adolescent preaching to the ragamuffins, street urchins, and anyone who would listen, William Booth had known he was meant for nothing else than to spread the gospel of Jesus Christ. His experience as a young Methodist lay preacher had given him a taste for the streets and for a heart for the unconverted.

His Methodist background had already played a part in convincing him that God wanted to know each person individually, not at a distance or through a saint or two, as other religious traditions taught. He was already committed to a theology of "holiness" and "sanctification" – which would become ever more important as his ministry developed.

Did he want to emulate his hero, James Caughey, under whose ministry his young heart had been stirred? Most definitely! He had admired the way the imposing American had stirred his audience and challenged each individual – man, woman, or child – to look deep within their heart, to analyse their status with God.

William's tenure at Binfield House in Clapham, where Catherine had first seen him preach, was only a three-month arrangement and it was unlikely to be renewed, even if William had wanted it to be.

At Binfield he found himself under the leadership of older men, who although wishing to see the world changed by Christ – they had, after all, stepped outside their comfort zone of Wesleyan Methodism to pitch their tents in the Reformers' field – were still held back by some of the traditions and structures of their day.

Young men like William Booth were expected to serve their time. They waited and learned, and matured in life and in theology. It was not enough for a young man merely to want to get out and "preach". There had to be deference to elders, training, followed by perhaps increasing responsibility in the church gained over several years, and then, finally, authority.

But William was young, and impatient. His life so far had taught him that there were no guarantees. His own father, Samuel, with his love of money and ambitious but ultimately disastrous schemes and business plans, had made little of himself and had died leaving his family not penniless, but with little support.

William's dear friend Will Sansom, with whom he had shared that early street ministry, had also died very young. It had been Will and other close friends who had first encouraged the young Booth to speak in public and together he and Sansom had stepped out in faith, offending the church leaders, and sharing a close friendship based on their common Christian conviction. When Will Sansom developed "consumption" he had been taken south to the fresh air of the Isle of Wight, but even that could not effect a recovery and he was eventually brought home to Nottingham, to die.

Tuberculosis, the pulmonary disease that took young Will, has been around since the dawn of time and in the early nineteenth century it was still endemic across many parts of the globe. Physicians were slow to identify the symptoms as one single disease. That only came in the 1820s, and indeed, the ailment that carried so many people off was not given the name "tuberculosis" until a decade later.[5] Although assured that Will had gone to meet his Lord in Heaven, William Booth was left bereft by the death of his friend and spiritual companion.

Now, in Catherine, he had found another close friend, as well as a lifelong love, with whom he could share his innermost thoughts and his spiritual ambitions.

*My Dear William,*

*I ought to be happy after enjoying your company all the evening. But now you are gone and I am alone, I feel a regret consonant with the height of my enjoyment. How wide the difference between heavenly and earthly joys! The former satiate the soul and reproduce themselves. The latter after planting in our soul the seeds of future griefs and cares, take their flight and leave an aching void.*

*How wisely God has apportioned our cup. He does not give us all sweetness, lest we should rest satisfied with earth; nor all bitterness, lest we grow weary and disgusted with our lot. But he wisely mixes the two, so that if we drink the one, we must also taste the other… .*

*But I have rambled from what I was about to write. I find that the pleasure connected with pure, holy, sanctified love forms no exception to the general rule. The very fact of loving invests the being beloved with a thousand causes of care and anxiety, which, if unloved, would never exist. At least, I find it so. You have cost me more real anxiety than any other earthly object ever did. Do you ask why? I have already supplied you with an answer! I think I see you looking puzzled to conjecture the cause of my anxiety after such a satisfactory interview, and so many kind words which as they fell from your lips sank into my heart and will never be forgot … The next cause of anxiety is that you should get cold going home too thinly clad, surely you will not; I hope if you come tomorrow evening you will bring your greatcoat. My candle is just going out, so I must say good night. May heaven's best blessing descend and abide with you sleeping and waking.*

*Yours in the fullest sense you can desire,*
*Catherine.*

In his weaker moments, William knew that he should have tried harder at education, but there hadn't been much to inspire at the local village school or later at Mr Sampson Biddulph's establishment. Books and study interested William little. All those around him constantly impressed upon him the need to train and study if he were to get on in church ministry. But there was so much to DO and so little time. What could he learn from a book that the Lord could not teach him?

That Catherine was better read, certainly in the Scriptures and theology, had worried him a little at first, but he had quickly realized that she might help him with his understanding of Scripture. Even though, despite her schooling, her spelling was atrocious, this just endeared her to him even more. And he was already becoming used to her loving, albeit determined way of sharing her thoughts with him. How precious that her love should extend even to advising him on prayer!

How wonderful that he had found someone who was so comfortable with him that they could share their deepest spiritual, as well as human, thoughts and dreams. How different their marriage would be from that of his eldest sister, Ann, and her brute of a husband, Francis Brown. What a disaster that was! As the man of the family, he, William, had felt uneasy about Ann moving to London when she had married some years earlier, but on paper the match had appeared to be sound. He recalled arriving in London, where there had been the promise of accommodation with Ann and Francis, only to find that his brother-in-law was far from the ideal husband! Not just materialistic, like his own father, Samuel Booth, but also a drinker and an agnostic who abhorred William's religiosity.

Suddenly William felt again the sadness and anger he had experienced when he realized that his loving sister had also been persuaded against matters of faith. He recalled the waves of loneliness that had overwhelmed him when, but a short while after arriving at what he had believed would be a family haven in an unfamiliar and threatening London, he was asked to leave, put out on the streets following yet another argument on faith and religion.

William laid his head back against the chair and remembered walking the streets and then, eventually, having to settle for the poor accommodation of the attic above Mr Fillmer's pawnshop opposite Kennington Common, where his lack of experience of anything but that hideous trade had led him.

William looked down at the note in his hand. So much had changed in the past months.

"Remember you are not on your own." William, for the first time in a long time, felt safe.

# CHAPTER

3

Miss Catherine Mumford was now a "lady in waiting". She was engaged, but no date had been set for a marriage because of the uncertainty of William Booth's future. Although he was confident that God wanted him to make a life as an evangelist, the chief difficulty was finding a church that would take him on. He had already had ambitions to become ordained in three different churches[1] yet he remained untrained, with relatively little knowledge or experience of church leadership. However, he was enthusiastic and was already making something of a name for himself as a preacher in London. The young couple were now intent on finding a "spiritual home" for William where he could gain experience as a preacher, pastor, and evangelist and earn enough to support a wife. It was unthinkable at this stage that Catherine and William would marry immediately; his financial prospects were still extraordinarily poor. This had been a bone of contention for him before the couple became engaged, as he worried about his ability to support a wife and potential future family. But although Catherine had assured him of her support, whatever the state of his finances, it was unlikely that her family would be happy for them to marry before he, at least, had an income.

Catherine was not as robust in health as she would have liked to be and even admitted to being something of an "invalid", which must have further worried William. He would want not just any work but a position that would enable him to provide for Catherine properly.

With this in mind, and knowing that the three-month bursary from his friend Edward Rabbits, which had enabled William to work in the Binfield chapel and ministry, would expire very soon, they were on the lookout for William's next employment.

William Booth's tenure under the Reformed Methodists at Binfield had been testing, more so than he had anticipated. In a pattern that would become familiar with him, he had happily and willingly embraced Mr Rabbits' offer of support to enable him to start his work as a minister, but the reality of church life was something different, as he found himself under other men's control, a situation that the headstrong young man found difficult to stomach. Now, having taken advantage of the goodwill of others, he was considering severing the relationship.[2]

Catherine began to formulate a way forward that would progress William into a preaching future, which would ultimately lead to employment and, God willing, their marriage.

PRINCES ROW WALWORTH ROAD
MONDAY MORNING LATE JULY OR EARLY AUGUST 1852

*My own loving Kate,*
*It has just occurred to my mind that I did not leave you a correct address to that poor girl, and less you should be prevented from your benevolent undertaking, I post this to inform you. If you leave the omnibus at the*

Obelisk at the end of the London and at the foot of the
Waterloo & Blackfriars Roads, you will be but a few
yards from your destination which is No 3 or 4 Duke
Street, next door to a Plumber & Glaziers shop. It is up
two flights of stairs. Take with you a smelling bottle. A
widow woman, who lives in the room as you enter from
the street, if you ask her for the poor girl of the name of
"Leach," will show you her room, I doubt not. Speak
pointedly to all you see of the family. Mention my name.

And how is my dear Catherine this morning? I
doubt not that Cotton End has already been in your
thoughts if not on your tongue, but not intending an
epistle I will not pause to moralise or discuss the pro &
con of College life.

… I have delivered into Mr Rabbits' own hand
the epistle you aided me in composing and penning on
Saturday Evening, after adding a lengthy postscript.
May God in mercy guide Mr R. right in aiding me, or
the contrary.

My love to you, with all my heart. I may or may
not see you this evening. I write this on purpose that
you may have the direction to that poor, dying girl.
Pray for me. Oh to be willing to take any path which
may promise most the diffusion of righteousness and
the Glory of God. Oh let us give ourselves afresh and
entire to him. Never was such a sacrifice as this needed
as now. I would make my choice under the influence of
deep piety and devotion & I shall not err.

My love to your dear Mother; I love not only you,
but her better than ever before.

*I pray for your entire consecration, and believe
me yours in the closest alliance of united Soul, Spirit &
Body, for Time & for Eternity, for Earth & for Heaven,
for Sorrow & for Joy, for ever & for ever, Amen.*

*William.*

Catherine took a piece of paper from her bureau and wrote down the
address of the "poor girl" whom William was wanting her to visit.
Was this the same girl to whom had he given his last sixpence the
other day? He was so kind, sometimes to his own detriment! She
would go to Duke Street, but not today, not in this overpowering heat.
She reached up with her white linen handkerchief and mopped her
brow and her neck. Perhaps if she just loosened the lace at the neck she
could feel a little less weak and ill. This had been a bad couple of days.
She prayed she was not sickening again but her headaches appeared
to have returned, along with a pain in her chest.

Although she knew in her heart that she had so much to look
forward to, with William especially, she still found herself once again,
as she had done so many times over the years, asking God to take her
to Heaven now, to put her out of her misery and remove the pain, not
just physical but emotional and spiritual.

Immediately Catherine felt a sense of guilt wash over her. How
could she still feel this way, when God had given her so much?

She looked again at William's letter.

"And how is my dear Catherine today?" he had written. He
had obviously taken time over her name, for it was illustrated and
adorned with pretty swirls and curls so that it had the appearance
of one of those illuminated manuscripts of ancient texts. How much
care he had taken over that single word! How much loved had been

*poured into the composition of those nine letters that made up her name – Catherine.*

*Why was her William being so thwarted by the church leadership at Binfield? Could they not see how sincere he was?*

*Well, if the Methodists and the Reformers wouldn't appreciate him, perhaps there was another congregation that might! She recalled something she had read in a pamphlet recently. Now, where was it? Yes, there it was, tucked away in her notebook, where she scribbled thoughts and comments on sermons and lectures she heard or read about.*

*Dr Campbell, of the Congregationalists and the Cotton End Training College. Maybe that was William's future?*

In later life, when recording her memoirs, Catherine was to describe the Revd Dr John Campbell as "the most influential man among the Nonconformists in London". He was a Congregationalist minister, and eventually the founder of various influential religious magazines and journals, including the *Christian Witness* and the *British Banner*. He was minister of two churches at the time – Tottenham Court Chapel on Tottenham Court Road and Whitefield's Tabernacle at Moorfields.[3] Catherine had heard him speak at the Congregational Stockwell New Chapel, which was near her home in Brixton and which, from mid-1852, she occasionally attended.

Although they had already turned their backs on friends in the Wesleyan Methodist Church for the revivalist Methodist Reformers, Catherine was very unhappy with the way that William was being treated by the Binfield leadership, particularly in that he wasn't being given his proper place as a minister or preacher. Years later she would write:

*The discipline of the Reform Society was very
unsatisfactory to us both, in denying the Minister
what we considered was his proper authority. The
tendency of human nature to go to extremes found
ample illustration in this particular. From making the
Minister everything, treating him with the profoundest
respect, receiving his word as law, putting him almost
in the place of God Himself – they went over to
regard him as nothing, denying him every shadow
of authority, and allowing him to preside at their
meetings when elected for this purpose, and speaking of
him in public and in private as their "hired" preacher.*

*In W's case it was worse than this. The leader of
the local movement with which he was connected, not
only denied him anything like the position of a leader,
but refused to give him reasonable opportunities for
preaching. They simply dealt with him as a cypher,
doubtless feeling that, did they give him any sort of
a position, he would earn for himself the leadership
which they were determined to keep for themselves.*[4]

So strained did the relationships become at Binfield that at the end of the three months that Edward Rabbits had funded out of his own pocket, William Booth parted company with the chapel and with his friend, whose heart was still with the Reformers. The friendship would later be renewed but for now William was without work and without many friends. He turned instinctively to Catherine.

Unemployment was not an option for William. He had already experienced the pain of being out of work. For a year after he had left pawnbroking in Nottingham he had struggled to find employment, in business and in the church. This period of inactivity, during which his male pride must have taken a knock as his mother and two of his sisters supported the family with shop work, had been resolved only by his move to London. No wonder that, many years later, when writing a book that proposed a strategy to abolish poverty, he did not just write about making the Christian gospel central, but also suggested that it could be linked to a "Work For All" policy, which would give men and women a purpose in life and a way of supporting their own families rather than relying on handouts and charity.

But where would he find his own new work? Did the answer lie in yet another move? This time to the Congregational Church?

*William picked up his Bible and, as was his custom, opened it to see what verse might present itself for inspiration. He scanned the pages in front of him. An obscure chapter or two from the Song of Songs. Nothing, or at least nothing that seemed appropriate. Maybe a walk would help. Walking was a necessity in his present financial situation but it was also beneficial to his thinking.*

*Perhaps he would walk to Brixton and visit Catherine.*

*Should he take her advice and pay a visit to Dr Campbell in Stockwell? Might THIS be a way into ministry? Could he really turn his back entirely on Methodism, which had been so central to his life and thinking?*

*He had heard that the Congregationalists – the Independents – were quite learned. Would he feel inadequate next to them? He had just about got away with his lack of formal training within the Reformed fellowship but would he be able to cope among the intellectual Independents?*

*William stopped to take in the sights and sounds of London around him. A bent old woman scuttled ahead of him, clutching a* thin scarf around her head and dragging a screaming child behind her. A horse and cart ambled by, the driver using the whip perhaps a little too liberally on the scrawny bag of bones that hauled his vehicle. A gang of men rolled out of a tavern.

William thought back to Nottingham, to the hours spent on the streets with dear Will Sansom. It was to people like these that they had witnessed. Did that old woman, the cart driver, or the men singing their way home to a poor wife and a hoard of starving children care whether William Booth had formal theological training?

Other doors might open to him, if he just had more patience. And if he were to go in with the Congregationalists, that would invariably mean study. Could he turn his back on his spiritual home? He knew that Catherine had his best interests at heart and was worried only about his well-being. That was, surely, why she was pressing him to think about a future with the Independents. Catherine could be so persuasive. She had already started attending Stockwell, just to expose herself to Dr Campbell's ministry, and had reported back favourably. Could he resist her counsel? It all sounded so simple. But it was not at all.

Catherine eventually won the day, as she invariably did where William was concerned. Despite his misgivings about rejecting his beloved Methodism, for which, Catherine would later admit, his love "amounted almost to idolatry",[5] William made an appointment with Dr Campbell to discuss his future.

William's indecision wasn't based solely on his commitment to Methodism. There was something much more fundamental that niggled and would just not retreat from his heart and mind.

At the centre of Congregational doctrine is the theological tradition of Calvinism, which includes belief in "election" and "limited atonement", an understanding that God has "prechosen" or "predestined" those who will be saved, and that only these "elect" will receive salvation. For William Booth, this was heresy. His belief in an all-loving God, who would save all those who called on His Name, was central to his thinking and his ministry. How could he consider throwing in his lot with a church that believed in "predestination" of just an "elect"?

Catherine wholeheartedly shared William's belief in salvation for all and his abhorrence for this Calvinist teaching. But she was practical and pragmatic. She had become convinced that the Calvinist doctrine was rarely preached and, indeed, was falling out of favour. She was sure that William, once within the Congregational Church, would be able to preach freely.

So William was persuaded to pay Dr Campbell a visit and one of his first questions addressed the subject of Calvinist doctrine, on which Dr Campbell apparently assured him that he would not be forced to preach any doctrine he did not honestly believe in, and then encouraged him to go to college to study.

William was introduced to various influential people and arrangements made for him to be interviewed by the Congregationalists Committee for Home Mission Works, where it was finally decided to admit William Booth for training at the home of the Revd John Frost at Cotton End, just outside London. His dream of ordination, and a ministry preaching the Good News of Jesus Christ, was within reach.

Although not an academic to whom study came easily, William passed his entrance examination and was admitted to the training school, where he immediately discovered, much to his disappointment, that the doctrine of predestination was certainly NOT off the Congregationalist agenda. Indeed, Dr George Smith, as the mouthpiece of the Home Committee and thus the man charged with ensuring that William Booth completed his studies satisfactorily, insisted that if he were to be considered for ordination in the Congregationalist Church he would be expected to conform on the question of Calvinistic theory.

William was furious, but he resisted the urge to give Dr Smith and his colleagues a piece of his mind there and then and instead accepted an essential reading list that included Abraham Booth's "Reign of Grace" and a series of lectures on "Divine Sovereignty, Election, the Atonement, Justification, and Regeneration" by George Payne.

Despite his spiritual and personal misgivings, but perhaps in one last attempt to prove to Catherine that he would give it go, he shook hands with Dr Smith and on his way home bought a copy of Abraham Booth's "Reign of Grace".

*William shifted uncomfortably in his chair. Barely thirty pages in, but already he had been at it several hours.*

"Chapter 3: OF GRACE, AS IT REIGNS IN OUR ELECTION.

*"Among the various blessings which flow from sovereign goodness, and are dispensed by reigning grace, that of election deservedly claims our first regard. It was in the decree of election that the grace of our infinite Sovereign did first appear, in choosing Christ as the head, and in him, as his members, all that should ever be saved. Election, therefore, is the first link in the golden chain of our salvation: and the corner-stone in the amazing fabric of human happiness…"*

*William read on…*

*"That those who in the volume of inspiration are called the elect, are a people distinguished from others, and that all mankind are not included under this denomination; are so apparent as hardly to need any proof…"*

*Now he found himself reading out loud, and he could hear his voice, full of disgust:*

"... the elect, as distinguished from others, are particular persons, whose names are in a peculiar manner known to God; that election relates to spiritual blessings and eternal enjoyments; and that the objects of it are dear to God, and forever precious in his sight...

"... It is equally clear that the elect were chosen of God before time began; for their election is one of the first effects of divine love. This love was from everlasting. The love of God to their persons, and their election to complete felicity, must, therefore, be eternal..."[6]

"ENOUGH!"

William snapped the wretched book shut, took it up, and threw it, with all the force he could muster, against the wall. It crashed with a heavy thud onto the wooden floorboards.

He moved to his desk, picked up his pen and immediately wrote his letter of resignation. Cotton End and the Congregationalists were not for him! Poverty or no poverty, Catherine would just have to understand.

WEDNESDAY 28TH JULY 1852

*My own dear Catherine,*

*I have just received a letter ... from my friend in the Isle of Wight. He says very plainly that he cannot give me up, and prays me to reconsider the determination expressed in my last. He calls upon me by all that is sacred not to go to be whitewashed at college, but to go to Ryde, where, as he says, I shall have superior opportunities for mental and moral training.*

*While I do not feel disposed to alter my views in regard to the position I should have to fill at Ryde, or even to reconsider my decision upon the subject,*

*still I must say this importunity considerably adds to*
*my perplexity. He looks upon our meeting as strictly*
*providential. He beseeches me not to go to college. I*
*give you a quotation: "We have a college ministry*
*already, and what are they doing in reference to the*
*salvation of souls? Their college whitewash is only*
*garnishing the sepulchre of dead souls. We want*
*a quickening, soul-saving ministry, affectionately*
*brought to bear upon the consciences and hearts of*
*sinners." Again he says: "Here is the place for your*
*social, and I believe loving, heart to expand and*
*quicken. Don't go to college. Your thoughts were*
*directed here. The experience of thousands of students*
*says, 'Don't go to college.' Their theology has become*
*stereotyped, their social and moral nature has lost its*
*vigour and power, while immured within the college*
*walls."*

*What say you to the matter? I hope you are*
*not making yourself unhappy. This is my reason for*
*writing. I am not miserable; do not fear that. I prayed*
*earnestly all the way home last night for guidance.*
*I believe it will be given. I am reading Finney and*
*Watson on election and final perseverance, and I see*
*more than ever reason to cling to my own views of*
*truth and righteousness.*

Soon after William Booth had rejected formal Congregationalist training, and word had got around regarding this audacious development, he was tempted for a final time to join the Independents by an unexpected letter from one Dr Ferguson, from the town of Ryde on the Isle of Wight.[7] Ferguson seemed impressed by the young man's determination not to train at Cotton End – there were others who also turned their back on scholarship – and was willing to offer him a place as his deputy minister and eventual successor.

This seemed an answer to prayer, a solid offer of work, with prospects for the future, including a salary that would have supported a wife and family.

But Ryde was still a Congregationalist church and William Booth was now dead set against throwing his lot in with that ministry. He declined the invitation. He must wait, it seemed, a little longer for a position to open up and his future to begin.

# CHAPTER

4

The whistle sounded shrilly a couple of times. The brakeman was alerted and the train began to slow as they approached the station. William peered out of the window to try to catch a glimpse of the landscape through the thick black smoke billowing from the engine ahead and the low light of a late November afternoon. A field here, a garden there, cottages, small houses – very soon this town and others in the vicinity would be in his care, the as-yet unknown residents of those homes his potential flock.

"Lord, help me to be the pastor and preacher You need me to be here!" William found himself instinctively praying.

"Sir, did you not say you are leaving us at Spalding?" Through his silent prayer, William heard the low tones of the elderly gentleman who had been his travelling companion since London and with whom he had shared several hours of stimulating conversation about industry, faith, and more.

"I am, sir. Thank you!"

William rose and straightened his coat, wishing that it wasn't such a poor garment and hoping that those awaiting him wouldn't think less of him for his lack of acceptable attire. He presumed not, as the reception party would be churchmen. He straightened the thick woollen scarf that Kate's mother had presented him with a few days *before his departure from London. It had been a real blessing on the long cold journey in the heatless carriage.*

*He reached down and picked up a carpet bag containing his few meagre possessions, took leave of the old gentleman, stood up, and steadied himself in the swaying carriage.*

*As the train pulled into the station the platform guard announced: "Spalding. This is Spalding!"*

In 1852 train travel in England was still relatively novel, especially for people of fairly limited means, such as William Booth.

Although the world's first public railway – the Stockton and Darlington Railway in the north-east of England – had opened in 1825, it had at first been designed merely to connect coal mines and factories for the purposes of trade. By the 1840s, however, railway transport had begun to capture the public imagination and a train network began to develop across the country to carry people.

The Great Northern Railway line, which William Booth would have used to travel to his new appointment as a preacher for the Methodist Reformers in South Lincolnshire, was relatively new. It was but six years since the Great Northern Railway Act of 1846 had passed through Parliament, after two years of lobbying from the company that wished to create a direct rail link from London to York. Despite opposition from competing companies, namely the London and Birmingham and the newly formed Midland Railway, which held the monopoly on London to Leeds and York traffic, the Act granted the GNR permission to construct the main line from London to York and loop lines, and gave rights to other companies to create branch lines. It took barely two years for the first track – between Louth and Grimsby on the East Lincolnshire Railway –to be completed, and the line opened on 1 March 1848.

The market town of Spalding, William's destination at the very end of November 1852, had over the centuries developed into a hub for the wool, coal, and timber industries. The trade from the town was originally dependent on water transport, but when the Great Northern Railway opened its loop line from London to Doncaster in 1848 it meant direct rail routes to important centres such as Peterborough, Boston, and Lincoln. In 1852 this loop line had been replaced by a direct link with London via Grantham.

Spalding was on the map! In 1851 the national census had established the population as 8,829. There were many souls out there waiting for William Booth! But he wasn't to be the paid preacher just for Spalding, but also for a number of other towns in the area, including Holbeach and even Boston, Catherine's childhood home, where he occasionally preached. It was an exciting time for William even if it had meant leaving his fiancée behind in London.

TUESDAY 30TH NOV./52

*My own dear Kate,*

*I have arrived safe. Two gentlemen met me at the station. Conducted to the house of Mr Shadford, a Chemist – very kindly received. Several friends introduced to me. Am going this afternoon to Holbeach. A friend I expect every moment will call for me to take me in his conveyance. My reception has been beyond my highest anticipations. Indeed my hopes have risen 50 per cent that this circuit will be unto me all I want or need.*

*Very, very cold coming down… feet so cold. I could not write in the train in consequence of it shaking so much. You may rely upon my writing you a long letter as soon as I can get opportunity. I hope you will make yourself as happy as possible. You are going to Mr Franks tomorrow, Wednesday; I will pray that you will reap great advantages from the application. Pray for me that that I may be preserved from levity and lightness and be enabled to conduct myself as becometh a minister of the everlasting Gospel.*

*… Oh, let us all give ourselves up entirely to the Lord. I prayed in the Railway carriage that God would secure his work in my heart. I believe he will. Oh, for simple, childlike confidence. Come Holy Ghost and breathe thy influences on my heart.*

*… I love you I think with an eternal love. I will pray that we may be brought together again to spend in company our days below. The people seem very glad to see me. I have been much expected, and the friends have been much disappointed. Oh, who is sufficient for these things? Lord help me; I know you say Amen. Another gentleman, a local preacher, has just come in; very glad to see me…*

*Heaven smile upon thee, my dearest love. I have brought with me to Spalding a far better likeness of you than the daguerreotype, viz. your image stamped upon my soul; that image, my dear, I never can forget.*

*I hope & trust that all is for the best. Mrs Shadford is indeed a kind lady. There are no young ladies.*

*But I must conclude. Do not take this as a sample of my future letters; it is written with a number of*

*gentlemen around me. It is market day & first one
then another keeps coming in. A nice old gentleman, a
farmer, has just come in … He is a leading Conference
man. I have had an argument with him & we have
agreed pretty well.*

*They are waiting for me, farewell. If you write
me at Mr Hardy, Draper, Holbeach, it will find me on
Sunday if not earlier.*

*I remain, my own dear Kate,
Yours very affectionately,*

*William Booth.*

Catherine Mumford was feeling unwell. Although this was not uncommon, especially during the long winter months, this time her illness was more of the heart than of the body.

How she missed William! During these past months they had grown so close. It had been a testing time while they sought the will of God for the future, and how unhappy William had been at times as he struggled with the decisions that had to be made. Although Catherine had continuously tried to reassure him, he had fallen into the Slough of Despond, as Bunyan would have put it. She watched as he sold all his belongings – first his beloved bureau and side table, then his wardrobe and finally even his chair and bed. He had held on to some of his books, of course, but had ensured he divested himself of the ghastly "Reign of Grace". At last, having got rid of virtually all his personal belongings, he had been invited to stay in the Mumford family home.

How glorious that had been! To see William each morning at breakfast and through the day and then at night as they went to their separate beds! It was almost like being married – a little glimpse into the future when they would be in their own little house and all would be perfect.

She thought of William now, all that way away in Lincolnshire. Oh how she wished she could have accompanied him, as his wife. But it seemed that the Lord meant them to wait longer.

Catherine reread William's note.

How like him to think to mention there were "no young ladies" in the house in which he was boarding. He knew she was concerned about the distance between them, the time they would be forced to spend apart, and the loneliness he might encounter. Yes, she had admitted to him, she was worried that another girl might capture his attention, at which he had fallen at her feet, kissing her hands, and declaring, "Never. Never! It is You and I. Forever, with God as our focus!"

Catherine determined to be strong, not to pine, but to support her William from afar. She resolved to continue her studies – she was already immersing herself in the works of one of William's heroes, Charles Grandison Finney. She was so pleased that William had come to her already convinced of the excellence of some of the American evangelists. Indeed, she had been thrilled to learn that it was under the ministry of the marvellous James Caughey that William had become certain of his vocation.

Now she must write regularly, to support William from a distance. William had so much potential and would be, she was convinced in her heart, a great man. She knew that she could assist his growth and development into the man whom God needed in the world, if only through the written word.

William Booth's arrival in Lincolnshire was nothing if not controversial. The Reformers, to whom William was still attached despite his and Catherine's recent flutter with Congregationalism, had only recently split from the local Wesleyan Methodists. There was infighting over which group owned which chapel and, as in other parts of the country, even families split as their loyalties diverged. In addition, within the local Reform Movement itself there was disagreement. Many wanted more change than others and half the Fenland members had moved over to another denomination, the Wesleyan Connexion.[1]

The outspoken young man from London was just what the Reformers in Lincolnshire wanted! William Booth's reputation as a maverick went before him. In Lincolnshire he could experiment with his evangelistic style and concentrate on what he desired most of all to accomplish – to see men, women, and children find Christian faith.

For William the invitation could not have been more perfectly timed. The ink had barely dried on his letter of resignation from the Cotton End Congregationalist Training College when the invitation to Lincolnshire was received. The Reformers, as the majority Methodists in the area, had formed their own societies and needed lay preachers and ministers. The churches that required ministering to were spread across a distance of twenty-seven miles[2] and it would be William Booth's job not just to preach, but also to oversee the business affairs of the circuit. This was just the experience he required to get him onto the next step of the church ministry ladder.

But William's sojourn in the east of England, although later described by him as one of the happiest times of his spiritual life, was not without its trials. Although he was welcomed in Spalding and indeed in the other towns for which he was responsible, from Holbeach to Donnington and beyond, and he was cared for by a series of landladies and hostesses who appeared to indulge their young minister, there were often long days and difficult journeys between appointments.

Most importantly, his time in Lincolnshire meant separation from Catherine. Their only means of communication was through their letters.

*My dearest Love,*

*I received your very kind letter duly yesterday morning. While it made me sad to think that you indeed feel so acutely a parting rather full of promise, I was delighted to hear of your improving health, your strivings after God and your continued love, nay, your absorbing affection for me, though so unworthy.*

*… All my fear now is whether I shall give satisfaction. Sunday will tell me, doubtless. Your letters will all reach me safely. If you would like to write before I write again, you must direct for me at Mr Shadford's, Spalding. I shall be there doubtless on Monday. Mr Shadford appears to be the Mr Rabbits of the Circuit, everywhere well-spoken of, of universal help to the movement. He and his lady resigned and brought out with them 33 out of 36 members.*

*If I stay, you may depend upon it, I shall be able to save nearly all the money they give me whatever it may be. I am rather fearful whether they will offer me more than £60. I am informed that the Circuit Preacher in the Wisbech Circuit has got married since he came down, but they only gave him £70. If I were to marry while in a Circuit of the extent of this, I should keep a house someway or other … I would not have a wife without one. It would be impossible to be at home much without.*

*... If you are not satisfied with the style of my letters, you must tell me, and I will try and do better. Nothing but deep piety will save me from ruin and disappointment, I am satisfied. Oh, my God save me with all thy perfect salvation. I want a clean heart and a restless anxiety to be made a great blessing to all around. I trust my health will continue good. I shall live well, have plenty of fresh air, and the week night congregations not being very large I shall not have to exert myself very much.*

*The roads are the worst, so very dirty and dark. When you send, that is if you do send them, my box, you must be sure & enclose my galoshes. I shall try to wear them, but I fear I should leave them in the mud. My love to Father, Mother and Mr Mackland, and believe me yours in full & true affection,*

*William Booth.*

Back home in Russell Street in Brixton, living quietly in a house which now included a lodger by the name of Mackland, Catherine had more than enough time for writing, so write she did.

There is also no doubt that she, the superior one in academic knowledge, felt that she had a role to play in moulding her future husband and keeping him on the "straight and narrow" while they were apart. She enjoyed letter writing and took enthusiastically to the task of advising William, reproving him, and instructing him in a host of subjects and matters.[3] So intensive was her letter writing that she often spent the whole day writing notes in between other duties such as church and teaching at Sunday school, and then continued the communication across several days. This was her way of "talking" to her beloved.

Although William Booth was far from humble and loath to take advice from others, from his beloved Kate, it seemed, advice and even condemnation was welcomed.

7 Russell St

Sunday December 5th / 52

*My dearest William,*

*Here I sit all alone in our comfortable little parlour. My dear Mother & Mackland have gone to hear Mr Thomas, while I, wearied with the previous exertions of the day, have been endeavouring to get good at home, and now feel a strong inclination to talk with you a bit.*

*You will be pleased to hear that we have spent a very comfortable Sabbath. We had a cold dinner and all went to chapel, and Mr T gave us an excellent sermon from the 49–52 verses, of John's Gospel. I wish I could send you an outline, but was not sufficiently collected either to take notes or write from memory; hope to be able next Sunday.*

*I went to school in the afternoon and was received with great apparent pleasure by my class. Hope some seed of truth sank into their minds which will germinate another day. Had a wet walk home and no beloved one to meet me.*

Have been praying earnestly for my dearest that his sermon may find its way to the hearts of the people, and that his own soul may be abundantly watered. Felt it very good to draw nigh unto God. Oh to live in the spirit of prayer. I feel it is the secret of real religion, the main spring of all usefulness; in no frame can the soul so copiously receive & so radiantly reflect the rays of the sun of righteousness as in this. I long once more fully to realize it, but oh what an accumulation of rubbish has to be cleared away ere this can be the case. I have been reading Finney's lecture on Isaiah Ch1 v 11. I have marked it for your prayerful perusal when you get your books. I trust it has done me good.

I wonder how you have felt today, your first sabbath in the circuit. I hope you have been a token for good, "the promise of a shower," not only on the people but on their pastor. How much I have thought about you I cannot tell, nay, I should say when you have been absent from my thoughts. I have struggled today determinedly against lowness & loneliness, & have gained a greater victory than ever before. Pray for me, my dearest love, that my over sensitive nature may be strengthened to endure trial in such a manner as becomes the Christian.

Mother & Mackland have just returned, highly delighted with the sermon. They both think it surpasses any previous one they have heard. I will try to get Mr M. to write me a sketch & send it to you. And now good night, another look at your portrait, and then I am off to bed. I have slept in your room ever since you went & have gone to bed much earlier.

*Have not dreamed about you once to my great
disappointment; was pleased to hear you had about me.*

*… Again, good night, or I shall fill my sheet. May
blessings of heaven above & on the earth beneath be
thine, as far as they would prove blessings indeed,
prays thy ever affectionate, Cathy.*

MONDAY NIGHT.

*My dear William will remember I often used to say
I should turn over a new leaf when he was gone, & I
am sure he must have thought it very necessary that I
should, and therefore will be very pleased to hear that
I have really done so. In consequence of going to bed
earlier, I am able to rise earlier and hope soon to reap
mental & physical improvement from it. For several
mornings I have sponged all over in cold water, &
dressed by the light of the lamp. I rest as many hours,
only I get it at the right end of the night.*

*I hope, my love, you will not sit up late. I am sure
it is most injurious. Try to get to bed every night by 10
o'clock. Don't let the pleasures of social intercourse with
the very kind friends with whom you stay induce you to
sit up late. Remember how it unfits you for early rising
& study in the morning, & if you rise late it will impress
them unfavourably as to your mental discipline.*

*… The post boy is just going past singing that
tune you liked so, about my "Master sell me," etc. He*

*frequently does & there is nothing seems to cast such a
shade over my heart. I hope it will soon be forgotten. It
makes me feel such a sense of loneliness now I hear you
sing it no longer.*

*Be sure to send me word how your poor heels are
… If they are no better, I do hope you will get a pair
of new boots. I will be sure to send your galoshes when
your box comes.*

*Good night, my own dear William. I shall
commend you to the love of Jesus & then retire to rest
with renewed determinations to love and serve Him.*

Catherine laid aside her letter. Would she send this off tomorrow or continue her writing for a few days more? There was so much in her heart and she wanted to share it all with William. He was moving around Lincolnshire quite a bit, it seemed, so perhaps it would be better to send one long epistle rather than a few short snippets. It would also save money, and money was always a concern for both of them.

Catherine thought back to her childhood, when writing letters and ensuring their prompt delivery (other than to addresses within walking or riding distance) was so much more haphazard. What had it been now, more than a decade since the introduction of the Penny Post, which allowed a letter to be delivered anywhere in Great Britain, and Ireland, for just a penny? She remembered the excitement of her first postage stamp, that plain black square which, once adhered to the front of an envelope or letter, guaranteed delivery and often by next-day post. 1840, was it? So much had changed for her since those days. Now here she was, writing to her future husband!

*I received yours this morning & felt very thankful you did not omit sending it because of the other being left in your carpet bag. I am delighted to hear that you had such a good day & gave such satisfaction. Let us give all the glory to God and be encouraged. I think you did quite right in saying what you did about salary. It is too little, certainly for the amount of labour required. Perhaps Mr H[ardy] was only probing you. Don't be in a hurry to cheapen your services. What the other young man offered to stay for is no criterion for you. He might be dear at any price. It is evident he did not suit them.*

*If they like you, they will not lose you for the sake of a few pounds. However, try them fair, but as you are so happy amongst them, I would not advise you to leave because of salary. I value your happiness far, far beyond any pecuniary advantages whatever. I am very sorry to hear you will have so little time for study. My dear, you must have it somehow, or you will wear out. They must lessen the labour; no man can sustain incessant toil without any restoring time, either mentally or physically, and you must tell them so after a time.*

*… I retire to rest, loving you as fervently as ever & rejoicing in your prosperity. I am yours in as full a sense as you desire, Kate.*

*I received your kind letter this morning & never since your departure have I more earnestly appealed to the throne of grace in your behalf than I did immediately after reading it. May the Lord save you where you most need salvation. My soul swells with gratitude & praise for his goodness in granting you such an auspicious commencement of your labour & in opening the hearts of so many friends to receive & treat you kindly.*

*… I rejoice in the kindness and attention you receive, but I rejoice with trembling. I know how dangerous it would be to a heart far less susceptible of its influence than yours, while a particle of the carnal mind remained. I feel how dangerous it would be to me, and it fills me with tenderest anxiety for your spiritual safety. You have especial need for watchfulness and much private intercourse with God.*

*My dearest Love, beware how you indulge that dangerous element of character, ambition. Misdirected it will be everlasting ruin to yourself and perhaps to me, alas. Oh, my Love, let nothing earthly excite it, let not self-aggrandizement fire it; fix it on the Throne of the Eternal & let it find the realization of its loftiest aspirations in the promotion of His glory and it shall be consummated with the richest enjoyments & brightest glories of God's own heaven…*

*I am glad you told Mr H[ardy] your desires as to the future. I appreciate your thoughtfulness for my future comfort & respectability fully. May the Lord grant you the desires of your heart as far as they would be beneficial to us both. The letters you sent to Spalding have not been* returned. Be sure to look into it … All yours have reached me safe, 5 in number, for which I sincerely thank you. How often they have been read I cannot tell. I still wear them all in my pocket.

THURSDAY AFTERNOON.

I am going to post this & may as well fill it up, notwithstanding its prodigious length. I lay awake part of the night thinking about you, which has not at all improved my health, but there is nothing to be anxious about. I am not much amiss. There is one thing I should like you to be particular in & that is to answer all my enquiries.

The plan I adopt is this: I take your letter, a bit of paper & a pencil & write down the subjects of all your enquiries & remarks which require observations. If we both adopt this plan, it will obviate the necessity of repeating our enquiries … I am glad to hear your health continues good. When you say it is good in every particular, I take it in its widest sense & therefore think there is no necessity to be minute in my enquiries. If you feel your chest pain, I hope you will consult some experienced surgeon.

And now, my dearest Love, I must again say farewell. I commend the later part of this letter to your deep consideration as an expression of my thoughts & feelings on some subjects on which I feel anxious. But I know there is no necessity for this.

Yours in tenderest affection, Catherine.

# CHAPTER

## 5

*My dearest Love,*

*This is a very easy week to me. My preaching laying in home distances about 4 miles away, but having no home I feel very uncomfortable. I told you in my last that Mr Dalton, where I sleep, wished me to lodge with him and asked me 9/- per week for cleaning boots & everything. Now, I thought I could do the thing cheaper than that, and so thought Mr Shadford. So some of the friends recommended me to one place & another, but all no use. Plenty wanted me as a boarder…*

*So at last I have found a home: a Mr Green, Baker, Red Lion Street. She is a Conference woman… They have a daughter about 6 years. She will be a Reformer & goes to the Reform school … However, I think all will be done to make me comfortable. I find myself food, soap, towels, candles, etc. They find me a snug,*

little bedroom, very small, but still large enough for
a bedroom, but no fireplace in, so would not do for a
study as well. And a nice little parlour that I am to have
when at home, to be mine, and coals for a fire. They
are to cook & wait upon me. I shall meal by myself, &
all for 3/6 per week, which I think very fair on both
sides. It will very near pay their rent, I know. I shall not
be above a 3rd of my time there and then only night
and morning, and not be a deal of trouble. The other
Methodist preachers have lived there.

I do not suppose my living will cost me on an
average over 6/- per week. I told you I would take care
of the ways & means…

And now, my dearest, I shall want my books, papers
& a few clothes. I do not know that there are many of
the latter to send. My expenses will be rather heavy in
that line at the first. I must have a new suit. I have split
the trousers I have on all out, & they are hardly worth
repairing, so that I must put my best on today.

I go away on Friday and do not return till the
Friday after for the watch night. I am going to Weston
tonight. A very rich farmer & land owner has invited
me to tea. I hear he is an intelligent man. I must have
Boots suited to this country, a small leather Bag to
carry about with me and by and by I shall want a
mackintosh coat & mackintosh gaiters to come right
up my legs. You will send some more shirts, if there are
any worth sending. I wish I had the Table and lamp
down here, but never mind. I will write & ask Mr
Panther, if he will have the lamp. The Table we may
want yet.

*I was reckoning up the other day, as I came from
Surfleet, that it would take about £60 pounds to
furnish a little house nicely; that is two bedrooms, a
kitchen & parlour, somewhat after this fashion:*

*Best Bedroom –*

| | |
|---|---:|
| *Bedstead (Mahogany Arabian)* | *4. 10. 0* |
| *Bed, Pillows & Bolster (we must beg)* | |
| *Bedding (perhaps we can beg)* | |
| *Wash stand & fittings* | *3. 0. 0* |
| *Carpet* | *1. 10. 0* |
| *Drawers* | *2. 10. 0* |
| *Dressing Table* | *1. 0. 0* |
| *Curtains for windows & bed (Small curtains for* | |
| *arabian bedstead)* | *1. 10. 0* |
| *(?) Glass* | *10. 0* |
| *4 Chairs* | *12. 0* |
| *Fender, fire irons, etc.* | *10. 0* |
| *Bed steps (Convenience)* | *1. 0. 0* |
| | *16. 12. 0* |

*The next Bedroom perhaps have a chest of Drawers,*   *6. 0. 0*
*would furnish very snug, so that it would do for a friend.*

| | |
|---|---:|
| *Best Bedroom* | *16. 12. 0* |
| *My study: some shelves & a chair* | *10. 0* |
| *Bedroom* | *6. 0. 0* |
| *Then the parlour:* | |
| *6 Mahogany, hair-seated chairs* | *4. 10. 0* |
| *Easy chair for you* | *1. 10. 0* |
| *Carpet* | *2. 10. 0* |
| *Glass* | *2. 10. 0* |
| *Table* | *2. 10. 0* |
| *Curtains for winter* | *1. 0. 0* |

*for summer (you have or you can beg them)*

| | |
|---|---|
| *Couch* | *2. 10. 0* |
| *Piano (you have)* | |
| *Fender, fire irons, etc.* | *15. 0* |
| *China, Glass, etc., Crockery, etc.* | *2. 0. 0* |
| *Knives, Forks, etc.* | *10. 0* |
| *Table Linen, perhaps secondhand* | *10. 0* |
| *Chiffonier we could do without.* | |
| *Kitchen perhaps would cost not more than:* | *5. 0. 0* |
| | *48. 17. 0* |

*To make all very complete it would take at least £11 or £12 more. I do not know whether I am justified by my circumstances to be so sanguine as to hope to marry in a 12 month, but time will prove it. I will write you again before you must contrive to get my things off. I do not know how you will do it. Perhaps your dear Father can tell. I have a horrid pen & scarce a drop of ink You must send me some out of that Bottle, if you can & if you please.*

Catherine's heart pounded as she read William's intense letter, unusually lengthy. He was obviously determined on marrying as soon as possible. Why else would he have been thinking about furnishing their new home?

Or had she been a bit pushy on the subject? Was he merely responding to what he thought were her expectations? Oh how she wished she hadn't even mentioned that they had hoped she would be married this coming January, but the idea of getting married on her birthday was so intriguing and she so wanted to be with him! William sometimes sounded so lonely, up there in Lincolnshire, travelling from place to place, catching chills, eating food that was probably far too rich – no wonder he was constantly complaining of feeling ill and sick to his stomach.

She was delighted that he finally had the prospect of a little place of his own but how much better it would be if it were THEIR home. How homely and comfortable she would make it for him, a real haven after his travels and stays in a series of strange accommodations, no matter how comfortable and hospitable his hosts.

Catherine looked at William's list of furnishings. Her brother John was in America – perhaps he could bring back an exciting gift for them.[1] She picked up her pen and continued writing where she had left off under "Friday afternoon":

> Your calculations about furnishing exactly meet my views. I like your notions about having things good & comfortable at first; there is nothing like it. We shall be able to pay the things you mention & also a bedstead for the 2nd room. I intend writing to my Brother to ask him to bring me a complete set of knives & forks, first rate ones … for a present, as he will doubtless bring me something, and perhaps might choose something which would cost him more & not be so useful.
>
> Mention in your next what clothes you want. I am glad you intend getting a new suit. I am sure you need them … I wish you had left an order for them in London. I think you would have done better.
>
> I hope you will have a good season at the watch night. I will meet you at the solemn hour, all well. Let us breathe each other's name with the last breath of

the old year; we owe it much. Let us part with it as an old friend. It has been a friend whose kindness we have sadly slighted & whose precious gifts we have often much abused. Let us bid it adieu with feelings befitting such solemn reflections & welcome our new friend with fixed determinations to make the most of its acquaintance.

We are a little busy preparing for Xmas. We shall dine off Hare. Send me word where you spend the day and how.

I am getting on with my short hand; I hope you are. Consider, my dear, what a pity it would be to lose all you have gained & thus throw away all the time you have spent in acquiring it. I hope you will soon begin to write sermons in it. In the course of your life it will save months of precious time, besides labour. I intend to write you some choice bits, extracts, etc. in short hand & send you them. Some I collected long since & some I shall keep collecting & I suppose you will have no objection to a little original sometimes, provided it be short.

And now, wishing you a happy Christmas in the fullest, best sense, and a New Year crowned with the loving kindness of the Lord.

I remain, my dearest William, affectionately yours, Kate.

Catherine Mumford was fastidious. She thought things through, and prayed intently about even the smallest matters in her life. She liked things done properly. That she had a theologian's mind was certain, in that her thinking was naturally collated in "main thoughts" and subsections. In the early days, before ever she was able to stand on a platform and preach, she would share her sermon "sketches" and outlines with William Booth, and he would gratefully receive from her superior biblical and theological knowledge.

Both Mr Booth and Miss Mumford liked order. William's correspondence, in which he outlined not just what they would need for their joint future home but also the potential cost, might have been a touch unromantic for some young lovers, but Catherine appears to have found it endearing

Their "list making" however, did not just extend to household management.

WEDNESDAY 9TH JUNE 1852
11 PRINCES ROW
WALWORTH ROAD

*My own dear Catherine,*
   *… Our meetings must & shall be salvation meetings. We will have a rule of conversation and action, somewhat after the following fashion.*
*1st Any general information to impart. Anything occurred since we last met. Inquiries into health etc.*
*2 What progress made in reading, shorthand, music etc.; exchange any information on the above subjects that may be required.*
*3 Inquire closely into our religious experience and give each other counsel and advice as may be needed afterwards.*
*4 Each pray earnestly that our meeting may be made a means of grace and for general prosperity.*

*5 Any desultory conversation and retire never later than ¼ after 10.*

*What think you? I have no doubt you will be perfectly willing and say that it is just what you have wanted all along but that I have stood in the way.*

*… And now, Catherine, shall we not solemnly give ourselves to God, to do his will and accomplish his purposes. Oh what happiness to know that we are working in sweet union with his providence and gracious dispositions toward us and toward the world. I tell you that nothing can afford me lasting and satisfactory and complete enjoyment but the work of winning souls, and how little I am doing therein just now, perchance account for my lameness. May God in mercy open a way and stir me up to duty & activity.*

*I trust that we shall yet be one in him as he and his Father are one. So may we be perfectly one in him, seeking in delightful harmony to fulfil all his commands and render perfect obedience to the letter and the Spirit of the Law.*

*… With an assurance of the high respect I entertain for you,*

> *I remain, affectionately yours,*
> *William.*

Just how Miss Mumford responded to her beloved's list of instructions for their meetings so soon after their engagement, when most young lovers are in the first flush of love, is not recorded. However, as from the very start of their relationship William Booth and Catherine Mumford believed that they must honour God in all things, even in their courting, it's likely the invitation to conduct their "meetings" in such an ordered manner was not entirely abhorrent to her.

Whether the couple kept rigidly to the list of requirements is also unknown. Certainly after months and months apart it's likely that Step 1, where they had pledged first to share *"Any general information ... to Anything occurred since they last met. Inquiries into health etc."* might have been somewhat forgotten in the sheer bliss of being together.

But William devised lists to keep him in line not just in life, but also regarding his spiritual well-being. A faded and worn document found in his papers after his death, more than sixty years after it was penned, was evidence of his utter determination that his whole life would be for God. It was written during his first year in London, when he was struggling with a heavy six-day-a-week workload at the hated Walworth Pawnbrokers, squeezing his street and church ministry into an already packed existence and desperately attempting to balance his life.

DECEMBER 6 1849

*RESOLUTIONS*

*I do promise – My God Helping –*

*1st. That I will rise every morning sufficiently early (say 20 minutes before seven o'clock) to wash, dress, and have a few minutes, not less than 5, in private prayer.*

*2ndly. That I will as much as possible avoid all that babbling and idle talking in which I have lately so sinfully indulged.*

3rd. That I will endeavour in my conduct and deportment before the world and my fellow servants especially to conduct myself as a humble, meek, and zealous follower of the bleeding Lamb, and by serious conversation and warning endeavour to lead them to think of their immortal souls.

4thly. That I will not read less than 4 chapters in God's word every day.

5thly. That I will strive to live closer to God, and to seek after holiness of heart, and leave providential events with God.

6thly. That I will read this over every day or at least twice a week.

God help me, enable me to cultivate a spirit of self denial and to yield myself a prisoner of love to the Redeemer of the world.

Amen and Amen.

WILLIAM BOOTH

I feel my own weakness and without God's help I shall not keep these resolutions a day. The Lord have mercy upon my guilty soul.

I claim the Blood.

Yes, oh Yes.

Jesus died for me.[2]

High expectations for a young man, but William's intention was sincere. Since his conversion he had already lived through a tempestuous spiritual time, having been knocked back in his ambitions and forced to work for at least two pawnbroking taskmasters, and having survived in a lonely, alien city.

His road to "salvation" had also not been entirely without struggle. William struggled with a particular "sin" which he felt prevented him from being completely "saved". As he was growing into adulthood back in Nottingham, he had got involved in a trading transaction with some friends and had come out of it with quite a profit, all the while giving the impression that he was being terribly friendly and generous. This "evil", as he described it, hung heavy on his heart, and when he became converted at the age of fifteen he was determined to make things right. He sought out the boy whom he had deceived most and handed over the pencil case that he had acquired through the deal and which was the subject of his guilt and remorse. From that moment he became determined to turn his back on the "godless world".[3]

By Christmas 1852 William's struggles seemed to be behind him. He was settling into life as an itinerant preacher in Lincolnshire, feeling quite pleased with himself and his developing Christian ministry.

SPALDING.
TUESDAY DEC. 21 '52

*My dearest Love,*

*… The meeting went off to middling last night. I do not think I have much to fear from a comparison with the Wisbech man. He is a little man, with a sharp, shrill*

voice; rather too light and trifling. They called mine the speech of the night, and a wretched thing it was, I know. I do not care what you say about me not being the best judge, I know it was a wretched, miserable thing. I put in 3 anecdotes & they went pretty well, or else I was shut up fair. I have to preach every day this week, Saturday included, & on Sunday 3 times. Next Sabbath week, as I intimated in my last, I go to Boston. I hear the Reformers are getting on middling. They are going to build a Chapel, a small one, I expect … However, I understand all is not smooth over there.

I shall endeavour, my dearest, to manage money matters some way without troubling you. My washing is to be done for 12/- per quarter, to average 1 Shirt, 4 White, 4 Collars, 2 or 3 fronts, 2 pocket & Hose, Drawers & Flannel Shirt occasionally – that is every fortnight. Cheap, is it not? The woman's own price! She is a widow… She does them very well.

… I will send you word how & when I use the sketch you sent me. It is a subject I intend preaching on…

… I think the box you have found & the green box will hold all my things. I shall not want only a few clothes, as I must buy me another Sunday suit as soon as I can obtain some money. My present are real shabby.

I want you to mark any mistakes in spelling in my letters, and put them down: how spelt & how ought to be in the next you write, and I wish you to put all your questions of a row, 1st, 2nd, 3rd. I will answer them in that way, as for instance:

*1. Have you seen Mr Rabbits since I left?*

*2. Have you found Mr Thomas' Bible class?*

*3. Have you learned any more tunes on the Pianoforte and if so, how many?*

*4. Did you hear Mr Grosjean? Did you like him? Was the chapel full?*

*5. Have you called at that Dyers in Commerce Place to ask for the book I lent to Mr Downs: "The Memoirs of John Smith"? There are two old books I borrowed. One is an old thing by Brown; I think it is in the bottom cupboard, and the other is the American Methodist Hymn Book. Will you put them aside and I will tell you how to get them home?*

*Send full particulars in your next concerning your health.*

*… My kind love to your Mother. Tell her I respect her highly & will forward my confession in a day or two, when I can find time to sum up the height, & depth, & length, & breadth of my delinquencies. The watch night I expect to spend at Spalding, the Covenant Service & Sacrament at Boston.*

*… I think about you and long for an hour's embrace. Oh, just to sit & talk things over for a little time, but Heaven knows best. Let us love one another & love God & all will be well.*

*… Yours in enduring affection and love, with many prayers, my dear Katy, William.*

William was determined to make his Kate a Christmas gift. But what to present to her, at this distance, and with only a few pennies to spare from his meagre allowance? Although the people he met and mingled with in Lincolnshire were generous with their hospitality and friendship, his stipend left little for luxuries.

He was aware that the best gift would be the settling of a date for their marriage, but 17 January – a mere three weeks hence – was certainly not attainable. Apart from anything else, he had only just arrived in Lincolnshire and had really to concentrate on his ministry. To head back to London so soon, and to make arrangements for his new bride here, where he didn't even have his own home, would be impossible. He prayed Kate wouldn't be too disappointed.

He longed to send her a parcel full of his love. Her last letter was filled with her pain, the pain of separation, the worry she had that he would misinterpret her darling "teachings" as bossiness.

Then his eyes lighted on her words. He raised his hand to his face and rubbed his eyes. Then, in a flash of inspiration, he had the answer.

"I am getting on with my short hand; I hope you are."

He pulled out his shorthand primer, grabbed a piece of paper, picked up the pen and began to write – in shorthand. He imagined her surprise when the envelope was opened. He imagined her laughing out loud with the pure delight of the effort he had put into this one little note.

SPALDING,
FRIDAY DECEMBER 24, 1852

*My dearest Love,*

*I write you a short note in shorthand, hoping that you will be able to read it. It will be practice for me. I have commenced writing a letter this morning. I intend writing a page or two every day until perfect. I am studying in my own apartments, a pleasant fire, a comfortable room, and a very pleasant person as my*

> *hostess. My dearest, I wish you the compliments of the*
> *season: a happy Christmas and a happy New Year.*

Why the fascination with shorthand? It seems an odd preoccupation for two people with hearts for God and each other and not much else. But Catherine Mumford, whose idea it originally was for the young couple to learn the system, was a woman of her time. Shorthand was all the rage in the mid-nineteenth century!

For centuries there had been systems of writing to help speed up communication. Writers such as Isaac Newton and Samuel Pepys had employed types of shorthand writing in their day and Charles Dickens had started out as a court reporter using something called "*brachygraphy*". In 1837 Sir Isaac Pitman had launched his shorthand system, which used a series of symbols based on phonetics and was destined to become the most commonly used shorthand system and eventually a staple discipline in the business world. But in 1852 and indeed for another twenty years or more it was not just the preserve of secretaries and reporters but was being promoted as a means of general communication.

That Catherine should become interested in this innovation, which could cut down substantially on time and effort when writing, is not entirely peculiar. She had a practical personality and would have been intrigued by this new way of thinking. Pitman himself associated his shorthand with "the dawn of *religious freedom*" and "the dawn of *political freedom*" because his system provided the facility to produce verbatim reports and transcriptions, particularly from Parliament. It prevented reporters from summarizing debates, which could involve favouritism. Indeed, among the early adopters of shorthand were many who were considered radicals – "spirit-rappers, teetotallers, vegetarians, pacifists, anti-vivisectionists, anti-tobacconists".[4]

Catherine was determined to master the system and she encouraged William Booth to do likewise. Imagine her delight when, a day or two after Christmas 1852, she received that short note, written entirely in shorthand!

*My dearest William,*

*As I did not feel in writing tune either yesterday or on Xmas day, I will this evening give you a sketch of our Christmas enjoyments. Father dined at home & tho' our number was so small we enjoyed ourselves very well.*

*Your representative on the wall seemed to look down on our sensual gratification with awful gravity, manifesting an indifference to the good things of this life, not at all characteristic of the original. I thought about you very, very much through the day. I could not but contrast my feelings with those of last year. Then my anxieties & affections were centered in objects whose love & care I have experienced through many changing years. Then I knew no love but that of a child, a sister, a friend, and I thought that love deep, sincere, fervent; perhaps it was; nay, I know it was.*

*But since then a stranger, unknown, unseen, till within the last short year, has strangely drawn around himself the finest tendrils of my heart & awakened a new absorbing affection which seems, as it were, to*

eclipse what I before deemed the intensity of love. Then
my anxieties were almost confined to home; now this
same stranger like a magnet draws them after him in
all his wanderings, so that they are seldom at home.
What a change in one short year! Can you solve the
mystery? Can you find the reason?

But I am forgetting to detail the day's pleasures,
etc. After dinner we all went on a walk, talked about
you, my dear brother, the changes which have taken
place in a few years, the changes which probably will
take place in a few more, etc. My dear father seemed
kinder and more comfortable than usual; he is still a
teetotaller & is abstaining altogether from the pipe;
there is a change for the better in many respects. Don't
forget him, my love, at a throne of grace. Help me &
my dear mother to pray for him … Oh, for a Christ-
like sympathy for souls, such as I used to feel when
I have sat up half the night to plead for them. My
dearest love, this is the secret of success, the weapon
before which the very strongholds of hell must give way.
Oh, let us try to get it again; let us make up our minds
to win souls, whatever else we leave undone.

But to return again, we spent a very pleasant
evening together. I lay on the sofa, working a little
watch pocket for the use of that stranger I have been
speaking of, which I hope he will use for my sake, even
tho' he may be provided with one already. I hope he
will not consider it murdered time. It did not take me
long. My dear mother & myself enjoyed a good season
in prayer & then retired to rest. Yesterday we heard
Mr T[homas] in the morn'g; liked him much. School

*in the afternoon; got on well; children gave signs of
serious interest. The evening spent alone, thinking about
& praying for your preaching, etc. Today have been
practising music, short hand, reading, working, etc.*

*Good night! I am very tired, or I would not send
such scrawl. I long for a letter to hear you have enjoyed
yourself and all particulars.*

Christmas 1852 would have been a quiet affair in the Mumford household in Brixton, and most likely an even quieter one for William in Lincolnshire.

The focus would, if anything, have been entirely religious. William had preaching duties over that weekend in Weston Hills, so was on the road and staying with various hosts. Although Father Mumford was still, much to Catherine's obvious anguish, in a state of indecision when it came to spiritual matters, his wife and daughter would have ensured that the birth of Christ did not go unmarked, although, in line with the times, this was likely to be done quietly and might not even have involved a church service on 25 December. There had been so much religious controversy over the centuries, with Puritans and others eschewing the frivolities of celebrating Christmas, that by 1852 Christmas was only just beginning to re-emerge as an important religious festival worth marking with the singing of traditional and new "carols" for the season.

By 1852 Christmas was generally accepted as a day off work – the only "public holiday" enjoyed at the time. The wealthier among the population were already beginning to exchange cards with special greetings – the first Christmas cards were illustrated by John Callcott Horsley in London in 1843. Thomas Smith had invented the Christmas cracker in 1847 and a new custom, of erecting and decorating a fir tree for the Christmas period, had been popularized by Queen Victoria and her German consort, Prince Albert, in whose homeland the tradition had begun. Certainly since 1848, when the *Illustrated London News* had published a line drawing of the British royal family with their Christmas tree at Windsor Castle, the idea of the festive fir had been catching on.[5]

In most homes, however, the Christmas trimmings would still have been few and far between and, as the Mumford home lurched from one financial crisis to another, with Father's uncertain income, there would probably have been few, if any, seasonal luxuries.

Catherine read widely, but her choice of literature as a child tended towards the classical and later almost predominantly the religious. Just nine years earlier a new book had been published, which was very proving very popular: *A Christmas Carol* by one Charles Dickens was reviving a "feel-good" Christmas spirit, based on merriment, compassion, and family values, but would Catherine have read it? It's likely that her thoughts were far more spiritual as she approached her Christmas.

*I should like to hear you breathe out your determination & desire that it may before the Throne to night, but as that cannot be join me on Xmas day (at any hour you will name) in asking for peace so to live.*

*Good night, my Love. Yours in the tenderest of bonds, Cathy.*

Catherine heard the clock downstairs strike the o'clock. Midnight. The start of a brand new year – 1853!

It was amazing to her that in such a short time one person should become so precious, almost the centre of her universe! How different were her emotions from the same time last year. She remembered how, twelve months exactly to the day, she had viewed the years ahead as if peering into a chasm. Feeling, as always, less than healthy with no beau, no prospect of marriage, nothing but a life at home looking after ageing parents.

Catherine shook herself at such evil thoughts … why should she not expect to look after her parents as they deteriorated? That was the way of life, the duty of children. But at least now she would not do it alone. Already William had shown such interest, compassion, and even love for her parents. Yes, now she would not have to bear the burden alone and, in addition, there was the dream of her own family.

William spoke in his letters of love and companionship, and now they were also beginning to discuss future children and how they might be raised. Catherine had very strong views on this; she hoped William would not be deterred by her opinions. However, judging from his recent comments following a visit to the friendly but chaotic Green family, where obviously even a devout Methodist couple were unable to control their offspring, William and she were of like mind on the subject of parenting, which was a great relief.

What was it he had written? She reached into her pocket for his letter.

*My dearest, one of the greatest troubles of my life is the awful manner in which children are dragged up in so many houses where I go. It is really fearful. Oh, if I had*

*not the most implicit confidence in your skill & loving*
*heart, I should really fear my hopes being realised in*
*that respect.*

She was so pleased that he had raised the subject. She felt so
vehemently that parents needed to guide and even rule their children
that William had to be in accord with this thinking. If they were to be
blessed with children the family would have to be well regulated and
the upbringing shared.

She sighed. She really must go to bed but there were so many
thoughts in her head. She was racing ahead of herself. It looked
unlikely that she and William would be married soon. But at least
now she had marriage, and a life with a man she loved, in the future,
whenever the Lord deemed good for them.

SATURDAY JANUARY 1ST 1853
20 MINUTES PAST 12 O'CLOCK

*A happy New Year to you, my dearest William, and*
*abundance of peace & joy.*

*I am all alone, my dear Mother having gone to*
*bed very unwell. I have just risen from my knees, &*
*as my first act (with the exception of impressing a*
*kiss of purest affection on the lineaments of your dear*
*features) I take my pen to salute you at this early*
*hour of this new year's morn'g. A cold unsatisfactory*
*mode of salutation, but one which I am sure (as*
*time and circumstances will allow no other) will be*
*pleasing to you.*

*If I could convey my feelings to paper, I would, but my heart is too full for utterance. The Lord only knows & can fully understand the indefinable emotions of my soul tonight. Oh, that I could see you & tell you all my heart. But if you were here I could not find language, I could only throw myself into your arms & sob out the agitated feelings of my soul. My whole frame is affected by their pungency. Nor is it mere sentimentalism. I seem, as it were, at this solemn moment to be poised on the ridge of time's highest billow, from whence I can see all the past & the possible future at a glance, and the mingled emotions of sorrow, gratitude, hope and fear, excited by the scene, almost overwhelm me. My spirit quails before the storms which seem to lower in the distance. If the Lord spares me, I have some bitter cups to drain. Death, which has hitherto spared all whom I best love, will one day visit us & I must then feel for the first time the bitter pangs of bereavement. Sorrow entwines itself even into the sunniest spots which the future presents; the purest & holiest earthly joys I ever hope to realize are linked with pain & grief. What a complicated thing is human life; how varied its phases, how short its enjoyments & trials. But, Oh, how important, how enduring its results.*

*The Lord has blessed me tonight. I trust he has blessed you. I have been committing you and all I love solemnly to his keeping & disposal, and when his will is painful I will expect grace to meet & strength to endure the stroke with patience & resignation, even according to his gracious promise, "as thy day, thy strength shall be."*

*And you, my own dear Love, will help me to bear the sorrows of life, will you not? And endeavour to brighten, by your ever watchful love, every dark dispensation, & increase the brightness of every hour of sunshine, & be it mine to share your cares & elevate & purify your joys. My soul rejoices to have one to repose in, one to love, & one who I trust will fully understand me & enter into my views & feelings, & sympathize in all my joys & sorrows, some of which have hitherto been peculiarly my own.*

*I must now retire, though I feel no desire to sleep… May the Lord save you body & soul, prays yours; till weeks & months & years with me, shall cease to roll.*

# CHAPTER

# 6

William Booth remained in Lincolnshire from November 1852 to February 1854 and in that time the couple saw each other only on about three occasions when William visited London.

For William this was a period of spiritual and personal development. At last, he had a busy ministry of preaching and teaching across a wide region. Catherine meanwhile supported her intended from afar, sharing not just her thoughts but also her strong opinions on many matters, physical, moral, social, and spiritual.

For Catherine, it was vital that William Booth get things straight on various issues, and that meant being in line with *her* views.[1]

As a child she had lived in an adult world with little contact with her peers, and been exposed to adult subjects – the whys and wherefores of the Temperance Movement, missions to Africa, and the involvement of Roman Catholics in politics (her father had a great interest in politics in the early years).[2] Catherine had a lifelong scepticism about the Church of Rome and its people and also developed a great compassion for animals, arising from an incident in her childhood that involved her beloved dog, a retriever called Waterford, who was an "inseparable companion"[3] for the rather lonely little girl.

While visiting her father at work one day, at a time when he was actually in employment, Catherine left Waterford outside. On entering the building, she stumbled and fell and her pet, probably running to his mistress's aid, crashed through a plate-glass window. Mr Mumford was so angry that the dog had damaged the property that he had the animal destroyed.[4] This was devastating for the child, and the result was a lifelong interest in animals and their suffering.

Growing into adulthood served only to strengthen her belief that animals were God's creatures, to be cherished and not abused. In later years the Booth household would be full of pets of all descriptions but even early on she was outspoken on animal welfare as on other matters. When she witnessed sheep being mistreated as they were herded through the streets of London en route to market, she shared her displeasure with the person closest to her.

JUNE 2 1853 WEDNESDAY EVEN'G.

*My own dear Love, I have spent the day well, feel happy, and what can I do better than talk to you a bit. It is astonishing how much more I can accomplish now I feel happier. If you had always written me such letters as the one I received this morn'g, what hours of gloom & unprofitable, soul chilling, Love cooling reasoning it would have saved me. But you did not used to feel so deeply & therefore you did not write so tenderly ...*

*I do indeed wish I could join you in your lovely walks amongst the blooming trees, green fields, & frisking lambs, pretty creatures. I sometimes see some in the Brixton road, but the sight makes my heart ache*

*& sometimes my eyes fill with tears. Poor innocents!
Instead of frisking in the joyousness of their young
being, they are being driven by rude, inhuman boys &
men with great thick sticks, and often so lame they can
scarce walk. Such sights remind me most forcibly of
the passage "driven as a lamb to the slaughter." What
more striking emblem of innocence & meekness under
suffering could the Prophet have selected? You will
think I am unaltered in my peculiar feelings towards
the brute creation, & so I am (except I feel more
deeply). I would rather stay at home than endure what
I often do in going a walk ... Surely, God must regard
these wrongs inflicted in such profusion on beings
which have not the power even to complain! Oh, if ever
I write for the press, I will not forget to plead the cause
of God's dumb creation.*

Was it a coincidence that, many years later, when William Booth
was intent on improving the lot of starving and homeless men
who could barely make a living to support their families, he would
couch his campaign in animal terms? In his book *In Darkest
England and The Way Out*, published in 1890, William pointed
out that London cab horses were treated better than people:

> *When in the streets of London a Cab Horse, weary
> or careless or stupid, trips and falls and lies stretched
> out in the midst of the traffic, there is no question of
> debating how he came to stumble before we try to get
> him on his legs again ... Every Cab Horse in London
> has three things; a shelter the night, food for its*

*stomach, and work allotted to it by which it can earn its corn.*

*These are the two points of the Cab Horse's Charter. When he is down he is helped up, and while he lives he has food, shelter and work. That, although a humble standard, is at present absolutely unattainable by millions – literally by millions – of our fellow-men and women in this country. Can the Cab Horse Charter be gained for human beings? I answer yes.[5]*

But all that, the development of William Booth's keen social sense and longing to improve not just the spiritual but also the physical lot of those around him, lay far in the future. For now, he was in Lincolnshire, developing his sense of vocation but struggling at times to feel confident in his Christian ministry, missing his Catherine and longing for a letter.

RED LION STREET, SPALDING.
MONDAY 10 JAN'Y '53

*My own dear, darling Kate,*

*I feel so lonely just now. You cannot imagine how much I would give for a kiss off those dear lips and an hour's chat, and ever so many other things that I could name only that it would be such a waste of time and paper because all is so impossible …*

*I was at Boston on Monday night and being as I had not the opportunity of speaking with Miss Elsey the last time I was there, I thought I would seize ½ an hour and call, and accordingly arriving in Boston at ½ after 6 I went to our meeting, spoke first and then left.*

The train by which I was returning to Spalding, having a day ticket, started at 10. I called on Mr Coulson for your sake, my dearest. Miss Elsey was out, but I asked myself in, being cold, and she came in. I talked to Mr Coulson about matters … However, I had a good look at Miss Elsey and I do not think much of her. At all events she did not manifest much affection for you by her kindness to me. So I left & for my part closed the acquaintance. They spoke very contemptibly of the Reformers in Boston …

However, my Katy, we have nothing to do with other folk; they can do as they please. You & I will be reformers and we'll stick to it & stick together, &, if the Lord's will, the sooner we get made into one, in my humble opinion, the better. If your health continues good, I have been thinking there would be no harm in your coming down to see Mrs Congreve of Holbeach. You would find them wonderfully kind, but I should not like you to go to Boston at all. You might come to Wisbech by the Eastern Counties Line, and that is 14 miles from Holbeach. I could meet you on the Saturday, that I preach at Holbeach on the Sunday, at Wisbech with a gig and bring you to Holbeach, and you could hear me preach three or four sermons and we could have a good bit of each other's company. I do not know after all whether this would look well, you know best. It would get out in the circuit. Your Mother is judicious; hear what she says and send me word. I have no doubt my friends would be glad to see you and would invite you to Spalding. Mrs Shadford gives me a great deal of advice on the subject of marriage. She is a *great favourite with me; a very nice looking lady. She is about 30, I should think, perhaps not so old. Was paralised 3 years ago; has no family.*

*It is well known in the circuit that I am engaged, & to a great many your name. But not to any person in Boston have I said anything & I do not wish to.*

*My dearest love, never did I love you more dearly, never with a calmer and more enduring affection, and never did I more earnestly desire its consummation. I do trust that this parting will not endure long. I have never looked upon any other female form to put into comparison with that I kissed and clasped that dark wintry morn'g when we parted. The lock of hair serves to call you up to my eye & heart even better than your portrait, and I looked upon it with a yearning for she who once wore it yesterday evening.*

*I have been poring over the plan today, getting it ready for the committee on Friday. I do hope you are doing something at the piano; you must not, you will not, neglect that for my sake. Your letters, their writing, diction and construction generally have given me great pleasure; and the remarks you made on woman's mission & its miscomprehension … I should much like my friends down here to know you, and I should much like you to know them.*

*… I have not as yet heard from either Mr Rabbits or Mr Panther, altho' I have wrote them. I can send your mama the money I owe, if wished particularly. What do you say? I think of writing to ask Mr P. to let the £1.0.0. I owe him be until another quarter and then I shall be in a comfortable position.*

> *Praying for every blessing on you, my darling,*
> *with my love to your Mother & Father & Mr*
> *M[ackland], and trusting that we shall speedily meet*
> *to live and love together.*
>
> > *I remain, my own dearest love,*
> > *Yours for ever,*
> > *William Booth.*
> > *For my dearest Love.*

Why is it, Catherine thought, that any young man who comes into a church fellowship immediately becomes the subject of attention not just from the young women around, but also from the older matrons who feel it's their duty to ensure he quickly marries?

Why would William not announce it widely abroad that he is engaged to be married – to one Miss Catherine Mumford of Brixton, London? Really, that would stop all the unwanted attention!

Catherine was surprised to find she was so jealous and, no matter how she castigated herself, she could not shake off the emotion. Quickly come the day when she and William could be wed!

WEDNESDAY EVENING.

> *I was very sorry, my love, to hear yesterday morning*
> *of your failure at Spalding on Sunday, tho' I am*
> *disposed to question your ability to judge in the matter.*
> *At least you should not despair of having done good*
> *because you did not see any. I feel sure there is some*
> *one or more persons in the Spalding congregation*

*[of] whose criticisms you feel afraid, & while this is
the case you will never have liberty before them. You
must, my dear, try to rise above all fear of man &
desire for his admiration. I hope the difficulties you
seem to anticipate will not prove so formidable as to
prevent your staying the time you mentioned in your
last. You must not expect to please everybody; there are
sure to be some dissatisfied & restless spirits in every
circuit, whom nothing can bring within the radium of
harmonious feeling…*

*I am glad you find Mrs Shadford such a nice lady.
I don't know whether she will think you any more
fortunate than the previous preachers of the circuit in
your choice of a companion, but this I know, that I feel
every day more deeply the importance of the position
before me and my own unfitness to sustain it.*

*I do want to be an example of all that is lovely & of
good report, & capable in head, & heart of commending
the religion of Jesus to all with whom I come in contact.
I am trying to live for the future. Pray for me, that I may
be prepared for the proper performance of every duty
attaching to my future relationships.*

William climbed the stairs, opened the door to his to room, and lay down on the bed. His stomach was growling and his head was aching. His hosts were grand people, but why did they have to speak so fast, and so loud? The food was good, but there was so much of it, and so rich. He really should have been more insistent on not having that second helping of beef and potatoes.

If only Catherine were here. She would help him, guide him right. She was so interested in every aspect of his being, from his diet to his attire. Across the room was the old trunk, received lately from London with all his books, some extra clothes and essentials, his old trousers, newly mended by Mother Mumford and all packed lovingly by his darling Katy. What a joy it had been to find a lock of her hair, cut from her own head with her exquisite little sewing scissors, tucked away safely in a little dressing case where he also found his old razors, suitably sharpened by Mr Mumford. Oh how that little dark curl had made his heart weaken with love.

He sat back down on the bed and reached down to untie his bootlaces. What could he do to encourage Catherine? His letters always seemed to be full of his own woes, his little illnesses, his busy and taxing schedule. As she was so far from him, he desired Catherine to know how much he longed for her. She seemed so insecure. Perhaps all his chatter about Mrs Shadford and the other attention that he sometimes got from girls and women, although only heaven knew why, wasn't helping matters. He must determine, as Catherine desired, to ensure that more people knew that he was "betrothed".

RED LION STREET
SPALDING
SATURDAY JAN'Y 15 '53

*My dearest, dearest Love,*

*Yours came safe to hand yesterday morn'g and gave me great pleasure. I am sure you will not allow the non-reception of a letter on the fixed day to trouble you again. When you hear me so repeatedly say that posts being sometimes far distant and business very*

*pressing etc., etc. You shall have two letters per week &
generally on a Tuesday & Saturday, but I cannot say
that the day will never vary… .*

*I was at the plan making committee yesterday;
not very first rate pleased with it. I was in the chair.
One thing in which they would not let me have my
own way (and you know that it is not the way to
please me), they would not let me go to Boston twice
during the next quarter. I believe that the interests of
the circuit demanded it; they, the majority, thought
different. I had to yield. In order to meet the wishes
of the people I have had to plan myself, as you will
perceive when you get the plan, 3 times nearly every
Sabbath and 4 times in the week, and I shall be four
weeks away from home & one week at home; that is, to
sleep at home. Poorish work to get married on, is it not,
my darling?*

*… If I had a wife & a pony I should be all
right. They are both very important things, and it
is supposing you can get them, which I very much
question my ability to get either just now. But it is
after all easier to get them, etc., than keep them when
they are got. I do not believe there is a harder circuit
than this in the Connexion, and I do not believe there
is another in which matters would be more to my
taste than this. You might soon raise a splendid class,
my darling. And you would have the best class in the
Sunday School and be a Benevolent visitor, and you
would have plenty of company when I was out. You
would be always out to tea & supper etc., etc., and
then the Holbeach Friends would be glad to see you*

when I was that side of the circuit. But I speak of you as first rate, and I have made Mr Shadford believe that you really are a first-rater by telling he & Mrs S. that you are on the Bazaar Committee, Exeter Hall, and about that letter to the Wesleyan Times, and that great meeting.

Of course you did not mean it to be a secret when you told it me, and he declared then that you was a deal older than me, and I declared that you were not, and so he has put you up very high. I mean to hint, when I have a favourable opportunity, that Mrs Congreve has invited you & I shall hear what he says, & he is, I consider, very judicious … You will really love some of the people. There is a liberalness about them that you will notice at first. Even the best educated say things rather plainer than the Londoner, and the people generally are much happier. They laugh & joke much more, and so do I. I know that will not please you. It does not please me, but it does me good to "'fess" as Topsy says, especially to you. You will always hear me, won't you my darling?

Bless you! I wish you a many happy returns of the day. Are you 24 or 23? Send me word. I told Mr Shadford that you were not older than myself, but I think you are 3 months. My time is gone; it is tea and post time and I want you to have it Monday morn'g. I have to pack up, for a week's tramp, my bag; a very respectable black leather one it is. I walk 4 miles in the morn'g when they meet me and take me 6 further to Donnington.

Be assured, my dearest, of my love … Expect another letter on Wednesday or Saturday. Write me

*one direct to me as Mr Booth, Wesleyan Minister, 218*
*Red Lion Street, Spalding.*

*My love to your dear Mama, Papa, & Mr*
*M[ackland].*

*And believe me your own dear, William.*

*For my own precious Katy.*

When William Booth arrived in Lincolnshire, it was to a Methodist circuit that had largely been persuaded for the Reform Movement. But, as he travelled around the county, he became aware that some were now reconsidering their decision to split from the main Methodist body and some were even contemplating reuniting with the main Wesleyan Methodist Church. This was a problem for William and Catherine. One of the attractions of his ministry for the Reformers in Lincolnshire was that he was largely his own boss. Although working alongside individual church members, he was largely able to determine his own diary and manage his own affairs.

The Methodist Church was developing more democratic patterns for church governance, according to which chapels were administered not just by the ordained ministers but also by local lay leaders and committees. If the Reformers in Lincolnshire developed along those lines, William would find himself beholden to those committees, which was not a particularly attractive proposition. *He* was the pastor, the leader, and if he was going to be forced into subservience then he feared for the effectiveness of his ministry. Catherine concurred with William that the minister should be the head of the church and not be controlled. To have to answer to committees was just not acceptable.[6] Catherine now began to wonder if the Reformers really were the best people for William or whether he should be looking elsewhere and casting his lot in with another denomination – the Methodist New Connexion.

This movement within Methodism grew after the death of John Wesley, the "founder" of Methodism, in the last decade of the eighteenth century. Methodism had originally been part of the Anglican establishment and indeed Wesley remained an Anglican priest until his death, and fought to keep his Methodist Connexion within Anglicanism. But the denomination he created eventually broke away and then separated internally. One reformer, Alexander Kilham, campaigned for change, desiring a more democratic Methodism, and for this he was expelled from the Methodist Conference in 1796. By the following year his ideas had grown into The New Itinerary, later to be renamed the Methodist New Connexion.[7]

By the time William Booth was in Lincolnshire, the New Connexion was well established and he and Catherine Mumford were becoming convinced that their security for the future may well lie there. The New Connexion had a sound Wesleyan theology, strongly emphasizing "revivalism", and although there was a democratic element to the governance, it was balanced. Control of chapels and the denomination lay with ordained ministers as well as lay leaders and local preachers.[8] William wouldn't entirely be under the control of local leaders who, to his mind, should have little spiritual authority over him.

Catherine encouraged William in his decision making and also asked around for other opinions.

*My dearest William,*

*... Miss Smith & her sister took tea with us yesterday...*

We had some conversation on the general aspect of the movement. Miss S. thinks the Reformers most injudicious in their expectations of their preachers. She says she is sure no man can sustain the incessant toil long. She was very sorry to hear you have to preach so often, & expressed her conviction that by the time the young men now employed reach the age of 35 they will find themselves worn out in body & mind, all their resources exhausted, their minds enfeebled & their characters anything but solidified.

I am, my dear, daily becoming more anxious on this subject. I see that it is absolutely impossible for you to sustain your position, to be whirling about incessantly as you now are. You may put it off & to a certain extent blind yourself to the future, but I am sure you will have to abandon it, if you cannot have time to replenish your mind, & there is, as you say, a fearful uncertainty about the movement, after all.

There is no security, no provision for the future, & now is the time to think about it. I hope, my dear, you will not let your present prosperity & your desire to get settled blind you to more weighty considerations. You must look about you & consider well whether it will be best to persevere in your present course; nay, whether it will be possible. You know you only determined to

*try it for 12 months, & you used to say that during
that time you would make your calculations & then if
you found reason to abandon it, you should be better
satisfied than if you had never tried it, & so should I.
For to tell you the truth, I feel differently with respect to
the ministry from what I used to do.*

*… Think about this, my love. Put aside your
predilections & silence the voice of ambition, &
enquire calmly & earnestly into your grounds of
confidence in the ministry as your proper sphere, &
whether you can possibly fill it as the reformers want
it filled, & look at the future, for it is only rational &
now is the time. It would be madness for us to plunge
ourselves & ours, more dear to us than our own souls,
into difficulties & sorrows from where a little foresight
might have saved us. We must consider beforehand &
do nothing rashly. If God gives us a family, they must
be provided for & educated, & to do this is the first
& most important of all duties. Nothing can claim
consideration before this. Herein is God glorified &
souls who have the first claim upon us saved.*

*The more I think of your present position the
more dissatisfied I am with it. I see it embraces only
one side of a good man's life, & if the reformers
expect such monstrous exertions from their preachers
& such incessant slavery, they ought to stipulate
with them never to marry. For I am sure there is no
time for the performance of domestic duties & the
development of a parent's solicitude. I consider it a
monstrous system of injustice to their preachers &
their families & a great hinderance to the prosperity*

*of the work of God, by lowering the tone of feeling &*
*deteriorating the preaching.*

*I like the independent system of a pastorate more*
*& more. After all, it is the way to cultivate practical*
*preaching, and all other is mere cant. I do hope, my*
*dear, that you will consider well. It will be easy to*
*change your position while single, & we can afford to*
*wait till circumstances are favourable. Act right. Be*
*activated by pure motives & use as much prudence as*
*you possess, & the Lord will guide you. I have never*
*reckoned fully on your continuing in the sphere you*
*now occupy. I feel so sure you cannot go on in this way*
*& continue to give satisfaction. But the Lord will guide*
*you… . There is time before you to settle it in. Then let*
*us act wisely, for, after all, it is an important matter*
*to throw ourselves on this movement under such*
*circumstances.*

*Good night. I am scrawling again. Never mind, I*
*have written it very quick & it is rather late.*

As William's conviction grew, he attempted to bring the Spalding circuit with him. In April 1853 he took a proposition to the Quarterly meeting, which was roundly thrown out.[9] He felt "a little insulted" and his natural inclination was to throw in the towel immediately and offer himself to the New Connexion. However, his close friends and mentors in the Spalding district, some of whom had supported the amalgamation of the Spalding circuit into the New Connexion and who obviously did not want to lose their talented evangelist, who was making good inroads into the heathen ways of many of those who came under his ministry, persuaded him to be patient. Catherine commiserated with him and urged him to write a "pamphlet" on the matter to try to draw others to his cause. He, in turn, encouraged her to do more reading on New Connexionalism and to become convinced of the merit of his joining that denomination.

In her usual manner, Catherine not only studied the subject but prayed earnestly about it and William's future. He wavered in his decision making as the prospect of leaving the Reformers who had offered so much in the way of financial security for the less obviously promising New Connexion preyed on his mind.[10] But he was beginning to be convinced and finally, on the day when she wrote so eloquently about the mistreatment of sheep being driven through London, Catherine gave William her blessing on a move to New Connexionism.

> *... I am delighted to hear that your mind is thoroughly satisfied about the constitution of the New Connexion. I only feared lest you should act precipitately and from impulse rather than principle. As you think it is scriptural and safe, by all means try to get into it, if you feel satisfied about the ministry being your path... I shall feel real happy & most heartily praise God, if he opens your way into a Methodism pure & scriptural in connexion with which we can both labour with undivided hearts. I feel no hesitation in saying that I can fully enter into such a sphere, & with far greater satisfaction than any in the movement, & should such a step tend to defer our union, don't let that weigh an atom with you.... I do hope and will pray that if it is consistent with God's will, He may open the way.*

As 1853 turned to 1854 William Booth had decided to leave the Spalding circuit, much to the disappointment of the people there. In a last ditch attempt to keep him they had offered more incentives – a permanent home, a horse, and the promise that they would be happy to see him a married man.[11] And there was to be more temptation yet.

HOLBEACH,

WEDNESDAY, 11 JANUARY 1854

*My dearest Kate,*

*The plot thickens, and I hesitate not to tell you that I fear, and fear much, that I am going wrong. Yesterday I had a letter asking me if I would consent to come to Hinde Street Circuit, London; salary £100 a year. I have also heard that the committee in London are about to make me an offer. I would give a great deal to be satisfied as to the right path, and gladly would I walk it, whether here or there.*

*You see, my dearest, it is certainly enough to make a fellow think and tremble. Here I am at present in a circuit numbering 780 members, with an increase for the year of nearly 200. Am invited to another with near a thousand. And yet I am going to join a church with but 150 members in London, and a majority of circuits with but a similar number.*

*I fear that, with all my cautiousness on the subject, I shall regret it. Send me a kind letter to reach me on Friday. Bless you, a thousand times! My present intention is to tear myself away from all and everything, and persevere in the path I have chosen.*

*They reckon it down here the maddest, wildest, most premature and hasty step that ever they knew a saved man to take.*

*I remain, my dearest love, your own, William.*

*My dearest William,*

*I should not write again today, only you ask me for a line, and as you seem so perplexed I will just put down one or two considerations which may comfort you. I have, with a burdened soul, committed the contents of your letter to God, & I feel persuaded he will guide you. I am pained that you seem to think me stoically or indifferently "brave" in the matter, & if I consulted my own feelings, I should say not another word on the subject, but for your comfort I do so.*

*First, then, you are not leaving the Movement because you fear not getting another Circuit or not getting as good a salary as the Connexion can offer. You are leaving because you are out of patience & sympathy with its principles & aims, & believe they will bring it to ultimate destruction. 2nd you are not leaving to secure present advantages, but sacrificing present advantages for what you believe to be, on the whole (looking to the end), most for God's glory & the good of souls, & the fact of Hinde St. offering even £200 would not alter those reasons. If it is*

*right in principle for you to leave the Movement &
join the Connexion, no advantages in the former or
disadvantages in the latter can possibly alter the thing.*

*But mind, I do not urge you to do it, & I do not
see even now it is too late to retreat if your conscience
is not satisfied as to the quality of your motives, but
I believe it ought to be. I am satisfied so far as I am
concerned, & then I look at several things which in
the nature of the case you cannot enter into. I look
at influences & circumstances in their effect on you;
of course you cannot do so in the same way. But I do
continually pray that God will settle it according to his
own will, & has he not promised to answer prayer? I
wish you prayed more & talked less about the matter.
Try it, & be determined to get clear & settled views
as to your course. Bare your heart before God & get
satisfied in his sight, & then do it, be what it may… .*

*I hope we shall have some sweet walks in the
spring if you come, but God's will be done.*

*I am living above; my soul breathes a purer
atmosphere than it has done for the last 2 or 3 years.
God lives & reigns & this to me is a source of much
consolation. With deepest interest & sincere affection, I
remain your loving, Kate.*

The decision was now irreversible. No matter what the future
might bring, William would leave Lincolnshire. He was heading

back to London. Catherine was, inevitably, delighted, but there was still the matter of what William would do next.

For some while he had been in correspondence with the highly regarded Dr William Cooke, who had been president of the New Connexion Conference before the age of forty, and twice subsequently. Ill health had taken him out of full-time ministry and he worked for the Connexion as librarian and archivist and as a highly regarded theologian. Dr Cooke ran a training school out of his home in Camberwell in South London and, the day after he returned from Lincolnshire, William Booth enrolled in the course of study under Dr Cooke's tutelage that he believed would lead to his ultimate goal – ordination in the Methodist New Connexion Church.

# CHAPTER

7

TUESDAY MAY 1, 1855.

*My dearest and most precious Love,*
    *May, that brings sunny days, soft breezes, and opening flowers, comes in cold and bleak with us. I was in hopes, especially for thy dear sake, that we were about to have some calm and continued summer weather. Perhaps it may be finer with you in the South than with us in the far North. I am all alone – far away from almost anyone who understands me or can sympathize with me. And yet I am not unhappy. Oh, that I could learn yet more fully than I have yet learned to lean chiefly on God. Oh, how much am I the creature of circumstances.*

William, along with the rest of the British Isles, was suffering in the cold of 1855. Although spring should have arrived long before, it had failed to appear. Indeed, history would put the winter of 1854–55 down as one of the driest, and the first few months of the new year as some of the very coldest, on record.[1]

William was still on the move, travelling from church to church, preaching and leading services.

He had returned to London from Lincolnshire in February 1854 to be near Catherine and presumably to prepare for marriage. Encouraged by Catherine, undoubtedly because of the need to settle once and for all the matter of which church William should be ordained in – and ordained he *must* be if he were to follow his Christian calling as an evangelist – he had opted to join the Methodist New Connexion as a student minister. His studies had kept him in London for a few months, which must have been a joy for Catherine especially, as she was able to have him near and get to know him properly, not just through his letters. Even though they had been engaged since May 1852 they had spent very little time together. But by June 1854 William was travelling again, visiting Nottingham and Caistor and returning to his old hunting ground of Spalding.

In the summer of that year London was hit by a cholera epidemic and panic was spreading. There were still fresh memories of the 1832 cholera pandemic in London, which had ultimately spread throughout the country, killing an estimated 55,000 people. Another outbreak in 1848–49 had sent 52,000 souls in England and Wales to their graves. In the overcrowded city, where many millions lived in squalid and unsanitary conditions, a disease such as cholera, which causes severe diarrhoea, dehydration, and death, spread like wildfire. The River Thames was like an open sewer – the innovative "new" sewers, the brainchild of Sir Joseph Bazalgette, were still in the future – and as cholera was transmitted primarily through contaminated food and water, once it took hold of the city it had devastating results.

The cholera epidemic of 1854, however, turned out to be an historical landmark. As a result of intensive study during this period, John Snow, a physician who was not inclined to go along with the current general belief that cholera was transmitted through the air, came up with a theory that ultimately led to the acceptance of the fact that the disease was spread through water. Snow isolated a water pump in Broad Street in Soho, where nearly 130 had died in just three days, and on examining a water sample found what he described as "white, flocculent particles". He concluded that the water was contaminated, he persuaded the parish guardians to turn off the pump, the cases of cholera began to fall, and London lost just 10,000 that year to the disease.[2]

For one as frail in health as Catherine Mumford, these were dangerous times. In August 1854 she arranged to spend a month in Burnham in Essex with her friend Miss Smith, in order to absent herself from the main area of contagion. In the days before modern rehydration treatment, the dangers of illnesses like diarrhoea were uppermost in many Victorian minds, so it's unsurprising that Catherine became a little obsessed with her family's bowel movements, especially those of the children who would arrive later. She knew that a bout of severe diarrhoea could cart a child off in a matter of hours.

Meanwhile, William was also suffering from ill health, perhaps owing to overwork, stress, and tiredness (which were to become common afflictions for him as the years passed), so he went home to his mother in Nottingham for a little nursing. In October 1854 he took the long and arduous boat journey south to Guernsey in the Channel Islands, at the invitation of locals who wanted his form of evangelism to help transform their island.

By early 1855 William Booth had been adopted as the New Connexion's travelling evangelist, although this was somewhat unofficial and experimental for the church. In this role, which he relished, he travelled extensively across the north of England and the Midlands.

Catherine, meanwhile, was still waiting to hear when she might be married. Several dates had been suggested since her first preferred option, her 17 January birthday in 1853, had come and gone. Two years had passed and now, finally, it appeared that there might be some light at the end of the long engagement tunnel. Catherine was preparing to become, at last, a bride.

BRIXTON,

WEDNESDAY MAY 2ND 1855

*My dearest Love,*

*... I thought much about you & the future after your Saturday's note. What you said about a year's pause, the importance of studying, getting more general knowledge, etc., was so exactly what I wrote you three months back that I could not but recognise the result I foresaw & forewarned you of, tho' perhaps at the time you thought me influenced chiefly by personal feelings. However, I shall be content whichever way it is, only I should not like you to be so burdened with anxiety & prostrate under a sense of inability as to make life a burden & destroy all domestic & social enjoyment. I hope you will consider the matter well & act for yourself. The conference are sure to wish you to itinerate, but you know your own resources best, & I should judge for myself in this matter of time.*

*Altho' in all probability the first year will be the most convenient for me to accompany you oftenest, yet I would not advise you to travel if you don't feel equal to it, for it would distress me to see you always burdened with anxiety & prostrate for lack of success. If you do consent to continue this life, on no account be tied for time. Let all minor considerations yield, & have time to follow up an impression once made on a place.*

*Bless you! Good bye. I might say lots more, but it would be too sentimental & some of it perhaps foolish, so good bye, & believe me thy betrothed & loving,*

*Katie.*

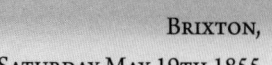

Brixton,
Saturday May 19th 1855

*My dearest Love,*

*Your letter this morn'g was most welcome and put an end to no inconsiderable anxiety respecting you. Since hearing that your head was so bad on Thursday I had been fearing that it might be something more than an ordinary attack & that you were ill. Do promise me in your next that if ever you should be threatened with inflammation of the brain or anything serious, you will at once let me know. Such a promise will save me from conjecturing & fearing things that are not probable.*

*I wish I could post this to reach you on Monday instead of tomorrow, but I cannot, & Tuesday would not be soon enough for what I want to communicate,* so you must only read the first part of this letter when it comes to hand.

Bless you, I cannot describe my feelings after perusing your letter. I could do nothing but pour out my full heart to God in solitude. Oh, that the prayers I then put up for you may be answered according to his riches in glory & in mercy by Christ Jesus. I am more than rejoiced to hear of your prosperity & success & its encouraging effects on your mind. I do unite with you in praising God, & I believe if you keep close to him, he will save you from being exalted above measure by this blaze of popularity. "Do I ever fear its consequences?" There are few evils that could befall thee which have not sometime been the occasions of fear & anxiety to me, then how could I overlook one so great & so fatal?

… God will save you if you will only seek his grace, but, oh, it must be agonised for in secret. Nothing but private intercourse with God can save you where so many mightier have fallen. It is far more important than reading, habits of thought, or study, or anything that can possibly claim your attention. Make it first & last; let neither the excitement of public labours, nor the pressure of private engagements induce you to neglect it.

Have time to be alone with God at least once a day, besides morn'g & ev'ng, & then I shall not fear much for you, and as to you becoming an effective & abundantly useful preacher I don't doubt. But oh, my precious, thou art walking on slippery ground. Take heed to thy steps & mind thou hast hold of the hand of him whose counsel standeth fast & the thoughts of

*whose heart endureth forever. Excuse this bit of advice.*
*It is some time since I sent you any, but thy questions*
*called it forth.*

… … For Monday.

*Father bought the Act of Parliament yesterday &*
*went to the Superintendent of the Lambeth register*
*this morn'g. The Act is too large to send you, which I*
*intended, but I can easily condense all the necessary*
*information if you have not got it.*

*It is necessary for us each to give notice in the*
*district where we have each resided not less than 7*
*(seven) days prior to giving notice. A notice may be*
*given as long as three months before the time, but*
*must not be less than 21 days after the day on which*
*it is given, so you must give notice before you leave*
*Manchester to the Super. of the district in which you*
*have been the last 7 days. I enclose a form of notice.*
*Forms unfilled are to be placed in the hand of the*
*register, but Father could not get one this morn'g.*

*It is necessary for one of the parties to appear*
*personally before the Super. of the district, in which*
*the marriage is to be solemnized, in order to sign his or*
*her name in the book of notices, so I shall have to go &*
*sign I suppose. It seems that we must be married in the*
*district where one of us resided for more than 7 days,*
*so I suppose you will have to borrow a chapel as Dover*
*Road is not in this district. It seems a strange bore. I*
*don't know how people do who go for miles away to*
*be married. I don't believe they all have licences …*
*If you decide for the 14th & have to arrange about*

the chapel, you have no time to lose. Don't let us have anything unpleasant about that. If everybody had as much trouble to get the information as Father has had, I think many would make less do. And the Act is so mystified that I cannot see clearly whether it must be in the district where one of us resides, but I think so, & I should think it will require a meeting of deacons & no end of fuss before the chapel can be lent, however, I shall leave it with you now. It has annoyed me enough one way or another. Write on Monday & tell me what place of worship you intend it to be in. As you will perceive the place has to be specified in the notice. I should think we might venture to name Stockwell New Chapel, & then afterwards try to borrow it.

It was generous of you to finish up your letter with such a sweet assurance, bless you. I can appreciate generosity of heart & feeling as well as most. And so it really is a fact that amongst all the fair & lovely & lovable ones thou meets with, there is not one whom thou couldst wish to supplant me with, but I am still thy "most precious earthly treasure."

Bless you! And you are mine! In tender affection I remain thy espoused Katie.

25 HYDE GROVE, SHAKESPEARE STREET, MANCHESTER
TUESDAY MAY 22, '55.

*My dearest Catherine,*

*Bless you! I shall soon, all well, change my address and call you my dearest Wife. It is astonishing how of late that name has gathered unto it in my estimation charms and sweetness which it lacked before. I intended writing you a long letter, but shall not have time.*

*I think if it be that we cannot be married at Brunswick Chapel we will let Mr Thomas marry us at his own chapel. I should like it much if it can be done without giving offence to Mr C[ooke], seeing that we have discussed the matter.*

*Write me per return how much black silk you will want for a flounced dress and whether you would prefer that to a satinet or satinture – I intend having a first rate one. If I buy it without your letter I shall get black silk and 16 yards.*

*I am very low spirited this morning. We are not getting on very well – not near so well as I expected. How are you? Are you happy? Write me all particulars about yourself. I am looking up; have been praying for you. You need not have any fear of my being over elated; I have almost as little self-confidence as ever. I wish I had more, I should preach far better. Look up, all will yet be well. I shall soon call you fully mine, and we shall be happy.*

*My dearest love,*

*Your letter came to hand this morning, & most willingly do I comply with your request to send you a few lines. I am sorry my last read unkind, tho' I felt deeply & perhaps spoke too strongly. I did not feel unkindly, however, if it was "unnecessarily severe," forgive me, there's a darling, & I will "forget the past as far as it has been painful & try to be happy now." I am sure I do not wish to create any mist between us, for I am never happy when it exists. I want our hearts to be in thorough harmony & sympathy. Our circumstances are so opposite that it is impossible for either of us duly to make allowance for the other. Thou art far away in the midst of popularity & excitement, which my imagination perhaps magnifies into greater danger than it really is, & I am here without anything to direct my thoughts from thee, thy circumstances, thy letters, our future, etc. But it will be over soon & then truly I think it will be a rest indeed. Bless you! I do think if you could come as you say "all the mist & gloom would disperse," yea, it has dispersed & my heart is full of tenderness towards you. Answer this part of my letter. Tell me you forgive me & whether your heart is right & loving towards me. Tell me.*

*I dreamt about you last night very sweetly. I thought I was reading to you, sitting on your knee, and you looked into my eyes with a look of unutterable affection & drew me tightly to your bosom. The book*

*of course was quickly laid aside, & with a full heart
I returned the loving clasp most warmly. I shall not
soon forget the thrill of love I experienced; even tho' a
dream it was very precious, & the sweet savour of it is
on my spirit now. I seem to realize your looks, voice,
and presence more vividly. Oh, how like a dream is
life. How soon its realities pass away. Let us try to
make them all as precious as this dream. Yes, I do
hope we shall do something real while we live, as well
as enjoy. We will try to bless the world. I will try to
help thee to do it.*

*... I am very sorry indeed about the chapel. It is
a pity, if we could have been married at Brunswick,
to have all that trouble. I think the people in office in
London are more stupid or particular than anywhere
else. Mother is sadly put about at the idea of having
Mr C[ooke] & Mr R[abbits] here, & I wish it could
be done without, but of course the least evil must be
chosen. Do just as you think best. It seems a pity when
you found it could be at Bruns'k that you did not
mention that chapel as you gave notice on Wednesday.
You did not know that I had mentioned Stockwell,
& perhaps I could have altered mine on Thursday.
However, it is done now & we will not make a trouble
of it. I am sorry you did not get the information
sooner. I should tell Mr C[ooke] how it is & see what
he says. I fear it will cause such a fuss to borrow the
chapel ... Do just as you think best about another
carriage, but we should be as economical as we can, if
we do have another...*

*Bless you, I hope your head is better & that you are resting. Look high, expect much happiness, & let us cast off every weight & realize a perfect & blissful oneness in the Lord.*

*From thy loving & espoused, Cathy.*
*For my faithful William.*

---

GREAT ALFRED STREET, NOTTINGHAM,
WEDNESDAY JUNE 6 / '55.

*My dearest and most precious Kate,*

*Thy kind note is just to hand. All well, Mr Thomas shall marry us. I do not know hardly how to write him on the subject. But I suppose I must. I would much rather call. I have not been very high spirited since Conference, so perhaps my last note or two have partaken of the colour of my feelings. Your last was quite satisfactory or I should have said so. I quite feel as you do with respect to the ceremony; in fact, the whole affair, and most heartily wish it was over. But that soon will be. Time flies most rapidly. I shall soon once more be sitting by your side.*

*I shall make no arrangements for the future, and should we not have any family, and should your health permit it, we will not encumber ourselves with a home. I have obtained an address for apartments at Ryde, Isle of Wight. I cannot understand how Mr Downs could say that I was not to preach on next Sunday, as*

*Mr Bates showed me a bill last Friday announcing
my preaching & tea meeting on the Monday. I have
written Emma to tell her of the same. I of course shall
be anxious to do all I can next Sunday and during the
week, as I do not wish this to be counted as my holiday,
having intimated that I expect a little rest after my
Guernsey expedition. The leading ministers in the
Conference were very cordial, and I have no complaint
to make, but I will tell you all about it and everything
else when we meet.*

*I am sorry you have not been sleeping so well.
Bless you, all will be well and I do hope and pray that
I may be enabled to make you fully happy. I am very,
very anxious about the matter, I confess to you, and
a meeting and a loving embrace will do a great deal
to ease my heart and make me happy. This will be on
Saturday. I shall get in about ½ past 6, I am afraid not
before – as I must travel Government train. If later, my
mind you shall know.*

*I intend writing to Guernsey today to say that
they may expect me to preach for them on the 24th
of June and following fortnight. I am afraid it will be
very hot for the services. Mr Piggin, one of the nicest
and most loveable men we have, is to be their preacher,
so I anticipate much pleasure from you making
the acquaintance & from our meeting under such
circumstances. Then Mr McCurdy is down for Bristol,
perchance he may go over to Guernsey for a week.
During the Summer rest I do not want any company
but thine. Quiet in some little village with thee and
a few books & papers would I think make me happy*

until I commenced work again, and should I be well and thou be happy & well, we will do all we can and rest when we are tired.

My Mother & Sister send their kind love. Mother is very anxious to see you and we will come to Nott'm the first opportunity. I suppose I shall not hear from you again. I must calculate on the joy of seeing you. The weather is more genial. It will prove beneficial to thee I trust …

For the present, my dearest, farewell. I have been praying this morn'g about thee and our union. Oh, may Heaven grant us happiness in each other. I ask no higher earthly bliss. I question if there be any higher.

Believe me, faithful & betrothed, affectionately for ever

William.

P.S. I think I shall postpone writing to Mr Thomas, at least I think I shall call and see him when I come up. It is rather a difficult matter to write. Supposing your Mother was to call upon him. She might, say Saturday morning, 10 o'clock, and I will call when I come up. Perhaps I may come earlier or Saturday, if it costs no more. I do not think there would be anything at all wrong if your mother would not object to call on Mr T., considering I am so far away.

The sun emerged from behind the early summer clouds as Catherine and William stepped over the threshold of the Stockwell Green Congregational Church.

Catherine clutched her new husband's hand, feeling small yet secure. William looked down at Catherine's sweet face and smiled. He could feel her shaking ever so slightly and a rush of protectiveness towards this woman overwhelmed him. He could hardly believe that, after all this time and so many obstacles, they were at last man and wife.

It had been a short and solemn service and blessing. Perfect. Catherine had been pale and had spoken quietly, her voice quivering as she repeated her vows of love and obedience. In contrast, William had found that his voice, which he was accustomed to using to rather larger congregations, had rung loudly around the church. As his "I do!" echoed around the building it had provoked a little giggle from his beloved. Then, in the cavernous chapel, William and Catherine had knelt at the altar and pledged themselves to God and to each other.

Behind Catherine, William noticed that his father-in-law, John Mumford, and his sister Emma, the only witnesses to the solemn ceremony, were now exiting the building and squinting in the watery sunshine. For a moment he regretted the absence of the rest of his family. Of course, it was unlikely that Ann would attend, but he had hoped that his mother and her namesake, his sister Mary, all those miles away in Nottingham, might have been able to make it, even at such short notice. However, he and Catherine had been thrilled when Emma had sent word that they would be able to afford for her, at any rate, to attend. He knew Catherine's day was also slightly saddened by the fact that her own mother had been disinclined to attend the ceremony, but, as he held Catherine's little gloved hand in his, he felt a rush of love and appreciation for her commitment to him.

Catherine pulled her shawl closer around her neck and shoulders. She shivered again. Even with layers of petticoats under her skirts she still felt the chill of the day. Maybe she should, after all, have worn her coat. The few days of milder weather in May hadn't lasted and it was still chilly, even for mid-June.

Catherine turned to the Revd David Thomas, who had so kindly agreed to preside over this most sacred of ceremonies.

"Mr Thomas, thank you!" she announced, grasping his hand and shaking it wholeheartedly. No simpering little handshake for this gentleman. She remembered their previous debates and discussions about the place of women in church and society, and she knew he would expect this forwardness from her, even on this day.

Father Mumford was calling from the street. The Stockwell New Chapel was tucked away from the main thoroughfare and he had a cab waiting. William, Catherine, and Emma took their leave of the minister and made their way to the horsedrawn vehicle. It was but a short drive back home to Russell Street in Brixton, where, regardless of her unwillingness to attend the actual service, William was sure that Mrs Mumford would be waiting with some light refreshments. Whatever her views on the marriage, and he still wasn't quite sure of her, she loved her daughter unconditionally and would, he was sure, come around.

William reached out his hand to Catherine. She grasped it and he helped her into the carriage. Whatever the future held now, they were one. The Lord would determine their way, and, whatever happened, they would face it together.

When William Booth married Catherine Mumford, they intended it to be a simple occasion, and it was. In common with many weddings of the time, theirs was a quiet ceremony in church, held in the morning. After the ceremony the couple would have signed the parish register in the vestry, the bride signing her maiden name for the very last time.[3]

As was common then, the venue was the bride's choice. This had been the subject of some discussion over the weeks, but despite her previous falling-out with the Revd Thomas over the matter of women's equality Catherine still greatly admired him, and despite the fact that she and William had rejected Congregationalism, she knew the Stockwell Chapel and it was quite near home. They had to marry in a local church and other options fell through, but the choice of venue may have been a reason why Mrs Mumford decided not to attend the marriage of her only daughter. Mrs Booth Snr's absence, along with that of William's youngest sister, was almost undoubtedly for financial reasons. They and Emma still only scraped a living in a haberdasher's shop in Nottingham.[4]

The wedding ceremony would have been followed by a small family celebration at home, perhaps with a specially made cake or perhaps not; perhaps in the company of a few friends, but maybe not. This was certainly a wedding on a shoestring budget.

Although William had earlier intimated that they would both have new outfits for the wedding, it's likely that they had better things on which to spend their meagre resources and the extravagance of new clothes may have been one step too far. "Sunday best" would have sufficed.

For the rich and well-to-do, marriage down the centuries had often been seen as a way of cementing helpful and even political alliances, and for the upper classes weddings afforded an opportunity to display their wealth. However, wearing white was not common for brides until it was made popular by Queen Victoria. When she married Prince Albert in 1840, some fifteen years before William and Catherine's wedding day, she opted for a white dress and, following the wide publicity of the day, this was copied by those who could afford expensive white fabric.[5] But even if Catherine Mumford had been romantically inclined to emulate her queen in this matter, her purse and that of her parents, who still appeared to stagger from one financial disaster to another, would have disallowed it.

Very few couples other than those with money could really afford a proper "honeymoon", but William had yearned for one, and had planned to take his bride "overseas" for that short "getting to know you" holiday. The reality was a week on the Isle of Wight, staying with friends. The couple then moved on for a mission campaign in Guernsey, from where Catherine wrote to her parents reporting crowds of people flocking to hear her husband but "not so many cases of conversion" as William had expected and hoped for. Their return boat trip included a short stopover at the nearby and larger Channel Island of Jersey, but the voyage home to England left Catherine violently ill. Very soon she was to discover that she was expecting their first child, but she remained determined to be with William whenever possible. She had waited this long for her husband and now she hoped not to be apart from him for any length of time.

Theirs was to be an itinerant life. On his wedding day, William Booth gave his "home" address as Ardwick, Manchester,[6] where he had lodged during his evangelistic work. He had very lately been confirmed by the Methodist New Connexion Conference in the post of evangelist with an annual salary of £100 for the year plus his travelling expenses. As he had proudly informed his fiancée just a few weeks before their marriage, "This, of course, is an advance of £30 or £40 on the young man's salary." He was to be employed directly by the Annual Conference rather than by any circuit, and this greatly pleased him and Catherine because it meant that he was not under the governance of local church leaders. After Guernsey he already had invitations to visit (among other places) York and Chester. As always, finances occupied his mind. He reported to Catherine that he had had to pay £5 for his Beneficent Fund Subscription but he hoped to receive £6 for preaching in London, so he had it covered.

Although they had no permanent home to move into once the wedding and honeymoon were over, William hoped to continue with his evangelism while Catherine would continue to live with her parents and join him whenever possible.

> 3 CASTLE GATE, YORK,
> SATURDAY AUGUST 4TH 1855.

*My precious Wife,*

*The first time I have written you that endearing appellation! Bless you a thousand times! How often during my journey have I taken my eyes from off the book I was reading to think about you – yes, to think tenderly about you, about our future and our home.*

*Shall we not again commence a life of devotion, and by renewed consecration begin afresh the Christian race? …*

*Oh, Kate, be happy. You will rejoice my soul if you send me word that your heart is gladsome, and your spirits are light. It will help you to battle with your illness, and make the short period of our separation fly away.*

*Bless you! I feel as though a part of my very self were wanting – as though I had left some very important adjunct to my happiness behind me. And so*

*I have. My precious self. I do indeed return that warm
affection I know you bear towards me.*

*Your faithful and affectionate husband,*

*William.*

*My own precious Husband,*

*Your two loving letters came to hand by the same
post this morn'g. Many a time yesterday did I wander
to the parlour window in search of the postman,
and numerous were my conjectures as to the non-
appearance of a letter. It is very tiresome there should
be such blunders. I wonder whose fault it is. There is
not a late mark on the letter, so it must be the fault of
the post office functionaries.*

*Well, bless you, when it did come it was very
welcome & very sweet. I am delighted that you are so
well & so comfortable in your home. It is very pleasant
to meet with such kind friends. I am glad also that
you have so many to help you in the work, because I
know what a comfort it will be to you. I hope you will
see much fruit in York and then our sacrifices will not
be in vain. Bless you for all your kind words and sweet
assurances. They are doubly precious to me now, in fact
they are almost all I have to think about, for I am too
ill to do anything.*

*The sickness continues very distressing at times. Sometimes all my meals come up again almost directly, but not often. I continue to drink the camphor water, but I fancy it makes my head giddy. Perhaps it is only fancy. I long to see Mr Franks, but it is of no use fixing any time. I must go when I feel able & he must see me without an appointment for once. I think he will. I begin to feel very weak and trembling, but Mother says she is sure I shall be better by & by, and everybody tells me it is only the common lot of woman, so I must be patient & wait, but it is wearisome work. I seem to want thee worse now than when I am well. But I will not be discontented. I will remember thy love for me and be happy & hopeful. Mother says when I begin to mend I shall very likely be better than ever I was and able to go about with you 4 or 5 months quite comfortably. Oh, if it please the Lord to let it be so, how happy we shall be.*

*I find myself thinking more about a nice home than ever I did before. I should like to make it a neat, tasty, clean, little paradise. I can just picture it to myself sometimes, the best bedroom, that room where our first born is to be ushered into the world. Oh, my precious one, let us pray about it. Bless thee, how I long to see thee, to hear thee say, "My poor, little wife" when I am so sick, but we must be willing to endure "as seeing him who is invisible."*

*I am very glad you will enquire about Father. I believe he is sincerely desirous of beginning a new life. May the Lord open his way... . Pray excuse this. I*

*have had to leave it here to be sick. I have been awfully
sick five times today.*

*Pray for me, & remember me as thy own loving,
& faithful wife, till death us do part,
Catherine.
My dear Parents kindest Love.
Bless thee, my darling*

Catherine's dreams of a permanent home were not just romantic
notions. She wanted her life to start properly and she had so
many aspirations for their future together, a life based on equality
of purpose and thought. She certainly expected to be an equal
partner in the union, something of which her new husband must
have been aware. He knew what he was letting himself in for, as,
many years later, Catherine revealed that her "rules for married
happiness" had resulted from a long time of consideration:

> *There were also certain rules which I formulated for
> my married life before I was married or even engaged.
> I have carried them out ever since my wedding day,
> and the experience of all these years has abundantly
> demonstrated their value.*
>
> *The first was, never to have any secrets from my
> husband in anything that affected our mutual
> relationship or the interests of the family. The
> confidence of others in spiritual matters I did not
> consider as coming under this category, but as being
> the secrets of others, and therefore not my property.*

*The second rule was, never to have two purses, thus avoiding even the temptation of having any secrets of a domestic character.*

*My third principle was that, in matters where there was any difference of opinion, I would show my husband my views and the reasons on which they were based, and try to convince in favour of my way of looking at the subject. This generally resulted either in his being converted to my views or in my being converted to his, either result securing unity of thought and action.*

*My fourth rule was, in cases of difference of opinion, never to argue in the presence of the children. I thought it better even to submit at the time to what I might consider to be a mistaken judgement, than to have a controversy before them. But of course when such occasion arose I took the first opportunity for arguing the matter out. My subsequent experience has abundantly proved to me the wisdom of this course.*[7]

### WEDNESDAY EV'ING, AUGUST 8 1855

*My own precious Love,*

*I feel better this eve'ng than I have done since thou left me, and seeing that I have sent thee two such shabby letters I will write a bit now I feel able, for fear I should be as bad as ever tomorrow.*

*Well, what shall I say? "Oh, just what comes bubbling up." Well, the first thing I feel is, bless you my* own precious husband, and the next, a few involuntary tears because I cannot throw my arms round your neck and tell you how dear you are to my heart. I have been pressing a fond kiss on each of your letters, but alas they are but cold, lifeless paper, tho' very precious for all that. I have been thinking about thee in thy lonely chamber, picturing thee going comfortably off to sleep without being disturbed by a little wife pottering about the room half an hour before she gets in. I can see thee sleeping nice & cool without anybody slipping into the middle of the bed and taking up all the room, and I can hear thee say when thou wakes up in the morning, "My poor little wife, I wish she was here." Ah, notwithstanding all the trouble & anxiety I brought thee, it is sweet to know that thou wouldst have me with thee.

Bless you, there is a better time coming. I shall get better soon & then I will try & reward thee for thy thoughtful care on board that Packet, for thy sympathy at that hotel, for thy back aching, limb cramping attention in the Train, and all thy other acts of kindness, not one of which is or can be forgotten. Oh, to meet again, won't it be sweet? I think our love will be more tender and watchful for these partings; absence will give us time to feel how dear we are to each other. I have written nothing, but my rebellious stomach warns me to have done, so good night, my darling. Kiss! Oh, how precious it is to feel that one is loved. "Bless the Lord, oh my soul."

# CHAPTER

8

*My very dear parents*

*You will see that I intended the enclosed to reach you this morning but I could not get it posted so was obliged to delay sending it. Yours came to hand yesterday … we were thankful to hear you are better but very sorry Mother has got no one to help her yet. <u>Have you tried?</u> I am glad you have got an order in for the person as I think it would be better to get someone to help in the house…*

*I am not very well, … and of course have little blessings to attend to in my new house, but I like it very much and never was happier. I have wished many a time that my dearest mother could come and see me every now and then. I want to get everything ready. Send all the napkins … There are two little pinafores that Miss Smith gave me, in the second drawer in the back room, send them and also two of those table napkins of Williams. Send the ointments you made* *for me and the marking ink out of William's dressing case, also the small <u>soft</u> brush out of his case. If I think of anything else between now and Wednesday I will write again. Pay the carriage and put it down to our accounts, which you must bring with you when you come. I should have sent a parcel to you before now, containing several things we don't want to keep about with us, but I thought they would go back with you … it is astonishing how luggage accumulates, but I suppose it will do more by and by.*

*I went to chapel yesterday evening, it is a very nice chapel, the largest in the circuit. William opened his mission very effectively…*

*Nothing more at present from your loving and affectionate daughter Catherine*

Catherine heaved herself up from her chair. Her back ached. Her ankles were swollen. Her extended belly pushed against her petticoats and the child lay heavy inside her, pressing on her bladder.

It could not be long now, surely. Perhaps another month? At least that was what the doctor had predicted. She longed for the day when she would hold her child – her and William's first child – but she also dreaded the experience.

William was anxious, naturally, and so attentive… when he was there! How she wished he could be around a little more, but that was being selfish. She'd known she must share her husband with others, perhaps even with the world.

If only they had their own permanent home. But that too was impossible. At least the people in the circuit had provided a little nest for the soon-to-be parents here in Halifax.

*My dearest Parents*

*I am very sorry I was prevented writing yesterday as I intended but a succession of circumstances and visitors prevented me. My precious husband left me for Hull at eleven o'clock and several friends taking compassion in my loneliness called to see me... I had five here at one time ... the Hull people have long been wishing William to join them one evening for a meeting and after several refusals he seemed compelled to do so.*

*I have received a line posted as soon as he got there to tell me of his safe arrival, and I am happy to say I expect him home in on hour or two, oh how thankful I am that we are not often called to part and that the horrid spectre of future separation is banished.*

*I am better than I have been, in fact I am fully recovered from the effects of a slight fall I had ... I should have named it before only I thought it would make you uneasy, and hoped to be no worse for it. One afternoon while we were staying at Brother H's a few friends were ranging themselves around the table for tea when in taking my seat as I thought on a chair behind me (which Mr H had at that moment removed) I fell backwards giving myself a little shake...*

*I can walk now as well as ever and with still a little pain in my hips feel no evil consequence. It has made*

me very low and poorly for several days and was the
occasion of such anxiety to us both, but we of course
made the best of it, for the sake of Mr H who was really
<u>distressed</u> about it. I felt as much pained for him as
for myself for his kindness and attention to me was
extreme, he has been over to see me twice since we left.

... I am very grateful for all your solicitude
and advice respecting my position and <u>do</u> try to use
every precaution and care and I think I am going on
alright. We have washed and got up the little things
and they look beautiful. I am proud of showing
them to my friends and telling them my Mother did
them. There are hundreds up and down the country
interested in me and my expected visitor. I often feel
almost overwhelmed when I remember the many
blessings and notlookedfor happiness crowded into
my pathway. I never expected to be <u>half</u> as happy. I
feel much more at <u>ease</u> in society than I used to do
and am often surprised and grateful to find myself
able to sustain a respectable position amongst the
educated and intelligent, it is a great advantage to me
in many respects.

My precious William has returned in safety and
as good health as when he left me, which I am sorry to
say is not very first rate. They had a very good meeting
at Hull and from what I can gather I am sure they
were very much delighted with his speech. Here ... the
congregation have uniformly increased, arrangements
are made for preaching in the schoolroom on Sunday
night to accommodate the overflow. They take from
10 to 30 names of a night. I wish you could come and

> *spend the Sabbath with us tomorrow, we are going to*
> *have a <u>beef steak</u> dumpling for dinner in order that we*
> *may all go to chapel, how <u>welcome</u> you would be to*
> *share it!*
>
> *… remember me as your ever loving daughter*
> *Cate*

Catherine put down her pen. William bent over her, kissing her neck in the process, which made her wriggle and giggle a little. She had been pleased to see him return home but he had brought in the cold wind and had spent a good ten minutes warming himself at the fire before the February chill was dispersed. He had returned in good spirits, and was now all smiles, and attentive.

"Let me write something. Please?"

He leaned over his wife and added his own greetings for her parents.

"And from your ever loving Son William

And from your future and obedient Grandson … "

"William!" Catherine scolded playfully. "It may not be a boy, don't you know? We may end up with a girl!"

"Never!"

He smiled and then took Catherine's hand to help her to her feet. He wrapped his arms around her and breathed in her sweet scent.

"It's a boy," he whispered. "It has to be a boy!"

William and Catherine's first child, a son whom they called William Bramwell, was born on 8 March 1856. He was named after his father and in honour of one Revd William Bramwell, an evangelist who had preached across northern England at the turn of the century.[1] From the start, it seems, Mama and Papa Booth hoped their little son, who was quickly dubbed "Willie", might emulate his namesake.

The commencement of family life would not halt their purpose, and God's work still came first. Seven more children would follow at regular intervals over the next nine years, but, despite her continuing delicate health, surprisingly Catherine not only managed to produce this large family but also often held the fort at home while William was away on his frequent travels.

William Booth's star was rising. He was gaining in popularity and notoriety as a revivalist and evangelistic leader, and demand for him was growing.

His period of study under Dr William Cooke in South London had been relatively short-lived. William had felt confined by the long hours of study, which he had started in February 1854, and despite Catherine's constant encouragement to be about his books, it was something of a lost cause. On William's first day back in London in 1854 he had been invited to preach at the Brunswick Street Chapel,[2] and even while trying to concentrate on his studies he took any opportunity to preach whenever and wherever he could.

Dr Cooke, who would become a lifelong friend, advocate, and supporter, had soon realized that William Booth's talents lay not in the classroom but in the pulpit. Undoubtedly much to William's relief, Dr Cooke suggested that the young Booth had probably had enough training and instead might become the superintendent of the Methodist New Connexion London Circuit. With the job came the role of the first minister, on probation, of the Packington Street Chapel in Islington in North London, which was just recently opened.[3] This would have brought some financial security but also a good deal of responsibility, not just for the pastoral and preaching ministry but also for the administration of the church.

William Booth declined this kind offer. He was set on a career in evangelism. So, instead, and thanks again to Mr Edward Rabbits, with whom he had now renewed his friendship, another minister, Revd P.T. Gilton, was recruited as circuit superintendent and Mr Rabbits agreed to fund a second post of assistant for William.

The funding came with the condition that the young Booth be allowed to marry within the year, rather than having to wait the obligatory four that most probationary ministers in the New Connexion had to endure, and there was an additional twist in the tale. Josiah Bates, another of William's supporters and a leading lay member of the church, wrote a letter to the New Connexion Magazine expounding Mr Booth's talents, and as a result William had been appointed as the denomination's full-time evangelist.[4]

By the time he and Catherine had become parents, William was well established and travelling the length and breadth of the country to preside over revival meetings, where he preached a simple gospel and encouraged people to repent of their sins, accept the death and resurrection of Jesus Christ for themselves, and be "saved". William himself had been greatly influenced by the American evangelist James Caughey, and with Catherine was enamoured of some of the American thinking not just in evangelism but also in holiness teaching. One theologian and evangelist, Charles Grandison Finney, was a particular favourite of theirs, not just for his innovative revivalist style but also as a pioneer of social reforms in favour of women and African-Americans.

Catherine, although sure that William was a great man with extraordinary potential, was concerned that he should not become ridiculous and should not, in particular, employ excessive emotionalism in revivalist meetings. As early as March 1853 she had urged him to be cautious, obviously spurred by some of the reports that he was sending back about the popularity of some of his revivalist meetings.

*I had no intention to write thus when I began, but it is out of the abundance of my heart. Oh my Love, I have felt acutely about you, I mean your soul. I rejoice exceedingly to hear how the Lord is blessing your labours. But as I stand at a distance & contemplate the scene of action & all the circumstances attending it, I tremble with apprehension for the object most beloved & nearest (except, I trust, the glory of God & the honour of my Redeemer) my heart.*

*I know how possible it is to preach & pray & sing & even shout while the heart is not right with God. I know how popularity & prosperity have a tendency to elate & exalt self, if the heart is not humbled before God. I know how Satan takes advantage of these things to work out the destruction (if possible) of one whom the Lord uses to pull down the strong holds of his kingdom. And all these considerations make me tremble, & weep, & pray for you, my dearest Love, that you may be able to overcome all his devices & "having done all, to stand," not in your own strength, but in humble dependence on Him who worketh "all in all."*

*Allow me, dearest, to caution you against indulging ambition to be either a revivalist or anything else. Try to get into that happy frame of mind to be satisfied if Christ be exalted, even if it be only by compelling you to lie at the foot of the cross & look upon him. If your happiness of soul comes to depend on the excitement of active service, what if God should lay his hand upon you and give you the cup of suffering instead of labour? Nothing but a heart in unison with his & a will perfectly subdued can then give peace.*

*Watch against mere animal excitement in your revival services. I don't use the term in the sense in which anti-revivalists would use it, but only in the sense which Finney himself would use it. Remember Caughey's silent, soft, heavenly carriage. He did not shout, there was no necessity. He had a more potent weapon at command than noise. I never did like noise & confusion, only so far as I believed it to be the natural expression of deep anxiety, wrought by the holy ghost, such as the cries of the jailer, etc., etc. Of such noise, produced by such agency, the more the better. But, my Love, I do think noise made by the preacher & the Christians in the church is productive of evil only.*

Concerning one revivalist of the time, Isaac Marsden, Catherine vowed not to attend any of his prayer meetings on account of their being "exceeding injudicious & violent". She did not believe that the gospel needed "such roaring & foaming to make it effective". Indeed, Catherine felt that antics made the gospel appear "ridiculous" and could even put people off it. Her own brother John Mumford (Jr) had apparently suffered spiritual damage, which Catherine hoped was not irreparable.

> *He went one Sunday evening to hear Mr Richardson*
> *at Vauxhall. He was quite unconcerned when he*
> *went, but was much wrought upon under the sermon*
> *and induced to go to the communion rail, where*
> *he professed to find peace. There certainly was a*
> *change in him for a short time, but, alas, there was no*
> *foundation & in a week or two the fair blossoms faded,*
> *and tho' he continued to meet in class, his conduct was*
> *far worse than it had ever been before. He was more*
> *impatient of restraint and reproof; in fact his heart*
> *was closed against conviction by the vain idea that he*
> *was converted.*

Catherine's overriding concern with the spiritual health of her family obsessed her, and when children came along she was determined to school them in the way of faith from the earliest age, and to show the example she believed was required in order that the children should choose to walk the road of faith:

> *In the early part of my married life, when my dear*
> *husband was travelling very much from place to place,*
> *I was frequently thrown into the houses of leading*
> *families in churches for three or four weeks at a time,*
> *and I used to say to myself, "How is it that these*
> *children seem frequently to have a more inveterate*
> *dislike for religion and religious things, than the*
> *children of worldly people who make no profession?"*
> *Subsequent observations and experience have*
> *shown me the reason. It is because such parents inform*

> *the head without training the heart. They teach what*
> *they neither practice themselves nor take the trouble*
> *to see that their children practise, and the children see*
> *through the hollow sham and learn to despite both*
> *their parents and their religion.*[5]

Catherine's views on child rearing had been communicated to William before their marriage and no sooner had they started reproducing than she began to implement them. Most important was raising them in the Christian faith:

> *Mothers, take the trouble to make your children true,*
> *and God will enable you to do it. If you work for him*
> *with your children, he will work with you in them,*
> *and you shall have the joy of seeing them grow up into*
> *Christ, their living Head in all things.*[6]

In this same address many years later, Catherine would write how, from when he was about two, she would take her eldest child – little Willie, who would later become the second General of The Salvation Army – place him on her knee and tell him the stories of the Old Testament in baby language, adapted to "baby comprehension" in order that he "thoroughly drank them in and also the moral lessons they were calculated to convey".

The Booth children, though clearly loved, were raised in a strict home where there was discipline from a very early age. As did most households of the time, the Booths firmly held to the principle of "spare the rod and spoil the child".

The Victorian family, with Queen Victoria and Prince Albert and their nine offspring as a national example, was focused on the home, at least for the upper and middle classes. Mother was in charge, with father playing a rather secondary role. In the Booth household both mother and father were sometimes absent as their evangelistic campaigns and ministry took them away from home. There would be a string of servants and governesses to look after the Booth clan, and in this aspect their upbringing wasn't much different from that of other Victorian children.

As in many homes at the time, although perhaps even more so as a result of both William and Catherine's obsessions with their health, there was an overemphasis on illness and treatments. Catherine in particular became increasingly interested in "alternative" medicine such as homeopathy and hydrotherapy, and William was bound to be recruited to the cause.

"Hydrotherapy", or "hydropathy" involved the use of water for pain relief and treatment and, although it had been used since ancient times, in the mid-1800s it experienced something of a revival in popularity.[7]

"Taking the waters" at bathing places such as Bath Spa was a common treatment and leisure activity for those who could afford it. William himself used this form of therapy and over the years became quite a regular at Mr Smedley's "hydro" in Matlock, Derbyshire.[8]

But the principles of hydropathy, the use of cold and hot water for treatments for a range of ailments, could also be employed more cheaply, at home or when away.

Clayton, Newcastle-under-Lyme, Staffordshire,
Monday Feby. 5, 1855

*My dearest and most precious Love,*

*Your letters are not quite as long as they used to be, but you are busy. I am sure I am very much delighted to hear of your industry, your improved health, and that you have adopted the cold water plan. I have very great faith in it. I have what they call a medical rubber, a towel made on purpose; almost as rough as though made of horsehair. I came from Nottingham with a dreadful pain at the bottom of my back – was very bad for two days. I bathed it once with cold water and salt and rubbed it, and never felt it again. I am not so well to-day. My chest is sore with yesterday's exertions. I intend being more careful to-night.*

*Yesterday was more successful than ever as a beginning. Altho' it rained in torrents, the chapel was crowded; many went away unable to obtain admission. We registered during the prayer meeting 40 names…*

Catherine's ill health was ongoing. It is thought that her own "back problems" were the result of curvature of the spine, and this was what had confined her to bed as a child. William's ailments were also many and varied, and the hard-hearted might even say sometimes exaggerated if not entirely imaginary.

This might have been linked with his mental health, because William was plagued by depression[9] throughout his adult life. There's no doubt that he suffered badly from "dyspepsia", or severe indigestion, from his mid-twenties, and this could make him rather difficult, some might say explosive, and even "censorious".[10] Unrelenting hard work, along with these illnesses, laid him low from time to time, with Catherine often picking up the pieces of family, church, and ministry life, even despite her own illnesses.

In an attempt to find remedies for their constant ailments, the Booths also turned to homeopathy, a system of alternative medicine that was relatively new at the time, having been originated in 1796 by the German physician Samuel Hahnemann. He developed a "like cures like" system of treatment wherein the patient receives minute doses of a natural substance which in a healthy person would produce symptoms of a disease.[11]

Catherine was greatly influenced by the American holiness teacher Phoebe Palmer, whom she looked up to on the subject of women's right to preach in church. Mrs Palmer ran a joint preaching ministry with her husband, Dr Walter Clarke Palmer, who also became quite famous as a homeopath!

During his 1857 campaign in Chester, when everything, it seemed, was going against him, William was feeling low and unwell, and inevitably turned for comfort not just to the woman he loved but also to a form of medical relief that she championed.

CHESTER, LATE JANUARY OR FEBRUARY, 1857

*If it does not get better, I shall go to the Homeopathic doctor. Chester is either blessed or cursed with three of them. But as you deem it a blessing, I am fain in this, as in many other respects, to pin my faith to your*

*sleeve, and with me there the controversy ends!*
*So I throw up my cap and shout, "Hurrah for*
*Homeopathy," with its infinite quantity of infinitesimal*
*doses, in whatever society I may be where the question*
*is mooted. All because I have such a blessed little wife,*
*in whose judgment I can confide on matters physical.*

Catherine was determined that the Booth home would not just be a healthy place, but also one of refuge and safety, as her own childhood home had been. Along with her inclination towards alternative medicine, Catherine also asserted the benefits of fresh air and exercise. She was determined that her own children would enjoy activities in which she had been unable to participate. Outdoor sports such as tennis, cricket, and football were insisted upon. There was to be, by and large, a home schooling regime, but whatever the merits of education and outdoor activities, spiritual instruction was at the centre of it all.

Despite the high expectations placed on them, the Booth offspring thrived under Catherine's rather austere view of child rearing. All eight of Catherine and William's children grew to maturity, and all became Salvation Army officers involved in the birth and development of the Army in its early years, although daughter Marian, who was known as Marie within the family, was an invalid who, although given the rank of "Staff Captain", did not participate much in her parents' work.

All the Booth children emerged from their childhood with a deep Christian faith and a commitment to mission, which was instilled in them from the earliest possible age. For William and Catherine, training their children to be first and foremost people of God was a priority.

*How is baby? Bless his little heart! Tell him his papa prays for him and hopes that God will make him a Luther to pull down the dreadful abuses under which the church groans. O Kate, ours is a solemn and important vocation, the training of that boy!*

*So you had to whip him to obtain the mastery, and now he is king, seeing that you are ill! I often think about him and imagine I see him lifting up his little arms to me. Bless him! Oh, may he indeed be great in the sight of the Lord, and whether esteemed or not by men, God grant that he may be holy and useful.*

William picked up his copy of the Chester Chronicle and read again the description of his revival meeting from the other night. The description of the "altar call" was so unfair and ill judged! Obviously it was written by someone who little understood matters of faith and repentance.

"The preacher next called upon 'all who want salvation to come out and kneel down at the rails of the communion table.' Presently, various persons have gone to the rail where 'leaders' at once fold them in their arms and commence close conversation. After a few minutes the 'penitents' are conducted to the vestry where their names are registered as 'converts'."[12]

William winced. Was that really how "outsiders" and onlookers perceived this work of God? Or was it just the cynicism of reporters? How dangerous the press could be, and yet how useful once on one's side. For all their sarcasm and irony, they could be useful for advertising events and happenings. It was something he would have to think on further.

But at least the article had got people through the doors, if only to view this spectacle that was Mr Booth, although William regretted that so many had been unable to gain access to the church and hundreds of would-be souls might not have been saved. So few. Just fifteen names taken in the vestry that evening.

But now he had something more positive to report to his darling Catherine, away in London and once again on a sick bed. While the news that another little Booth was on the way was welcome – they had after all intended to have a large family, hadn't they? – the accompanying illness was not.

### CHESTER, FRIDAY 13TH FEBRUARY 1857

*Mr Radcliffe, a solicitor from Liverpool, was here last night. He is a rather singular, and at the same time a very devoted man. He consecrates his life and efforts and fortune to the great work of saving men. I am informed that he goes up and down the country preaching the gospel anywhere he can obtain an opening. He especially attends races, executions and such like gatherings of people.*

*For instance, the other day a man was hanged at Chester. Mr Radcliffe came over two or three days before the day fixed, drew up a plan of the different routes by which people would approach the gallows, and when night came he placed a man with a supply of tracts at each road, and thus put some papers on Salvation into the hands of every person who came. In addition to this he had four or five preachers at work besides himself.*

> *It appears that he had heard about me at*
> *Macclesfield and Nottingham, and last Sunday he sent*
> *one of his preachers to see me with an invitation to*
> *Liverpool. He proposes taking for me a large theatre,*
> *capable of holding between two and three thousand*
> *people, the effort to be unsectarian and no collections,*
> *he undertaking to meet all expenses, and allowing the*
> *New Connexion to take the converts.*
>
> *He is a nice fellow, a brave man, and a true*
> *Christian. I like him much. But of course I cannot at*
> *present entertain anything of this character.*

The idea of revival meetings being held outside church buildings was certainly not novel, but for William it was something of a departure from his usual course.

Later, William Booth would deliberately go for buildings where the "ordinary" people felt comfortable – tents, music halls, and theatres. He understood that, for the unchurched masses, entering a church building was not an attractive proposition. This was quite apart from the fact that the "church people" of the day sometimes looked down on those whom they perceived as rather ramshackle and even dirty, and those who could not afford to buy their pews in church were left isolated and standing at the back. William Booth himself had experienced just this at home in Nottingham many years before. He and his friend Will Sansom, with their little band of evangelists, had preached on the streets and gathered a gang of street boys together whom they had persuaded to attend "church". However, when they entered the back door of the Wesley Chapel and sat in a pew, the elders had been furious.[13]

This injustice made William Booth determined never to turn a penitent away and to offer opportunities for them in places in which they did not feel like aliens. This became one of the calling cards of his ministry, which developed into the Christian Mission and later The Salvation Army. The prospect of leading a meeting in a 3,000-seat theatre in Liverpool must have been very enticing, despite the ongoing trials of the Chester campaign.

CHESTER, WEDNESDAY, 18 FEBRUARY, 1857

*We had a tremendous struggle at the chapel. I never saw anything like it in my life. We were crowded above and below, and having been out all day, I was poorly prepared in mind and much fatigued in body, yet I was pressed in spirit and the Lord helped me to preach as I very, very seldom do! Oh, the words seemed like jagged daggers running into the hearts of the people! And yet, though the great mass of them stayed to the prayer-meeting, we had only twenty-one souls. We ought to have had fifty or more. That abominable paper has helped to raise all this opposition. It has encouraged a lot of ignoramuses to come and mock. They have no shame. You cannot make them feel.*

CHESTER, LATE JANUARY OR FEBRUARY, 1857

*We had a good night. I preached from, "What must I do to be saved?" We had not much power during the first part of the sermon, but during the appeal,*

*"What must I do to be damned?" I don't remember*
*ever having more. In fact Mr Round said this morning*
*that he never felt so much under any appeal before in*
*his life, and that he could have knelt down and wept*
*his heart away at the conclusion. George Fox said*
*he could not sleep after it. It was indeed terrific. I felt*
*astounded at it myself. Of course I can only talk in*
*this way to my wife.*

*… I never was better pleased with people than I*
*am with the poor country folk. They come four, five,*
*six, seven, eight and nine miles night after night, and*
*many of them have found the Lord. Thank God, the*
*common people hear me gladly. I believe I should be*
*a great deal more useful among the simple-hearted*
*country people than I am among the fashionable,*
*hard-hearted, half-infidel townsfolk, with their rotten*
*hearts and empty heads, and yet full-blown conceit*
*and pride!*

Support was growing for William, with advocates such as
Reginald Radcliffe, who was just four years older than William.
He operated as an independent evangelist for most of the second
half of the nineteenth century and was partly responsible for
William adopting similar work.[14]

But, as William ploughed through the Chester and other
campaigns, it became clear to him, to Catherine, and to his
supporters, that although many of his peers in the Methodist
New Connexion saw the benefit of his revival meetings, not
everyone liked his style and not everyone was happy about his
rising popularity.

# CHAPTER

# 9

*My precious Mother,*

*Your very kind and interesting letter came to hand this morning would that I could find to answer it as my heart prompts but I feel as tho' I could far easier lay my head on your bosom and weep with fatigue and weakness. However I must send you the patterns as you are so kind as to make Willie a frock, bless you. The making is far more to me than the material. The enclosed patterns fit him nicely ... and the length of the shirt is written on. His Father likes his things so short that I shall be obliged to let him wear drawers ... Keep account of the cost till I settle with you. The pattern is a very pretty one the back and front are <u>alike</u>.*

*Baby is wearing that little old red frock you made for Willlie ... he looks quite a sight but I cannot let him wear white any longer. I was going to buy a bit of scarlet*

*and make him one. I don't like any other colour for*
*babies and hessian wears better than anything and is*
*cheapest in the end, but don't hurt yourself to make one*
*… The nurse girl I parted with was not good for much*
*as a nurse and I had no confidence in her work, the*
*one I have got seems a sincere girl but almost useless at*
*present, knows nothing about nursing or children; my*
*servant does not do amiss so far as the work goes but I*
*am in doubt about her nurse work. Oh for a thorough*
*good Christian girl and one who can work.*

*Don't put yourself about to write. Let Father*
*write when you are busy. It is post time so excuse more*
*and believe me as ever your loving Kate*

Catherine Booth was settling into the first of what would become a succession of "new homes" over the following decade or so. After a couple of years as the wife of the Methodist New Connexion's itinerant evangelist, at long last she had a "home" of her own. But she wasn't a happy woman, because she and William were there under sufferance.

William's evangelistic ministry was growing, as was his popularity. But with this came jealously from older and more experienced ministers[1] who felt that the young Booth – William wasn't yet thirty – undermined their rather dull ministry.

At the 1857 New Connexion Annual Conference, held in William's home town of Nottingham, there was a proposal to take William out of his ministry. According to some, it was rather costly and it wasn't preparing William for his eventual ordination as a minister. He was not really being "tested" in a church, with all the responsibilities that entailed. But the underlying theme of the motion was that William Booth was having far too much influence on the denomination for someone quite so young.[2] He should be assigned to a regular circuit and put in charge of a church. Despite his protests, the vote was carried and it was decided that he would be sent to the Halifax Circuit in Yorkshire, with responsibility for Brighouse.

William bowed to the will of the Conference but, as he told his in-laws, he remained sad and angry:

> *For some time I have been aware that a party has been forming against me. Now it has developed itself and its purpose. It has attacked and defeated my friends, and my evangelistic mission is to come to an immediate conclusion. On Saturday, after a debate of five hours, in which I am informed the bitterest spirit was manifested against me, it was decided by 44 to 40 that I be appointed to a circuit. The chief opponents to my continuance in my present course are ministers, the opposition being led on by the Rev PJ Wright and Dr Crofts. I care not much for myself. A year's rest will be very acceptable. By that time, God will, I trust, make plain my way before me, either to abide as a circuit preacher, or by opening me a door which no man or number of men shall be able to shut. My concern is for the Connexion – my deep regret is for the spirit that makes manifest, and the base ingratitude it displays.[3]*

Unfortunately William's appointment to the Brighouse church was far from restful. The Halifax Circuit was uninspiring and

Brighouse, which Catherine described as a "low smoky town", one of the most unsuccessful and obscure parts of it.[4]

There must have been opportunities for revival-style meetings, but the response to that ministry was underwhelming. The next twelve months weren't particularly happy for the Booths, apart from the birth in July 1857 of their second son, Ballington, who was named for one of Catherine's uncles. One highlight of the inauspicious year was the baby's baptism by the man who had most influenced William, the evangelist James Caughey, who visited Britain in early 1858.

But, for all its inadequacies, it was in Brighouse that Catherine first became actively involved in the life of the church, running classes for children and for mothers, despite her continuing back problems and a busy life as a wife and mother. As she reported in a letter home to her parents, motherhood was proving to be a joy but also a test, as she trained her little ones:

*Willie gets every day more loveable and engaging and affectionate. He manifests some very pleasing traits of character. You would love to see him hug Ballington, and offer him a bit of everything he has! He never manifests the slightest jealousy or selfishness towards him, but on the contrary he laughs and dances when he caresses baby, and when it cries he is quite distressed. I have used him to bring me the footstool when I nurse baby, and now he runs with it to me as soon as he sees me take him up, without waiting to be asked, a piece of thoughtfulness I seldom receive from older heads! Bless him. I believe he will be a thoroughly noble lad, if I can preserve him from all evil influences. The Lord help me! I have had to whip*

*him twice lately severely for disobedience, and it has*
*cost me some tears. But it has done him good, and I*
*am reaping the reward already of my self-sacrifice. The*
*Lord help me to be faithful and firm as a rock in the*
*path of duty towards my children.*[5]

A year later and the Booths were on the move once again, and the father of the house was now officially the "Revd William Booth". At the 1858 New Connexion Conference, held in Hull in May of that year, William was finally ordained into the ministry in a formal ceremony which marked the end of his four years as a probationary minister.

He had hoped this might herald a return to his evangelistic work, but in spite of his pleadings, and those of several circuits to allow Revd Booth to resume that work, he was instead appointed to a church in Gateshead near Newcastle-upon-Tyne in the north-east of England.

For Catherine this was a release from Brighouse, where she reported she felt "imprisoned", and although she still yearned for William to be allowed to go back on the road, regardless of the fact that it would leave her without a permanent home, she was happy to move north with him.

Gateshead immediately stole her heart. The parishioners were friendly and welcoming and the house was a vast improvement on their previous abode.

GATESHEAD

TUESDAY AFTERNOON SEPT 1858

*My very dear Parents*

*I know you will be anxious for a few lines from me and I am as anxious to send a few or I should defer it a little longer for we are in a bad muddle at present and I am very much fatigued and harassed. I like the house much better than I expected, it is in a lovely situation and has a nice piece of grass in front nearly as large as grounds at the back where Willie can play on the grass for hours ...*

*They had a social meeting last evening to welcome us into the Circuit and we were highly gratified. I assure you, you could not conceive of a more marked contrast than that between our reception here and at Brighouse, in fact it is all we can desire and the leading men ... think that they have got the best appointment in the Connexion ... The people here seem unanimous in their satisfaction and cordiality. I like them very much as far as I have seen them, they seem so intelligent and warm hearted.*

The fact that Gateshead had far more spiritual potential than Brighouse was obvious from the moment the Booths arrived in the town. Methodism had first come to Gateshead with John Wesley himself and there were Methodist chapels of various types, including New Connexionalism. Most importantly, there were opportunities that had not been open to William in Yorkshire for trying out his evangelistic work at a very local level.[6]

William's predecessor at the Bethesda Chapel in Gateshead had proved to be a bit of a maverick and an "infidel lecturer", so the Revd Booth was welcomed as something of a deliverer.[7] The chapel would soon be full to overflowing as people responded to William's ministry.

Within a few weeks of his arrival, in July 1858, he was presiding over a "Camp Meeting" on Windmill Hills to the south of Gateshead[8] – an open-air meeting of the sort that, not too many years in the future, would become his stock-in-trade. William Booth enthusiastically embraced, reinterpreted, and employed ministry tools from past eras. The "Camp Meeting" had been introduced in the eighteenth century by John Wesley and his friend and fellow founder of Methodism, George Whitefield. Successful evangelists such as the American Charles Grandison Finney had also used outdoor ministry very successfully.

Back at the chapel Catherine was leading classes, and they had instituted a system of "house-to-house visitation", which supported the congregation in their homes. There were special prayer meetings with a focus on revival as well as the street ministry.[9] William had already tested some of these strategies but at Gateshead it all began to come together. It was not uncommon for thousands of people to flock to Bethesda Chapel for the Booths' Friday night meetings. The chapel was one of the biggest buildings in Gateshead, and so numerous were the souls being brought to Christian faith there that the ironworkers in the town dubbed it "The Converting Shop". This success was recognized by the New Connexion, who elected to reappoint William to Gateshead at the 1859 Annual Conference in Manchester.

This was just as well, since the family was now settled, and still growing. On 18 September 1858 the Booths welcomed the arrival of their third child and first daughter, Catherine, named after her mother and always called Katie. The plump little girl soon became the apple of her parents' eyes.

Gateshead

Oct '58

*My precious Mother*

*... I suppose you will think me like all mothers when I say she is a little <u>beauty</u> tho' I don't think I ever said so of Ballington because I did not think so, he was a much larger child but not near so pretty a baby nor so fat, that is, when he was born; <u>now</u>, I consider him a fine and beautiful boy.*

*Baby is more like Willie. Her hair is exactly the colour of his and her eyes just the colour Willie's were, she has ... a fine forehead and a plump round face. William thinks she is more like me than any of them but I think she will be nicer looking than ever I was, she has a beautiful hand and a nice little ear. She is the picture of health and happiness and thrives daily. Now I hope this description is enough even for a Grandmama.*

*Willie is very pleased with his baby "tissa" as he calls her, he gets in to my room as often as he can and when he does get in he lets me know it. He is a merry sunny little fellow so full of life and spirits he does not know how to let it out fast enough. I think he is one of the loveliest children I ever met with, he attracts everybody's notice at once and is becoming a general favourite in the Circuit...*

In common with most middle- and upper-class Victorians, the Booths employed servants to help in the house and with the children. "Service" was one of the most reliable sources of work for many women in particular, and there was never a shortage of people wanting to work for a well-connected family, even if, as with the Booths, there was not always a great deal of money in the house.

As the years progressed, the "help" became increasingly important as both William and Catherine spent more and more time away from home as they immersed themselves in Christian ministry. But in the early years of her marriage, and when her first children were very young, Catherine sometimes struggled with the servants. Perhaps she was unlucky with her choice of help, perhaps she was far too finicky and even controlling in her household management, but she seems to have had some very poor experiences.

### March 1859 Sunday afternoon

*My dearest Mother,*

*… I think never anybody was so unfortunate with girls as I am; I get such looks they seem to have neither thoughts nor judgement. I often wish you were here just to blow them up well for me. That is the nurses I refer to, my servant is a good servant but neither truthful nor honest.*

*I sent you word a little while ago that Ballington was thin and fretful and yet he seemed to have no symptoms of ill health beyond looking ill and appearing thin and feeble compared with what he was; the thought struck me one day that perhaps he did not get all the food that I sent into the nursery for him so I took him more under my*

own care … and soon had my suspicions confirmed for I
found he would always eat a second meal when I gave it
to him indeed he never seemed satisfied. You would have
been surprised to see how he improved in a week and how
much more lively and spirited he became; whether it was
eaten from him or wasted to save the trouble of feeding
him I don't know but I am sure he had not had enough.
You see I cannot be in two places at once and he sleeps
until our dinner time when I am obliged to be at table.

    This will give you an idea of the vexations I have to
endure. A month ago I stayed for dinner with William
in the town to save me walking up to chapel twice and
had baby brought. The next day I perceived Ballington's
bottom all over black marks on one side just like the
stripes left between anyone's fingers and I have no doubt
that one of them had done it during my absence. It
continued so for several days but I did not accuse her of it
because I knew she would deny it … is it not trying when I
am giving them every privilege and paying them well, but
we all have our trials and these are mine? Oh for patience.

    I think William told you about Willie's head, poor
little fellow. It was a frightful gash just on one side of
his forehead. It was an incised wound opened right to
the bone, I fear it is not doing as well as it might do but
the Doctor said at the time that it would never close but
would have to heal from the bottom and would probably
mark him for life tho' not seriously he thought. In all
other respects Willie is well…

    Baby, I do wish you could see her, she is as fine strong
and fat as ever Willie was and I think bigger than he
was at her age. I never had half as much enjoyment from

*either of the others, she is such a good happy contented little creature and then I can suckle her with comfort. I tried her with her bottle the other day but her Ladyship would not have it any way. I persevere with her a long time but she lets me. You should have seen what a piece of work she made about it. She was very hungry at this time she kept catching hold and when she perceived it was not the titty she spit it out and cried a "goodern". I have not given it to her again… everybody says what a <u>sweet</u> little creature and so she is and she has one of the <u>smallest</u> and most beautiful hands I ever saw …*

MONDAY AFTERNOON

*My dearest mother*

*… the lass I got as nurse has turned out good for <u>nothing</u>. She came a month on trial fortunately so I sacked her on Wednesday and I intend to do <u>without</u> one while my present servant steps up, for if I have a dozen she will win them.*

*I fully believe she has been robbing us ever since she came in … having found out that she prigged the bacon, tea, sugar and I began to keep a sharp look out and to lock up pretty tightly when I found my things lasted about half as long again. I have my groceries by half stones of each thing at a time. This has annoyed her and made her very disagreeable and she has managed to bring the others over to her side and this one is a saucy impudent hussy so I am pretty well tired and assume you pray for me.*

# CHAPTER

# 10

The odour of the house was what assaulted them first, being a combination of dampness, urine, and old cabbage water. The building was dark, depressing, and rotting. The rickety wooden stairs creaked as Catherine and her companion trod carefully up to the first floor.

In the corner of the poor, pathetic room overlooking the street they found the woman they had come to see. On top of a decrepit wooden bedstead, a thin mattress, and a pile of rags, she lay half dead with exhaustion, a babe in each arm, both of whom were whimpering. The place reeked of birth and blood and sweat and worse.

Catherine Booth had never seen anything so appalling in her life. Her stomach heaved and for a moment she thought she would be sick. Then she looked again at the woman on the bed. She remembered her own four labours, in clean fresh bedding with a midwife in attendance and a loving husband waiting downstairs for news of the new arrival.

"Where's your husband, dearie?" she asked quietly, bending her head to the bed, breathing in the stench. The woman slowly shook her head. Did that mean he wasn't around? Or dead? Or maybe drowning his sorrows at the alehouse? Whatever the case, it was up to them to sort out the situation.

Catherine and her friend, who had come to her house a short time earlier to tell of this woman's predicament, got to work. Catherine opened the small window to let in a little air but the woman shivered. She removed her own coat and placed it over the woman. They hadn't thought to bring blankets, but some must be brought from home, and immediately. Catherine looked around for a broom, but could not see one. There were no plates or knives, so, opening her basket, she pulled out a clean cloth and on that laid out the bread and cheese she had quickly grasped from her own kitchen.

Catherine's colleague from the Bethesda Chapel returned with a bucket of water collected from the rain barrel in the yard below, and then, together, they helped the new mother to sit up slightly to take a little water from a chipped cup, and to try a little bread. Catherine took the tiny newborns, both poor pathetic pieces of humanity, and washed them, as carefully as she could, in a broken pie dish which she had found under the bed. It had more than likely been used as a bedpan, but it was empty now and the rainwater was passably clean, so it would have to suffice as a baby bath. She washed the birth debris off the scrawny infants and then she and her friend cleaned the mother up as best they could and reunited her with her babies, both now wrapped safely together in a shawl which the friend had produced from her own basket.

Too weak to speak her gratitude, the woman gazed at these angels of mercy, her large eyes filling with tears that then rolled down her wan and shrunken cheeks.

"Don't worry, dear. We'll look after you. Sleep now."

Catherine had seen poverty before, of course, but nothing like what she experienced in Gateshead. In Brighouse they had lived among the poor and, although the growing Booth family itself had precious little in the way of financial resources, which was an ongoing concern for her and William, in comparison to those around them they were rich.

In Brighouse, Catherine was first exposed to children who were forced to work in the mills from the age of seven or eight, for long hours and for just a few pennies a day. Although Catherine had had a social conscience from a young age, she now witnessed first-hand the dangers of child labour and became more and more convinced of the need for Christians to champion causes such as the introduction of laws to restrict the hours that children might work. Years later William Booth would campaign for the rights of girls forced to work in extremely unsafe conditions making sulphuric matches, which would often result in a terrible disease called "phossy jaw", and through this he, among others, would be at the forefront of ensuring better working conditions for workers.

But it was in Gateshead that Catherine witnessed the severe effects of dire poverty. As a centre for coalmining and ironworks, the town was feeling the full force of Britain's Industrial Revolution. As industry expanded so did the necessary urban population, most of whom lived in overcrowded back-to-back houses with little in the way of sanitation bar an open sewer running its filth through the streets.

For Catherine Booth these were revelatory days, as she was exposed to human misery caused not just by lack of finances but also by moral decay. She saw the effects of alcohol abuse, which she had long advocated against as a member of the Temperance Movement. She witnessed fathers and mothers wasting what few pennies they had on beer and worse, as they sought to blot out the squalor and hopelessness of their existence. It would be some years before care and compassion for the physical well-being of men, women, and children would be incorporated into William and Catherine's ministry for souls, but in those desperate homes in Gateshead the seed from which grew the work of The Salvation

Army was beginning to be sown in Catherine's, and consequently William's, heart.

For now, William's concentration was still on leading the unconverted to Christ, and although many thousands flocked to the Converting Shop in Gateshead, it was tough going. His health was failing once again and in August 1860 he was forced to take a rest, leaving Catherine to hold the fort. While William was indisposed, she would take care of the administration of the church and the business of the circuit, deputizing for her husband.[1]

GATESHEAD, TUESDAY
AUGUST 28TH '60

*My precious William,*

*Your kind & welcome letter is to hand, and as I have a letter I want to forward & a little news which will gladden your heart, I write again today.*

*I need not tell you how thankful I am to hear of your satisfaction in the place of your abode and with the general arrangements. I should think from your account that you are pretty well occupied with dousing & scrubbing, etc. from morning till night. I presume it is what one would call pretty vigorous treatment, & yet I suppose it will be only what the Hydropathics call mild. Well, I do hope it will prove the right thing. I must say I feel a little anxious lest they should overdo it, but I am trying to commit you with all I am and have to the care of my Father in Heaven, and I am not without faith that he does take you at my hands. May He bless you and then you shall be blessed.*

*I did not forget your class. There was but a poor attendance, but we had a blessed season. I never felt so much liberty in leading before. I think all were blessed. I stayed the prayer meeting in the school room, and Mr Firbank called on me to pray. I did so as I have not been able to pray for years. Truly, the Spirit of intercession was poured out & all present seemed to partake the glorious influence. I felt unspeakably happy after I ceased, & could have shouted, "Glory!" if I had given expression to my feelings. I never felt like it before in my life in a meeting.*

*Oh, why could I not believe for the blessing of holiness? I tried but I have not yet learnt to take the naked word as a sufficient warrant for my faith. I am looking for "signs." Oh, pray for me. I have solemnly pledged myself to the Lord to seek till I do find this pearl of great price. Will you not join me in seeking it too?*

*I am so glad you find religious society. I trust the fellowship of Xians will be made a lasting blessing to your soul. Oh, my love, I cannot tell you how bitterly I regret that I have not been a greater help to you in spiritual things. I see how I might have stimulated you to fuller consecration, but alas I fear my influence has been all the other way. But if God spares us to meet again, by his help I will do better. I will try to get filled with the Spirit before you come back.*

*What am I to say in reply to the enclosed? I feel inclined to go for night but not for afternoon. I think if I mistake not, they have wanted you two or three times & you could not go, so I think on that account*

*I should like to comply, and there is plenty of time. What do you say? Write by return, & if I am to go, may I say that as you have not been able to serve them as you would have liked you wish me to comply with their invitation?*

*I hope you will send me an outline for Bethesda. I cannot get rid of the care and management of things downstairs, and this constantly takes of my thoughts, but I must try to possess my soul in patience & do all in the kitchen as well as in the Pulpit to the glory of God – the Lord help me.*

*I will attend to Mr Jackson's account as soon as I get some money. I wish you would drop a line to that Shoemaker and order a pair the size of the last largest. Willie wants a pair so bad. The children are all well except Willie. He complains of his head & throat, & seems chilly & feverish at night, but I think he is better today. I put a bandage on his head & gave him Belladonna last night. I felt afraid of scarlet fever last night, but he is better this morn'g.*

*Be sure and write to Father & Mother the first opportunity, but you need not particularise the treatment. I fear it would frighten them. I am grateful for your wish for me to come, but if you don't get any reduction, that would be out of the question. You must doctor me yourself.*

*The spice kisses were fully appreciated, but they cost 2d, the letter being too heavy. Katy was specially gratified & gave you one of her sweetest "Pa's" in return. Willie wants to know when you are coming back. He seems to think it is quite time.*

*And now my dearest I must say farewell. I think*
*I should be happier with a letter on every day for a*
*while, till you see how the treatment seems to affect*
*you. I hope you won't do too much. I am rather afraid*
*it is too active, but I hope all things, and remain your*
*loving & faithful wife, Catherine.*

For a woman to stand in a pulpit and preach to a mixed congregation was revolutionary for the times and it was during their stay in Gateshead that Catherine Booth got her first taste of it. Soon after the birth of her fourth child in January 1860, a second daughter, called Emma Moss, named for William's sister and his mother's maiden name, she delivered her first public address.

Since her girlhood, when her mother had insisted on and taught her about the equality of men and women, Catherine had become increasingly convinced not just that women should be treated equally but also that they should have a right to preach in church. This was much against the practice and the theology of the day, and had been a bone of contention with William when they were first engaged, as they disagreed on the matter most fundamentally.

In April 1855, just a few weeks before their wedding, she had set out in the strongest possible terms her views on (among other subjects) teetotalism and the equality of women.

*... I have searched the word of God through &*
*through, I have tried to deal honestly with every*
*passage on the subject, not forgetting to pray for light*
*to perceive & grace to submit to the truth, however*
*humiliating to my nature. But I solemnly assert that*
*the more I think & read on the subject, the more*
*satisfied I become of the true & scriptural character of*
*my own views.*

*I am ready to admit that in the majority of cases*
*the training of woman has made her man's inferior,*
*as under the degrading slavery of heathen lands she*
*is inferior to her own sex in Christian countries. But*
*that naturally she is in any respect, except in physical*
*strength & courage, inferior to man I cannot see cause*
*to believe, & I am sure no one can prove it from the*
*word of God, & it is on this foundation that professors*
*of religion always try to establish it. Oh prejudice,*
*what will it not do?*

*I would not alter woman's domestic position*
*(when indeed it is scriptural), because God has plainly*
*fixed it. He has told her to obey her husband, &*
*therefore she ought so to do, if she profess to serve God;*
*her husband's rule over her was part of the sentence*
*for her disobedience, which would, by the by, have*
*been no curse at all if he had ruled over her before, by*
*dint of superiority. But God ordained her subjection*
*as a punishment for sin, & therefore I submit. But I*
*cannot believe that inferiority was the ground of it. If*

it had, it must have existed prior to the curse & thus have nullified it. Oh, I believe that volumes of light will yet be shed on the world on this subject. It will bear examination & abundantly repay it. We want a few mighty & generous spirits to go thoroughly into it, pen in hand, & I believe the time is nor far distant when God will raise up such. But I believe woman is destined to assume her true position & exert her proper influence by the special exertions & attainments of her own sex. She has to struggle through mighty difficulties too obvious to need mentioning, but they will eventually dwindle before the spell of her developed & cultivated mind. The heaving of society in America (that birthplace of so much that is great & noble), tho' throwing up, as all such movements do, much that is absurd & extravagant & which I no more approve than you; yet it shows that principles are working, & enquiry awakening.

May the Lord, even the just & impartial one, overrule all for the true emancipation of woman from the swaddling bands of prejudice, ignorance & custom, which almost the world over have so long debased & wronged her. In appealing thus to the Lord I am deeply sincere, for I believe that one of the greatest boons to the race would be woman's exaltation to her proper position mentally & spiritually.

BRADFORD,
THURSDAY APRIL 12, '55

*... The remarks on Woman's position I will read again before I answer. From the first reading I cannot see anything in them to lead me for one moment to think of altering my opinion. You combat a great deal that I hold as firmly as you do, viz. her equality, her perfect equality, as a whole, as a being. But as to concede that she is man's equal, or capable of becoming man's equal, in intellectual attainments or prowess – I must say that is contradicted by experience in the world and my honest conviction.*

*You know, my dear, I acknowledge the superiority of your sex in very many things; in others I believe her inferior. Vice versa with man. I would not stop a woman preaching on any account. I would not encourage one to begin. You should preach if you felt moved thereto; felt equal to the task. I would not stay you if I had power to do so. Altho' I should not like it. It is easy for you to say my views are the result of prejudice; perhaps they are. I am for the world's salvation; I will quarrel with no means that promises help.*

William's initial reply to Catherine's lengthy epistle, in which she had outlined all the biblical precedents that she could find to back up her claims for the equality of women in all matters, must have been slightly disappointing, but she was not deterred.

She had already taken up her cause with Dr David Thomas of the Congregational Chapel in Stockwell, who would later marry her to William Booth. A couple of years before their wedding Dr Thomas had preached about the role of women from his pulpit; Catherine had taken exception to what he said and had written to him, ever so politely but still strongly objecting to his viewpoint:

> *Forgive me my dear Sir if I have spoke too boldly, I feel deeply on this subject. Tho' God knows it is not personal grounds, I love my sex and desire above all earthly things their moral and intellectual elevation. I believe it would be the greatest boon to our race, and tho' I deeply feel my own inability to help it onward I could not satisfy my conscience without making this humble attempt to enlist one whose noble sentiments on other subjects have so long been precious to my soul...* [2]

The right of women to preach was something that was at the heart of the message of one of Catherine's heroines, Mrs Phoebe Palmer. She and her husband, Dr Walter Palmer, were leading lights in the American Holiness movement, which had its roots in Methodism and in particular in the teaching on "Christian perfection" by John Wesley. It was this Wesleyan theology which William Booth had chosen above Calvinism when he flirted with the Congregationalists.

The Wesleyan-Holiness tradition starts with the concept of "original sin" and maintains that a person cannot save him- or herself through good works. Only God, through His Son, Jesus Christ, can save an individual, and by God's grace a person who repents of their sin and believes in Jesus is "saved". They are "born again" in what is described as the "first work of grace". But this theology goes a step further. Holiness adherents believe that there can be a "second work of grace" in which the believer is cleansed of the tendency to commit sin. The experience of "sanctification" enables the Christian to live a holy life entirely without voluntary sin. And this whole experience doesn't have to take decades of trying; it is available instantaneously to those who ask and seek it from God.[3]

Wesleyan teaching was at the heart of the Booths' theology. Holiness would, eventually, become a focal point of The Salvation Army. So there was great excitement in the Booth household in Gateshead in 1859 because the Palmers, who had long been the main proponents of the holiness tradition in the United States of America, were about to visit the north-east of England.

Although she was a woman, at a time when women in any form of leadership, let alone in church authority, were extraordinarily rare, Mrs Palmer's views were gaining ground and not just in America. In years to come, when his Salvation Army was in its infancy, William Booth would give his female recruits and officers the recognition they deserved with his purported announcement that "Some of my best men are women!", but in 1859 he was also taken with other elements of her theology.

Phoebe Palmer had simplified John Wesley's "doctrine of entire sanctification", modifying it so that it was identified with the concept of the "baptism of the Holy Spirit". This sat well with William Booth because it relied not on any intellectual theology

– William's attitude to theological study remained much as it had been at the start of his ministry – but on a simple step of faith. It was available to anyone, even to working men and women, illiterate and unschooled.[4]

"Have you seen this, William?"'

Her husband was barely through the door when Catherine threw a rather plain-looking pamphlet at him.

"What, dear?"

"It's that Rees man again! It's just outrageous. How dare he rail so at Mrs Palmer?"

William Booth took up the leaflet and began reading. The Revd Arthur Augustus Rees, whom he knew as an independent minister from Sunderland, had obviously taken great exception to the fact that Mrs Palmer had visited the area, and had the audacity to stand up and preach to the congregation. Of course, it had all been done properly. Dr Palmer had stood first to lead the service. The main sermon came from the church leader but then Mrs Palmer had walked forward to the Communion rail and urged those listening to throw themselves on the grace of God and repent of their sins. Many had come forward and hundreds of souls had been saved, something which warmed William's heart.

"You're taking too long to read it. Can I just tell you what he says?"

There was no arguing with Catherine when she was in this kind of mood. William sat down and prepared to listen.

"The title gives it away. See here – 'Reasons for Not Co-operating in the Alleged Sunderland Revivals'. Alleged Revivals! That's just insulting. Was he not happy that so many sinful men and women came to Christ under Mrs Palmer's ministry?

"But, William, this is the worst of it. I could understand if Mr Rees objected to the message – to her thoughts on holiness, abstinence, and even conversion and sanctification. After all, we're used to this doctrinal disagreement. But no! His main argument is against Mrs Palmer herself. She's a woman and she's had the audacity to stand and preach! That's what he objects to!"

"Well, darling, you know that lots of people feel the same. I once also thought that way. Even after I'd heard the wonderful Miss Buck speak all those years ago, and been so impressed, my pride still wouldn't give way. Even though you had me read accounts of Caughey and Finney both encouraging women to stand to speak in their services ... you've been so patient with me. But Mrs Palmer's abilities, I think, have finally persuaded me."

"And did you listen closely to her teaching on total abstinence? As you know, I've long maintained that we cannot live a holy life if we continue to resort to a substance which takes our senses from us. The rejection of drink, as Mrs Palmer says, has to be an essential part of our holiness!"

"Yes, you know, dear, I'm convinced of that now. But not, I tell you, entirely because of Mrs Palmer's teaching, but more as a result of your own guidance."

Catherine smiled across at him.

"So!" William broke the silence. "I suppose you've decided what you're going to do about this Mr Rees?"

"Of course! I'm going to write a reply!"

Catherine Booth's retort to the Revd Rees was published as another pamphlet with the less-than-snappy title "Female Teaching or The Reverend A.A. Rees versus Mrs Palmer, Being a Reply to the Pamphlet by the Above Named Gentleman on the Sunderland Revivals". Although in later versions it became known simply as "Female Teaching" and then "Female Ministry"; or "Woman's Right to Preach the Gospel", in its original concept it was from the start a confident, scripturally based and theologically well thought out and robust rebuttal:

> *Whether the Church will allow women to speak*
> *in **her** assemblies can only be a question of time;*
> *common sense, public opinion, and the blessed results*
> *of female agency will force her to give us an honest*
> *and impartial rendering of the solitary text on which*
> *she grounds her prohibitions. Then, when the true*
> *light shines and God's words take the place of man's*
> *traditions, the Doctor of Divinity who shall teach that*
> *Paul commands woman to be silent when God's Spirit*
> *urges her to speak, will be regarded much the same*
> *as we should now regard an astronomer who should*
> *teach that the sun is the earth's satellite…*
>
> *We have endeavoured in the foregoing pages*
> *to establish, what we sincerely believe, that woman*
> *has a **right** to teach. Here the whole question hinges.*
> *If she has the **right**, she has it independently of any*
> *man-made restrictions which do not equally refer to*
> *the opposite sex. If she has the right, and possesses the*
> *necessary qualifications, we maintain that, where the*
> *law of expediency does not prevent, she is at liberty*
> *to exercise it without any further pretensions to*
> *inspiration than those put forth by that male sex.*[5]

The chapel was packed to the rafters. Revd Booth's sermon on this Pentecost Sunday had been inspiring and had uplifted the souls of the faithful again, and stirred those of the not so faithful! He was concluding now. He banged his fist on the pulpit. All eyes were turned towards him.

"So, my dear brothers and sisters. We must be SAVED! SAVED from sin and by the power of J… "

Revd Booth had stopped. What was this? Mrs Booth had risen from her seat and moved to the front of the chapel, just under the pulpit. Was she ill?

Revd Booth looked up at the congregation.

"Friends… if you'll forgive me… "

He stepped down and began to talk quietly with his wife. A few moments later, the Booths returned together to the pulpit, he so tall and she so small.

"Friends. Please bear with us. My wife would like to say a word."

And so Mrs Booth began to speak. Quietly at first and then more confidently.

The Bethesda congregation would not have known it, but they were witnessing a piece of history that Pentecost Sunday morning in 1860. Catherine Booth, after months and perhaps years of struggling with the conviction that she, like Mrs Palmer, should stand and speak and even preach in church, had finally got up the courage to do so.

In that first address she did little more than confess to the packed meeting that she had been struggling with this conviction for a long time and had been disobedient to God because she hadn't previously stepped out in faith. She who had such vivid dreams had felt the Holy Spirit speak to her in her sleep around the time of Emma's birth in January, and now, as she later remembered, she had finally taken the first step into ministry.

> I said: "I dare say many of you have been looking upon
> me as a very devoted woman, and one who has been
> living faithfully to God, but I have come to know that

*I have been living in disobedience, and to that extent
I have brought darkness and leanness into my soul,
but I promised the Lord three or four months ago,
and I dare not disobey. I have come to tell you this,
and to promise the Lord that I will be obedient to the
heavenly vision."*[6]

Catherine returned that very evening to deliver her first sermon at Bethesda, preaching on the theme "Be Filled With the Spirit", and she did not look back.

By August of that year, when William was once again ill and away receiving treatment, Mrs Booth was not just running the business of the church and the circuit but was also preaching on a regular basis. Although not everyone agreed with it, she was in demand and proving quite popular in the vicinity. Now the tables were turned. It was not Catherine advising William on his sermons, but she seeking his help and advice.

NORMANBY TERRACE, GATESHEAD
FRIDAY AUGUST 31ST '60

*My very dear Husband,*

*I was rather disappointed this morn'g that there
was no letter. I am getting anxious about the outline you
promised me. I have undertaken the Teams morn'g &
night for Sunday week, & they say they will want me at
Bethesda the Sunday after, and Mr Scott was here last
night to get me to promise for Sherriff Hill anniversary
the Sunday after that, three weeks next Sunday. I
promised to go if you thought it the best, so you must let
me know. I suppose you are planned there on that day.*

*George Young has also been at me for their anniversary, but they wanted it on the same day as Sherriff Hill, so I don't know how they will arrange it. But I don't think I can undertake any more at present. They expect me to meet the 4 classes, two together. & this together with my own meeting & preparing two new subjects, which I must do, seems almost more than I dare think about. So if you don't send me some help, I shall faint. I have been busy all this morn'g rewriting & improving the Prodigal ready for Sunday. I think I have materially improved it, if it is not too long. But if it is, I must leave it unfinished & make an application at the time. I intend to rewrite & improve the Pentecostal one also.*

*But oh, you don't know the distraction of mind I am subject to. The children have been extremely trying today; both Willie & Ballington are poorly & very fretful, and nobody can or will supply my place. I have to jump up & down incessantly & I am obliged to sit to write in the parlour because I am so cold in the Study, and consequently the noise is forever in my ears … My back has been very bad the last two or three days. Writing does not suit it.*

*Now try & revise that outline & get me one on the 5 v. of the 22 c. of Matthew, or some other that will do for night at Bethesda, and pray much for me that I may keep the prize in view & labour alone for the glory of God.*

*Bless you, I should like to see you.*

*Believe me ever your loving & faithful wife,*

*Catherine.*

# CHAPTER

# 11

The conference hall was bubbling with quiet conversation. On the platform the Connexion president, Mr Crofts, and the others had their heads together. In the front, seated rather nervously next to him, the Revd William Booth waited anxiously.

Joseph Love had seen the signs before and knew that it did not look good for the young Booth. They had worked so hard behind the scenes these past few days – he and Edward Rabbits, Booth's long-standing friend and supporter. William had taken the time to speak to those he needed to consult, and Joseph knew that he'd been unusually restrained. Perhaps it was the fact that Mrs Booth was here in Liverpool with him. He'd presumed she was a quietening influence – that was until last night when he had the opportunity to talk with her over dinner.

They had sat next to each other – not by coincidence, he was sure. It had not taken Catherine Booth long to launch into her questioning of him.

"So, Mr Love, I must say it's very generous of you to offer pay for my husband's salary should the Conference decide that he can return to his revival work, but what do you think are his chances this time around? Will the Conference at last allow him the freedom to follow his God-given employment of evangelism to the masses? Or do you think there are still those who are so jealous and spiteful that they will continue to thwart the will of our Lord in this?"

Joseph Love had been rather taken aback by Mrs Booth's directness. Despite the warnings from Mr Rabbits that Catherine was no shrinking violet, she had appeared on all occasions to date rather quiet and demure. However, he was aware that in the past twelve months she had taken to public speaking and even preaching in Gateshead, so she was certainly not to be taken lightly.

She was direct on this subject too.

"Do you think, Mr Love, that my own preaching ministry may be damaging my dear husband?"

"I know, Mrs Booth, that there are those who frown upon your speaking. But I also believe that the Connexion president and his advisers will be guided more by what they think is good for the denomination and for Revd Booth himself. The argument is, of course, that he requires more experience at local… "

"More experience? I am sorry for interrupting you, Mr Love, but that is just nonsense. William, my husband, has proved his worth. He has proved his experience! Even in Gateshead the evangelist in him will not be still and we are weekly seeing souls won. Sinners saved by grace and coming into a new relationship with the Lord! God will not be held back, Mr Love. He will not!"

Today at Conference, the behind-the-scenes discussions had continued. Revd Booth had been interviewed again at length. Would he not be prepared to continue in a circuit for at least one more year? What if, as Revd Booth's old friend and mentor Dr Cooke had suggested, they made Booth up to Superintendent in the Newcastle Circuit, and then allowed him to be invited to conduct revival meetings?

The huddle on the platform, Mr Crofts at the centre, was now involved in a heated discussion. Someone was pointing out the flaw in the proposed compromise solution to the dilemma. Who would give permission for Revd Booth to conduct these occasional revivals but the Superintendent of the Circuit? And who might that Superintendent be but Booth himself? This was tantamount to giving in to the would-be evangelist. No, he should be required to submit. He should be given another appointment and all this talk of launching out into revival meetings should be ended. Now!

"William!"

Mr Love and Revd Booth looked up. Mrs Booth was shaking her head and mouthing something to her husband from the balcony, where she and the wives and other onlookers were expected to sit quietly throughout the business of Conference.

Revd Booth cocked his head as if to enquire what his wife was about. Mr Love could see she was exasperated. If he had been able to hear the discussion from the platform, then so had others, and so had Mrs Booth. Her face was red with frustration and anger, and she was obviously struggling to control herself. She stood up and leaned over the balcony and directed her next word at her husband, and for the benefit of the whole congregation.

"Never!" she said. Not a shout but certainly loud enough for all to hear.

Catherine was by now, as she wrote to her parents, "sick of the New Connexion from top to bottom". As certain as they had been some years before that this denomination held the future for William, she was now just as determined that they should leave it. The May 1861 Conference eventually turned down William and his supporters' pleas to allow him a return to itinerant ministry. Although initially he ceded, moved his family to his new appointment as Superintendent of the Newcastle Circuit, and even moved into the Superintendent's house, it was not to last long.[1]

The situation was far from ideal. First, the house was inadequate, dirty, and, like the one at Brighouse, in a very poor part of town. The circuit itself was not in a particularly good financial state. William undoubtedly could see the next year or more stretching out in front of him as he buried himself in administration and church governance with little time to travel and preach.

But he was still receiving invitations to lead revival meetings, which he could not resist accepting. He preached in Alnwick, Northumberland, and then travelled to London, where his supporters encouraged him to think of life outside and beyond the New Connexion.

LONDON, 19 OR 20 JUNE 1861

*I saw Mr Hammond yesterday. Found him in a beautiful mansion, after a long and weary search. He is a very agreeable gentleman and welcomed me cordially, giving me all the information and counsel he could. He starts for America on Monday in the Great Eastern. His success has been very considerable in Scotland, and they have acted most generously towards him. He has only been a public evangelist for the last twelve months – held three services a day until his health broke down. The people then sent him to Italy, meeting all his expenses, and numbers of first-class ministers are doing him and his work honour.*

*I should like to lay the noble conduct of these men before our Conference, and contrast it with the drivelling opposition with which they have met my movements and convictions.*

*Almost his first advice after hearing my position was, "Cut the denomination and go to work for Jesus, and He will open your way." He says there is a committee at Glasgow who are only too glad to get the right sort of men and to find them a sphere. But he adds, "If you go to Scotland, you must not go as a Methodist. If you do, you will very largely, if not entirely, block your way."*

*I must say I was pleased with him, though I far from agree with all he said. Still, the interview was such a contrast to the discouraging looks and desponding words of everybody I have come in contact with for the last two months, save one (my Kate), that it quite cheered me. I shall not, of course, decide on any plan until I see you.*

*Mr Hammond said, "If you have power to hold a large audience and to exhibit the truth and bring home the Gospel to their hearts, you may go forth, and God is sure to provide for you. All Britain is open to you!*

*Well, whatever comes, we must live to God, close to God.*

---

FRIDAY NIGHT, JUNE 21ST '61

*My very dear Husband,*
*... Thou talks silly about my fears proving groundless. It is beyond a doubt now. I am just in the old fix, but I think worse than with either of the two last, sick, languid & spiritless in the extreme. But as you say perhaps it is all right. Oh, for more faith*

*& patience. My heart is so rebellious, or Satan is continually injecting rebellious thoughts. I don't know which it is. But it makes me very unhappy to feel so.*

*I am very pleased with the contents of your letter. It seems remarkable that you should meet Mr Tomlins, but I should think you will not find much help from his class of friends. You will occupy quite a different sphere to him. I shall be very anxious to hear the result of your interview with Mr P. It seems to me that Scotland is the place to begin at, and we should soon be there from here. It is of no use talking about me doing much now, or else I don't doubt but I should soon be popular in London. You see, I am not so fearful of myself as you are. But that cannot be now, at least for 12 months. So you must do all your calculations apart from me, & I have no fear about you alone getting on first rate.*

*My only difficulty is I shrink from long & distant separations, & something has suggested today, what if your husband by being so much away from home & you should become indifferent to it & prefer the luxuries & attentions of other homes to yours, etc., etc.? This would indeed be bitter, but I cannot think it can ever be. I think God, who knows why I offered you for the work, will spare me this & keep your heart & affections fixed, and I think the union we have realized for six years past will make such a thing all but impossible. You will forgive me for telling you my heart is rather sad. I have never yearned for your presence since you went as I do tonight, & it seems a long time to look forward to Wednesday. Nevertheless, I would have you stay Sunday over by all means if you can get* some services; not in any of our chapels, that would not be worth staying for, but in some large place where you will have somebody to hear you.

I don't know whether a six month's engagement with the Theatre committee might not be a good beginning. It would publish you the world over & we could be in London & you be much at home, & perhaps I might do a little if I feel better in a few weeks.

Give my kindest love to dear mother & father, & ask father if he will please to get me 2 or 31b of nice smoked bacon, the belly part, & three or four real bloater herrings, & you must bring them with you. Now, don't think it a bother. There are no nice ones here & I should much like some. Tell mother if she has got a bottle of that wine that she wants to dispose of, she can put it in too, but not if she has not it to spare. I can do without that. I am living on fish at present. I have only indulged in one half pint of shrimps. They are so dear – 10d per quart. Is Mother wearing that dress? Just ascertain, & if not & if she does not intend, you may as well bring it. I want to show it to two or three friends & we shall get it back again before long.

Excuse more now & ever remember me as your loving & faithful wife, Catherine.

---

PROBABLY MONDAY 24 JUNE 1861

Yesterday, accompanied by father, I went to the Garrick Theatre. We arrived there at half-past three *and found about forty "workers," who were receiving an address. Then prayer was offered for God's blessing on the work, and afterwards they went off to the surrounding neighbourhood. Some went to the lodging houses, where about sixty persons were found in one room, others from door to door, and others to the open air for meetings at the corners of the streets. I joined the last and gave two short addresses. At five all came back to the theatre for tea. Then there was more prayer, and all went forth again to bring people up for the service at seven. The attendance was not large. I preached; had a little liberty in talking to the people. I found that a sermonic address is but of little service. A random talk is the most effective. A meeting for conversation with anxious persons was held afterwards. Several were much concerned and with some of the cases I was pleased. But it was a very different affair altogether to what I have ever taken part in.*

*I feel very much easier in my mind. In fact, I have a measure of trust and confidence that all things are working for the desired end, to a degree that I have never had before.*

On 18 July 1861, less than a month after that preaching engagement at London's Garrick Theatre accompanied by his father-in-law, William Booth officially resigned from the Methodist New Connexion. For Catherine, it could not come quickly enough. Although they were now, once more, afloat without a church and without any means of financial support, she felt that this was God's will for their lives.

Catherine was pregnant again, although this child was miscarried. The family moved out of their secure accommodation in Newcastle but there was a warm welcome for them back at the Mumford home in Brixton. And while the prospects looked rather bleak at the time, Catherine and William would not be idle for long. Over the next four years the couple developed their own separate ministries, becoming evangelists of note.

The first invitation came from Cornwall, and although there was no guarantee of any payment, the couple left their four little children with their grandparents and headed west, to Hayle. More invitations followed and they moved on to St Ives and St Just, Camborne and beyond, leading revival meetings and witnessing hundreds of unconverted people come to faith and turn their backs on alcohol. This was the holiness they preached and it captured the imagination of those around them. Revival was in the air across Cornwall and Catherine, having recovered from her miscarriage the previous year, was pregnant once more and awaiting the arrival of another little Booth.

*Catherine felt rather frustrated. Although the imminent arrival of yet another little Booth was, of course, warmly anticipated, it meant she was indisposed and could not help William with this work that they had started together.*

*Will had been thrilled at the news of the new baby and at last the children had joined them from London, although this had been something of a mixed blessing because Catherine had felt rather overwhelmed by the whole brood. Thank God for the provision of nurses and governesses, though how they managed to pay them all was still a mystery. God always seemed to provide when the money was due.*

*She opened the window and let in the warm August air, touched by just a little sea breeze. If she stood ever so carefully on tiptoes she* could just about glimpse the ocean, blue against a cloudless sky. This little house at 6 Cornwall Terrace was lovely and would do well for her confinement and labour. She had already, on Mother's strict instructions, sought out the local midwife, who appeared to be a clean and sensible woman. Now it was just a matter of waiting.

Herbert Henry Booth's safe arrival on 26 August 1862 while his parents were billeted in Penzance was a blessing, although he proved something of a sickly child and, as Catherine later reported in her memoirs, "We really had fears at times about rearing him."

But she was soon up and about again, getting actively involved in the Cornwall campaign, which was producing some encouraging results, as Catherine's memoirs record:

REDRUTH SEPT. 28 1862

*Redruth was to be our next sphere, where we had been personally invited by the Methodist Free Churches, and accordingly we packed up, and with the latest interesting addition to our family removed there. It was not a very long journey, being only some 10 or 12 miles. An empty house had been taken as in the case of St. Just, and supplied with furniture on loan, either from the upholsterer's or from the different friends who were interested in the visit …*

*Redruth is a town of 10,000 inhabitants, mostly occupied with the tin mines of the neighbourhood… It was on Sunday Sept. 28th that the first meetings were held. The chapel in which we came to labour was in the centre of the town and belonged to the same body*

that we had been with at Mousehole and Penzance,
and which had been formed out of the division that
had taken place when we ourselves left Wesleyan
Methodism. The building was not a very large one,
still it would seat 900 and would hold at a push, I
should think, 1100 or 1200 people. Indeed, I know
that number was crowded in at the majority of the
meetings that we held there, seeing that it was packed
in every corner at almost every service during the seven
weeks we held meetings in it. One of the results of our
visit was to replace it with one of the largest and most
commodious and beautiful chapels in the county.

I was enabled to take quite as active a part in
the services here as I have done in any place hitherto,
so soon as I was strong enough to do anything. It
would be, I should think, about a fortnight after the
work commenced that I took my first meeting, and
from that time I went steadily forwards to the end,
doing at least one Sabbath service, with two and
three weekday meetings, besides assisting in the other
services. As the work progressed and the crowds
increased, a large hall was taken in another part
of the town, where I conducted the services on the
Sunday night, while William preached in the chapel,
which, together with the cares of home and the dear
children and my dear Herbert, who already made
some considerable demands upon my attention, I was
kept very fully employed.

The cooperation on the part of the leaders of the
Church, with which we laboured, was not as complete
and perfect as it had been with other societies … with

which we had worked up to this date. A handful of
the principal people had been opposed to our visit and
from the onset these took up a position of antagonism,
which was neither agreeable to us nor helpful to the
work. It is quite true that as the meetings went on the
prejudices of at least some of these gave way and they
were added to the roll of our helpers, while others
continued their opposition to the very last. From the
ministers of the circuit and from the entire staff of office
bearers, with one or two exceptions, we received warm
sympathy and cordial assistance.

… I held two meetings here for women only,
similar to the one I held at St. Just, which were both
crowded and useful after a similar manner. My views
then, of course, were somewhat … contracted in
comparison with what they are today with respect to
women's opportunity of labouring for God and her
ability to answer to it, but I was still far ahead of my
time, and it would have been useless so far as any
practical consequences would have gone for me to have
advocated anything beyond.

… The transformations of character produced
after the consecrations in members of long standing were
almost as striking as those produced in the most godless.

… One evening a young man who had been living
a very random life yielded to the Spirit's call, and gave
himself up to God and was made, as they say here,
"right happy". The news of his conversion was carried
straight from the chapel to a public house that was one
of his regular haunts. A group of his old companions
at the moment were sitting playing cards, but when

*informed that their old mate had been converted and*
*was now shouting the praises of God, threw down their*
*cards and all scampered off to the chapel. While there,*
*looking on the happy face and listening to the joyous*
*voice of their old companion in wickedness… Some of*
*them yielded on the spot, and before the service closed*
*were numbered among the converts.*[2]

When William and Catherine were settled in London and The Salvation Army was developing out of their Christian Mission, the idea of new converts being employed to attract other potential new converts with their "testimony" of a changed heart and altered life was a vital evangelistic tool. During these months in Cornwall William and Catherine used this tactic to widen their circle of converts and supporters.

After eighteen months in Cornwall, during which it is estimated that around 7,000 people had their souls "awakened and saved",[3] the Booth family moved on to pastures new in Cardiff, Wales.

In the days before there was a road bridge to span the River Severn between Bristol and South Wales, and before direct or even indirect rail routes (the Severn Tunnel was completed only in 1886), the journey from Cornwall to Cardiff was tortuous. The cheapest way to get there was by boat, and William, the children, and the nurse made the winter journey from Hayle in February 1862. Catherine, who on her own admission was "so wretched a sailor" that she had taken the train to Bristol, joined them on the second leg of the boat journey, by steamer across the river and around the coast to Cardiff.[4]

The Welsh people extended a warm welcome to the whole family and the revival meetings got under way almost immediately, with hundreds of conversions reported. There was no thought then, or even as they developed the Christian Mission in the East End of London and later The Salvation Army, of the Booths creating a new church or denomination. The idea was to see people converted and to send them back to existing churches, where they could make a witness and a difference.

> *Almost every class of society has been found among the converts, and there is scarcely a church which has not had its numbers increased by the instrumentality of these services. The moral condition of the town is greatly improved, and, at a season of the year when crime is generally on the increase, the magistrates have very little to do.*[5]

Although some churches welcomed the Booths, William was also keen to use other venues that were less intimidating for non-churchgoers.

> *Our meetings were commenced in the Circus, a building capable of containing some 2000 people, which was usually crowded. We continued here a good many weeks on the Sabbath and usually had crowds. The meetings on the weekday were usually held in the Baptist, Wesleyan and other chapels, and the "Gospel" and other halls.*
>
> *William was somewhat disappointed with the results of this movement, as far as he was concerned, but especially with himself. He went through a period of depression during the weeks we were here, which*

was most distressing. I thought at the time, and on looking back have been confirmed in the opinion, that it was very largely the reaction from the frightful strain of the previous two years. He thought otherwise, but his health and the management of it has always been one of the few points on which we have disagreed. Anyway, he was very dissatisfied with his work in Cardiff. Still, he toiled on and reaped much fruit, which I have no doubt we shall find again in the great harvest home.

For myself, I never appeared without a crowd and seldom spoke with other than pleasure to myself and I think profit to those who heard me. Some of those morning meetings I shall never forget. It was quite a common thing for me to see ministers, local preachers, deacons, elders/leaders of churches, and people in very respectable positions of society, even magistrates, kneeling at the communion rail, bewailing their past unfaithfulness, seeking restoration from backsliding and crying to God to have mercy on their souls and pardon their sins. I believe that God used me to stir up the hearts of many leading Christians and set them to work for Christ after a fashion they had never done before.[6]

As William and Catherine moved around the country, they had opportunities to make new friends and supporters. In Cardiff they were introduced to Mr and Mrs J. E. Billups, he a wealthy contractor and she destined to become a close friend of Mrs Booth. A few years later their daughter, Mary Coutts Billups, would become converted under Catherine's ministry in the east-coast town of Margate in England and Miss Billups would lodge with the Booths. When, on 4 May 1864, Catherine produced her sixth child, she was named for her friends – Marian Billups Booth, known as "Marie".

The Billups family would provide emotional, moral, and financial support for the Booths for years to come, as would John and Richard Cory, two brothers whose family had grown wealthy as coal merchants and shipowners. As a token of respect and gratitude, William and Catherine named their seventh child after their friends. Evelyn Cory Booth was born on Christmas Day 1865 and would many years later, as Evangeline Booth, become the first female General of The Salvation Army.

# CHAPTER

## 12

By 1863, with Wales behind them, the Booths were travelling the country leading revivals. After a few days' rest and recuperation in the coastal town of Weston-super-Mare with their new friends Mr and Mrs Billups, their next stop was Walsall near Birmingham, for an eight-week campaign.

The Midlands town was already bubbling with spiritual excitement. In recent times the American evangelist James Caughey had been invited to preach there, Dr and Mrs Palmer had also preceded the Booths, and the community of revivalists had a brand new chapel which had just celebrated its anniversary.

Now William and Catherine Booth headed up a series of meetings, both outdoors and in church. The Booths had a reputation for drawing in people who would not normally see the inside of a chapel, people considered the worst of "sinners" but whom William and Catherine believed to be precious souls. They flocked to the June 1863 "Camp Meetings", where they heard a gospel of "salvation for all".

> *One of them had been a prize-fighter, a drunkard and*
> *a gambler, having tramped all over the country... So*
> *desperate had he been that five or six policemen had*

*been required to take him to prison, and then from the grating of the lock-up he had waved his hand to his comrades, shouting, 'This is the boy that will never give in!' Now he shouts, "The lion's tamed! ... The sinner's saved! Christ has conquered." By his evil ways he had nearly broken his parents' hearts, but, being pious, they had never ceased to pray for him. Now they rejoiced over him, and the other day he sent them his portrait with a Bible in his hand instead of the boxing-gloves. All this and a great deal more he testified with great simplicity, while his face, covered with smiles, told of the happiness which now reigned within.[1]*

In Walsall, William coined a phrase that would stick to those who had found faith during the revival – "The Hallelujah Band" – and when he and Catherine finally departed, the spiritual momentum continued in theatres, music halls, circuses, warehouses, and sheds across the region. Although The Hallelujah Band movement eventually died back, in its time the group from Walsall, and others that also sprang up, saw hundreds converted to the Christian cause.[2]

Walsall was also notable because it was there that Willie – William Bramwell, the eldest Booth child – would be "converted".

He was about seven and a half years old, and his parents were thrilled. They, and later their Salvation Army, would recognize that a child can come to faith just as an adult may, and that that faith can be a true and lasting experience, despite the youth of the penitent. Catherine had already spoken "seriously" to her eldest son about accepting Jesus as his Saviour back in Cardiff, but then, when asked if he would accept the offer of salvation, he had quite bluntly and deliberately announced, "No!" Yet, the following summer, in one of Catherine's children's meetings in Walsall she looked up to see Willie, along with a crowd of other children, kneeling at the Communion rail "confessing his sins and seeking forgiveness". There was rejoicing in the Booth household and Catherine wrote the news to her parents with utter delight:

> *Willie has begun to serve God, of course, as a child, but still, I trust, taught of the Spirit. I feel a great increase of responsibility with respect to him. Oh, to cherish the tender plant of grace aright. Lord, help!*

Catherine and William held out a great deal of hope for their children, desperately wanting them first to love God and serve Jesus, and then to join their parents' mission and ministry, however young. From early days they prayed with them and encouraged them to pray, although Catherine had strong thoughts about forcing young children to go to religious meetings:

> *I never allowed my children to attend public service till they were old enough to take some interest in them…*
> *I deemed it an evil to make a child sit for an hour-and-a-half, dangling its legs on a high seat, listening to what it could neither understand nor appreciate, for alas, there is little in the ordinary services of our day to interest or profit children, and I am satisfied that a great deal of the distaste for religious services so common amongst them has been engendered in this way. My experience has been that my children have*

> *come so highly to appreciate the privilege of attending*
> *service, that a promise of it during the week would*
> *ensure extra good behaviour and diligence.*[3]

Undoubtedly, though, as the Booth children grew they had little choice but to follow their parents and the faith they espoused. They knew little else, as they were mostly taught at home by a series of governesses and tutors while being hauled around the country, which must have been somewhat unsettling.

However, there must have been some concern about a lack of formal education, especially for the Booth boys, because a few years later, when the family at last settled in London, Bramwell would be sent briefly to the City of London School. He was a rather quiet child, which may have had something to do with the fact that he suffered from deafness, and at school he was also apparently bullied for his faith.[4] He lasted just a few months there, although his younger brother Ballington did benefit from a period of more formal education.

However, even when away at school in Bristol, a letter from his mother around 1876 shows that she was determined that Ballington should not forget the main purpose of his existence.

> *… Your letter to Willie has been forwarded to me. I*
> *am delighted to hear that you are going on so well, and*
> *that the Lord is using you amongst the boys. Nothing*
> *could rejoice me more than to hear that you are*
> *prospering in your soul; only keep right with God and*
> *everything else will go well i.e. for your good, though*
> *not always as you would like…*
>
> *My dear boy, walk consistently. It is the greatest*
> *source of strength, next to the Holy Spirit, and we*

*must be consistent in order to keep the Spirit. Cast*
*yourself afresh on the Lord for strength. Try simple*
*trust a moment at a time. Mind and observe all the*
*laws. Keep your own counsel. Never allow any boy to*
*approach you with a secret which you would not like*
*me to hear. Then you are safe.*

   *I am in haste how, so good-bye.*
   *From your loving, anxious Mother.*[5]

While they were certainly dutiful, the Booth offspring were no angels. There was the inevitable sibling rivalry and bickering, which Catherine especially found irritating and disturbing. Although they submitted to William and Catherine during their upbringing, the Booth children were being raised to be not just people of faith, but people who could lead. This bred strong, single-minded individuals, which did not bode well for future harmony within the family.

Like gypsies with no permanent home, moving from revival to revival, the Booths now travelled the country. Money had been and continued to be a constant worry. On departing Walsall Catherine reported to her mother that they had not "at present received as much as our travelling expenses and house-rent".[6] Although the Mumfords themselves were also frequently in financial straits, they often came to the rescue.

Debt and money worries were to plague the Booths for years and could not have helped William's depression as he struggled to acquire the means to support his growing family. Although their ministry was usually successful and in public they put on an optimistic face, under the surface there was often a touch of despair, especially during the times the couple were separated.

*… I wish I were in a more satisfactory state spiritually. I feel almost dead – powerless. Consequently my preaching and praying in public has but little effect on the people. But wishing produces no improvement. O, that God would come and give me some new light or some new power. Will you pray for me? I never felt less emotion and power in prayer in my life. And I am sure I don't know what to do…*

*It is no use me talking about my rebellion of heart against this separation. I must submit and say, "Thy will be done." I wish I was sure that it was His will. As I turned into my lonely lodgings last night a young gentleman with a lady on his arm knocked at the door of the house opposite mine, and I could not help asking why I was parted from my young and precious wife. I know why, and for a season it must be so. Perhaps we shall grow accustomed to it and not feel it so much. I do feel a measure of comfort from the thought that we are securing our own livelihood by it and not hanging on to anyone. That thought has been like a canker at my heart of late. It must not be after that fashion. We will work and then rest together and then work again…*

*… The people are as cold as an ice-house. I am much disheartened … I don't feel disposed to persevere*

*much longer in a life, the results of which are really so trifling…*

*I need not tell you how I should like to see you this morning, and how lonely life is without your precious society. All the people appear only just tolerable. I don't know how it is, but quick, interesting folks seem very rarely to cross my path.*

*… Give my love to my dear children, bless them. I think much about them. Dear Katie's merry voice and laughter are often ringing in my ears and so are the pretty ways and tricks of them all. I forget their troublesomeness when away from them.*

In the parlour Mama was waiting, and she was waving a piece of paper as the children bounded into the room, followed by the governess, Miss McBean.

"A letter, from Papa?" Willie asked.

"Yes! And there's a little message in there for you children. A very special message! Shall I read it to you?

"'I am delighted with your account of Miss McBean. Strange and good that she should have heard of us. Of course she had an idea of what she was coming to. Hope the children will be good and respectful. Tell her she must exact uniform obedience. Tell Willie that if he does not obey and set his brothers and sisters an example in this matter, he must prepare not only to lose his dog, but to live in the attic while I am at home, for I will not see him. On the other hand, if they are good and obedient, they shall have a party again on the Friday evening, and have Patience etc., and we will have a great many more nuts and have some nice games, etc.'"

Willie's little face fell. The message, apparently, was all directed at him. Oh why did he have to be the oldest? Why couldn't Papa see that so much of the trouble he got into was down to Ballington? He was such a little bully, always pushing his sisters around. Thankfully Mama was alert to it now, but it didn't stop Willie feeling the weight of family responsibility and the displeasure of his adored father.

"Does that mean Papa is coming home on Friday?" Katie's eyes were burning bright. She had heard none of the reprimand, but just the words "party" and "games".

"Yes, my dears. Papa is coming home! But just for a short while, then he'll be back to Manchester and then on to Sheffield!"

### Sheffield, mid-October 1864

*I am rather afraid that I am not going to be very comfortably located. There is much knocking about. They come in and out of my room and sit in it occasionally. I like privacy. I want no company but yours. I was woke up this morning at six with someone at the house bell and could not sleep, so I thought I would get up and talk to you. But they are homely, nice people from the neighbourhood of South Lincolnshire. If I am not right I shall change…*

*… You may rely on it, my dearest, that I shall be most thankful once more if possible to abide at home and to abide with thee. But we must be careful. We could not come here much, if anything, under £10. We shall want £21 for assurance directly, and the extra expenses for winter clothing, sable victorine, teeth, etc., etc. will be £6 or £8 more. So we must look before we leap. Still, I think there is a sphere here, and I shall do my utmost to*

*work it, and we will all live together again so soon as the
Lord shall make it possible… My poor little children,
bless them, and dear Willie; I am afraid we are rather
hard on them sometimes… Goodbye for the present.
Cherish yourself. Always wear the respirator.*

*I had a slight throat affection last night. Pray
for me. Live in and for Jesus. I have little else but this
paper with me and I want to use it and get it out of
the way. I fancy it would suit your writing; try it. It
does not suit my old quill a bit… How very much I
should like to see you today, to hold you in my arms
and look at you, right through your eyes into your
heart, the warm, living, beautiful heart that throbs so
full of sympathy and truth for me and mine, and then
to press you to my heart and hold you there and cover
you with kisses, warm and earnest kisses. Bless you! I
send you two kisses; you understand me, and you will
keep your promise with them.*

*Kiss the children for me. Tell Willie I got him a
penknife this morning, and Ballington that I am going
about the white mice. The white mice and pigeon man
is coming with the Hallelujah Band to Leeds. I have
not time or patience to write more. Somehow I am
nervous. The day is damp and sultry, and my room is
hot and close, and I am out of sorts for writing … I
feel lonely and nervous. I don't like the folks much I am
with and I am tired. I shall be better in the morning.*

William huddled up against the cold as he left the hall. It had been a
good evening, with many saved and their names taken so there could

be some visits afterwards. Just as it had in Sheffield, the Hallelujah Band was waking people up. He liked the way they had taken to turning up in red shirts to sing and jump. It was a sort of uniform, which appealed to William's sense of order.

He picked up his pace and turned up his collar as he rounded the street corner and made for his accommodation. Oh how he would love to just turn the handle and be home with darling Catherine and the children. It had been weeks since he'd seen them. Sheffield, Nottingham, Batley, Pudsey, Gateshead… it had been a tiresome and gruelling schedule in the past months and years and Catherine had been so supportive, accompanying him when time and commitments allowed.

How disappointed he was, though, that the church leaders were still insisting on treating his wife with such contempt. She worked so hard on her ministry, her sermons were so well thought out, and the people crowded into the chapels where she spoke.

William felt a pride when he thought of his wife, and defensive against her detractors. He walked faster as his anger grew. In ten years, when this period was past and just a poor memory, this treatment would be as nothing, while his and Catherine's treatment of the work of God, their forbearance and humility, meekness and perseverance in the face of this persecution would be everything!

If he and Catherine could be together more, he would be more settled. This year – 1865 – surely might see them more permanently settled. Catherine was, as always, inclined towards London, to be nearer her parents. It would certainly help having Mr and Mrs Mumford on hand to help with the children. Catherine's own preaching was developing wonderfully but she found the children quite a handful. The invitation from the Rotherhithe chapel had been interesting. It was a good chapel, with some of the warmest-hearted people in London! Maybe that would bring something different for the family.

# CHAPTER

# 13

Catherine Booth stood to speak, clutching her Bible in her right hand. She looked down on the hundreds of expectant faces in the chapel, and could not help but feel a little nervous and overwhelmed by the responsibility of it all.

When she had received the invitation from the Southwark Circuit Free Church Methodists to conduct their evangelistic campaign in Rotherhithe, it had provoked mixed feelings, which wavered from "Yes, I'm absolutely fed up with being God's gypsy and it's time I went home to London" to "What will William think?"

As usual, her darling had left the decision to her, although she was well aware of the side glances he received in some polite societies whenever her name was mentioned as a woman preacher. And she knew that in his heart he was not for moving back to London.

"The Provinces, Catherine! The Provinces! That's my battleground!" he had said some years before, but now he was prepared to allow her to return to London and to take up this wonderful opportunity for her own ministry. The past weeks had been chaos. She had come on ahead and, if this campaign proved worthwhile, the rest of the family would follow.

As she had passed through the doors she'd seen the notice "Come and Hear a Woman Preach", and she knew that many of those staring up at her from the pews were there out of pure curiosity. But no matter. They were there, weren't they?

It was Catherine's appointment to the evangelistic campaign at Rotherhithe that brought the Booths eventually, in February 1865, back to London. Catherine proved an immense success, and was very popular among those who heard her. Following the conclusion of the Rotherhithe meetings in mid-March, she was immediately engaged to preach at the Free Methodist Church in Grange Road, Bermondsey.[1]

Catherine's thoughtful and straightforward style of preaching had proved very attractive and effective over the last few years and had even been described by the *Wesleyan Times* as "more in the manner of Finney than of many revivalists". It must have given her great comfort to be compared to one of her heroes, but although she went down a storm in South London, there were still those who thought it inappropriate for women to preach to mixed congregations.

On 8 March 1865, as the Rotherhithe revival meetings were entering their final week, the editors of the weekly newspaper *The Revival*, which would later become *The Christian*, wrote that, although they were hoping to hear Mrs Booth at least once, they had grave misgivings.

> *Let us say now a word on the subject of female preaching.*
> *We quite feel that it is to be defended in principle, but*
> *we are greatly led to question, from circumstances which*
> *have come under our notice on different occasions of late,*
> *whether it be right for mothers or families to be away*
> *from their home duties on any account, not excepting*
> *this most important work.*[2]

With the children still in Leeds – William would bring them down to London shortly and they would become settled in a house in Shaftesbury Road in Hammersmith in West London – the editors in question, Mr Morgan and Mr Chase, were not to know that Catherine had completely abandoned her family, albeit briefly, to undertake the Rotherhithe speaking engagement. It was a pattern that was to be repeated over the years. The year before, just five days after giving birth to her daughter Marian, Catherine had resumed her preaching.

Soon after settling the family in Hammersmith, William was back to his beloved "Provinces" – an appointment in Ripon in Yorkshire and a new revival campaign in Louth in Lincolnshire took him north again. But it soon became apparent that with London as his main base doors were now beginning to open for him there.

*Outside on the street a tall man with a thick dark beard mounted an old box. Oh, not this again!*

*Couldn't a man enjoy a couple of ales without having that noise outside? If the pub wasn't so handy for home, he'd find somewhere else to sup. But the Blind Beggar was perfect, especially when he'd had a few too many – all he needed to do was stagger round the corner to the old woman who'd be there, as always, waiting to put him to bed.*

*The drinker rubbed the dirty window pane to peer out.*

*"George!" he shouted to the aleman behind the bar. "Can't you get rid of 'em?"*

*"It's a free world, Joe. So long as they don't step over the doorstep we can't do nuffink about 'em!"*

*"Shut the door!" someone yelled.*

*"Don't you dare! It's bloody boilin' in here!" shouted barman George.*

He was right, of course. Even this late in the day, it was still warm. Well it was midsummer, after all, and the inn reeked of sweat, stale beer, and the stench of the open sewer in the road outside.

Joe looked out of the window again. He'd lost count of the times his drinking had been interrupted by these religious fanatics. There seemed to be an endless stream of them, all spouting about God and how he needed "saving".

Saving from what, that's what he wanted to know. Who could save him from the misery of gruelling hard work and grinding poverty?

Maybe another pint might help. He searched his torn pocket. Just a penny left. Enough for one more, but then he'd go home empty-handed again and he'd get it in the neck from the old woman. He'd done that many a time before, even though it meant the kids went to bed with empty bellies. But a man had to have his fun, didn't he? What with spending all day at the docks, hauling all those sacks of whatever it was they were loading the ships with. Maybe he'd just spend the ha'penny.

"Another half, George!" Joe approached the bar, where the crowd had thinned out a bit. A few of his mates had ambled outside and seemed to be listening to the tall man. A few were heckling from the door, but a couple had moved forward.

Just to get a bit of air, Joe took his half across the threshold into the street and stood there under the Blind Beggar sign.

"Not seen this one afore, Will!" he said to the man next to him.

"No – new, I think! Looks a bit fresh, doesn't he?"

Not just fresh, but not posh either, Joe noted. He wasn't dressed particularly sharply; his frock coat looked a little worse for wear. In fact, he appeared more frayed around the edges that the other missioners who usually turned up outside the pub. This one's thick black hair was all over the place as he waved his arms around. He was sweating profusely and occasionally mopped his brow with a grey-looking kerchief. And what was that accent? He wasn't from London, that was for sure.

Joe was intrigued. He found himself listening to this one as he hadn't listened before. He was, of course, a religious nut, but he seemed to be a bit more normal than the rest.

"What's 'is name, Will?"

"That's right!" came the reply, followed by a hearty laugh.

"Don't muck me about, mate! What's 'is bloody name?"

"You said it! 'is name is Will! William Booth!"

Although William had rather reluctantly joined Catherine in London and at first merely expected to use it as a base for his continued work in the rest of the country, as he walked about the poverty-stricken eastern reaches of the city he had quickly recognized the desperate spiritual needs of those around him.

Although the term "East End" would not be coined for a few decades more, this part of London was already notorious for being desperately poor, overcrowded, crime-ridden, and disease-stricken – cholera, typhus, typhoid, and influenza were virtually endemic. In the nineteenth century London was fast becoming the first "world city", with a large population that was almost daily added to by immigrants, most of whom arrived poor and even destitute. It was a city of contrasts, with all the trappings of the beginnings of a "modern" society lying cheek-by-jowl with almost medieval poverty. Transport systems were developing to bring people into the city from the suburbs for work and play – the first London Underground line, the section of the Metropolitan line from Paddington to Farringdon stations, was already two years old by the time the Booths were setting up home in the city.

Shipbuilding around the ever-expanding docks along the River Thames brought goods and people in from all around the world.

There were sugar refineries, iron foundries, tanneries, glassworks, dye shops, and other industries, which required hordes of unskilled workers – dockers, builders, chimney sweeps, rag collectors, garment workers – most of whom worked for subsistence wages, on daily contracts with no job security. These "labouring poor" sat at the bottom of the social heap, and just above them was an elite group of well-paid and privileged craftsmen and a fast-growing "white-collar" or lower middle class, who sat just below the "higher middle class" – among them the lawyers, doctors, and churchmen of the day. The "upper class", often landed and titled gentry, were perched at the very top of this rigidly stratified society.[3]

The eastern reaches of London, which were once a selection of small villages surrounded by fields to the east of the medieval walled City of London and north of the River Thames, were by the mid-1800s a mass of streets with open sewers running through them. Millions of people were crammed into the East End, displaced by slum clearances around the St Katharine Docks in the late 1820s and the building of the Central London railway stations, which was taking place when William and Catherine arrived in the city in 1865.[4]

Years later, when he was devising plans not just to help save souls but to rehabilitate individuals and give them a practical as well as a spiritual future, William Booth's Salvation Army would establish one of the first labour exchanges to help people find work. And the seeds of that programme were being planted in William's heart in 1865 as he mixed with the hordes of displaced persons in the eastern reaches of London. As he walked through the streets he was captivated by the place and the opportunities that it afforded his ministry. He bounded home to Hammersmith one night, burst through the door, and announced to his wife, "Darling! I have found my destiny!"

In the summer of 1865 outside the Blind Beggar pub, William Booth was doing what came naturally, preaching to the unconverted in their own environment. Under a pub sign, risking ridicule and even some physical danger – it wasn't unusual for street preachers to have things thrown at them by a heckling crowd – William was part of an evangelistic tradition that was growing rapidly in mid-nineteenth-century London. There were numerous chapels and small missions, many of them Methodist, across this part of town. By the 1850s there were around 144 charities at work in London,[5] many of which were already mixing religion with practical works and good deeds.

William's street preaching impressed a group of churchmen and evangelists known as the East London Special Services Committee. Among them were Mr R. C. Morgan and Mr Samuel Chase, the editors of *The Revival,* who, despite their misgivings over the preaching antics of the Revd Booth's wife, were still determined to have William join them for their next evangelistic campaign.

The Special Committee didn't come from or belong to one single denomination, and William Booth had already preached for them at the Garrick Theatre some years before.[6] Now they wanted him for more radical work, and on 2 July 1865 – the date that is now noted in history as the "start" of The Salvation Army – William Booth stood to preach for them in a tent on the Mile End Waste, on the old Quaker Burial Ground in Whitechapel, East London.

Although the old tent blew down that autumn, there was no stopping the Booth mission. The East London Christian Revival Society was born and in the winter of 1865 it moved indoors. On Sundays the meetings were held in a local building – the Assembly Rooms on New Road, Whitechapel, otherwise known as Professor Orson's Dancing Academy, its main function in the week. Even on the Sabbath the evangelists had to share their meeting hall with a photographer,[7] and on weekdays the Booths and their expanding group of supporters rented other venues: an old chapel, a warehouse, a stable, a carpenter's shop, a skittle alley. By 1867 the group had moved into more permanent "Sunday headquarters" at the Effingham Theatre in Whitechapel Road.[8]

When, in November 1865, William's daily walk from Hammersmith to East London proved excessively strenuous, the Booths had moved to Mare Street in the East End. The family was growing again, with the birth in 1865 of Evelyn and then, on 28 April 1868, the arrival of their eighth and last child, Lucy Milward, who was granted her maternal grandmother's maiden name.

# CHAPTER

# 14

Papa Booth bounded into the schoolroom where the older children were waiting in great anticipation.

"Now listen," he said. "I have a wonderful piece of news for you. God has sent us a most beautiful present."

"Is it alive?" little Katie shouted.

"Yes, it's alive!"

"Is it a dog?" asked Emma.

"No," Papa shook his head. He looked across at Willie and winked.

"A donkey?" Ballington burst out.

"No!"

The little group went through a list of other livestock until, at last, their father could hold himself back no more.

"It's a baby!" he declared, "And if we're very, very, quiet, Mama says we can go up and meet your new sister."

"A girl?" asked Katie.

"Yes, my darling, another little girl!"

The children crept quietly upstairs, from where they had been banned all day. They entered their parents' bedroom and found Mama sitting up surrounded by thick white pillows. She smiled at them.

Baby was in the crib by the side of the big bed. Ballington peered down at her, his eyes shining.

"That's what I've been praying for – a baby!" he declared.

"Liar!" said Katie. "I heard you last night – praying for a donkey!"

The whole clan burst into laughter, even Mama, who looked so pale and tired.

"Quiet now, children!" said Miss Short. "Mama needs to rest. Let's go downstairs and have our supper, shall we?"

By the time of Lucy's birth, Miss Jane Short was a lodger in the Booth household and helping to care for the children. She was a recent convert who had made her Christian commitment during one of Catherine Booth's campaigns, for while William was establishing himself in the eastern reaches of London, Catherine's own reputation as a sought-after speaker and preacher was also growing.

Mrs Booth led revival campaigns across the south-east of England, including in Tunbridge Wells in Kent, and Ramsgate and Margate on the east Kent coast. It was at Margate that Jane Short became a Christian, along with Miss Mary Billups, the daughter of the Booths' friends from their Cardiff days. Both would become Booth lodgers.

In 1867, when Jane moved into the Booth household as a family helper, she also became involved in the work of the Christian Revival Association, which by 1870 had been renamed "The East London Christian Mission" and then simply "The Christian Mission". Now the evangelistic campaigns for which The Salvation Army would soon become renowned were being augmented by mission work.

At Rotherhithe in 1865 Catherine Booth had first come into contact with the Midnight Movement for Fallen Women, a Christian ministry to prostitutes. The Booths could not help but be overwhelmed by the poverty of those around them, certainly once they moved the family home from Hammersmith to Hackney. The Booths' Wesleyan background had emphasized "loving God and loving one's neighbour".[1] With Christian faith came "good works", and Miss Short would eventually become a visitor for the Mission and an important part of the Booth household, as well as a keen observer of all the goings-on.

Years later, she would recall her move into the Booth home, about which she was at first rather nervous because of previous bad experiences of living in the home of "religious people":

> *I was terribly afraid of going to live with these dear folk,*
> *because I had been so often disappointed, grievously*
> *disappointed, in religious people. It seemed to me that*
> *the Booths could not possibly be in their home life what*
> *they were in their preaching. I thought I should see*
> *things and hear things which would distress me; I could*
> *not imagine that it was possible for them to live their*
> *ideals. You see, I loved them so well that I quite shrank*
> *from finding my hero-worship an illusion.*[2]

However, she was not disappointed, and both the Booths came up to scratch, although in later years she was somewhat more critical of Mrs Booth than of the "General", whom Miss Short obviously idolized.[3]

> *People who say that Mrs Booth was the greater of the*
> *two do not know what they are talking about. Mrs*
> *Booth was a very able woman, a persuasive speaker,*
> *and a wonderful manager; but the General (William*

*Booth) was a force – he dominated everything. I've never met anyone who could compare with him for strength of character. You knew the difference in the house directly he opened the door. You felt his presence in every department of the home life. He was a real master … We used to call him "The General" long before there was any Salvation Army. He couldn't bear beating about the bush. Prevarication, like stupidity, exasperated him. Everything had to go like clockwork, but very much faster than time. I always say that he got forty eight hours' work out of the twenty four.[4]*

Although they had to meet the demands of a young and growing family, the Booths' workload was expanding. Their reputation went before them and people of all classes were beginning to be attracted to the cause. While William preached to the poverty-stricken in the East End, Catherine could often be found sharing her faith and challenging the more affluent sinners in the more prosperous parts of the city. Some joined the ranks of the Mission helpers and there was much work to be done.

By October 1868 William had produced the first copy of *The East London Evangelist*, aided by his friends Mr Morgan and Mr Chase, to share the good news of what his mission was about. By 1868 the Mission had thirteen preaching stations with a capacity for accommodating around 8,000 people. There were also various "ministries" including soup kitchens, mothers' meetings, reading rooms, and "penny banks". Although there was no centralized co-ordination of what effectively was "social work", the Booths' followers provided, in Christian love, what the local community needed – food, clothes, boots, blankets, and much more. Somewhat ironically for a movement that expounded the benefits of (and insisted upon) abstinence from alcohol, the Mission had its first "headquarters" at the old Eastern Star beer shop in Whitechapel.[5]

The Mission was growing organically. Much as, in later years, people converted in The Salvation Army would take their new faith with them and establish new Salvation Army centres wherever they went, so it was with the Christian Mission.

Catherine had ministered in Croydon and in September 1868 the Mission took its first hall outside central London, in Norwood.[6] An enthusiastic supporter invited the Booths to Edinburgh in Scotland and a centre was set up there. Catherine was invited to Brighton, and so the work spread to the south coast. Although some of these stations did not survive, or eventually became independent, the Christian Mission was spreading.

But all the work, family tragedy – Catherine's mother died in December 1869 after a long battle with cancer – and continuing money worries for both the family and the Mission took its toll. For a long time the family had no steady income. What little the couple earned came from the sale of a hymn book that William had compiled, popular sales of Catherine's rewritten pamphlet on "Female Teaching", and fees from some of her preaching engagements for more affluent congregations.

For months William had prayed for the money to acquire a large building for the Christian Mission. An old People's Market was available, which once converted would seat in excess of 1,500. It had a number of smaller adjoining rooms, which could be adapted for a shop, soup kitchens, and other social needs, but it would cost a large amount of money to buy and renovate.

William was convinced that they now urgently required permanent and more substantial headquarters. The family home was overflowing with growing children and servants but also doubled as office space for the Christian Mission. So, although he had not secured all the funds, he went ahead and bought the lease to the People's Market.

When renovation work went over budget, William found himself in a quandary. As he had several times in the past, particularly in the early evangelistic days, he considered stepping down from his ministry and taking a job in business, just to secure a wage.[7] But, as in the past, this notion quickly passed and, although impoverished, they looked to the future.

There arose the prospect of financial rescue in the form of a supporter, a rich Australian called Henry Reed, who, when William somewhat reluctantly approached him, agreed to donate £10,000 to the mission. But with the donation came conditions. Mr Reed was not in favour of the old People's Market and instead encouraged William to buy land to build a new building. His money would also only be good as long as *he* agreed with what the Mission was doing, and he insisted that Revd Booth devote himself entirely to his London work and rule out any other commitments. To take Mr Reed's money would have placed the Christian Mission in the benefactor's control, and to this William could not agree. As in the past, when he had declined the offer of some support because it would entail compromise and the relinquishing of some of his authority and control, William turned down his would-be benefactor.

Mr Reed was infuriated and on 15 April 1870 he wrote strongly to William Booth, advising him on the "sin" of going into debt.[8] Although Mr Reed later became one of the Christian Mission's major supporters, it must have been a hard pill for the Booths to swallow, not least because, just days before, the People's Mission Hall had been officially opened. The ceremony was held on William's forty-first birthday – 10 April 1870.

Stress had affected William once again. It was Catherine who preached that day at both morning and evening services and then William took a leave of absence. His overstretched and overworked wife was, once more, in charge not just of the family, but also of the Mission.[9]

During these early years of The Christian Mission, while William and Catherine were often completely caught up in the spiritual work they had started, at home they were often also handling crises and chaos.

Eldest son Willie, who now at least in public had taken to using his second name, "Bramwell", had his run-in with school. Marian had proved a sickly baby and was an ill child, suffering from fits. This sixth Booth child would remain an invalid who had to be cared for by other members of the family and would be the only member of the Booth clan who would not become actively involved in their parents' work and mission. In early 1871 Marie, as she was always known in the family, went down with smallpox and threatened the well-being of the whole family. The other children were dispatched to a big country house owned by that most benevolent of friends, Mrs Billups.[10]

FEB 9TH 1871

*My Dear Willie,*

*Your somewhat graphic epistle cheered me a good deal this morning. I am glad to find you in such good spirits. What a pity you lost your hat! However, it was better than losing your head, which would not at all have surprised me, seeing that you are so fond of poking it where it ought not to be!*

*Mr Billups has sent a telegram which is
an unspeakable comfort, for we have been very
apprehensive about Herbert and Emma. I trust now,
if it be the Lord's will, that you are all safe. I hope you
will in this emergency show yourself to be a true son
of your mother, and a consistent disciple of the Lord
Jesus. Very much depends on you as to the ease and
comfort of managing Ballington and Herbert: do all
you can. Be forebearing where only your own feelings
or comfort are concerned, and don't raise unnecessary
controversies; but where their obedience to us, or their
health, is at stake, be firm and unflinching in trying
to put them right. Mind Emma's medicine – two
teaspoons twice a day – and her feet kept warm. I
will send over-boots for her in the house. Mind you
don't take cold. Remember how unpleasant rheumatic
fever is! If you will take care and let reason guide your
conduct you will get much benefit, but if you will not,
why, you will help towards the very undesirable result
of invalidism for life!*

*The Lord bless you all. Pray for us.*

*Your loving and anxious Mother.*

*PS – Papa says you are to mind the children with
the dogs! You are to read this bit of print to them, and
knock it well into Ballington and Herbert.*

Fifteen-year-old Bramwell, as the eldest child, was not just
expected to take responsibility for his siblings but was already

being groomed for leadership in his parents' mission. A century before the term "teenager" came into being and allowed young people more time as children before they became adults, Bramwell was already being expected to be mature beyond his years, despite his sheltered upbringing. If Bramwell's brothers, in particular, took exception to their eldest sibling being put in charge of them and being "in loco parentis", it would be years before the resentment built up enough to blow the family apart.

Emma, the fourth Booth child, was considered the healthiest of the batch, so it was a shock when Catherine had to rush home from an engagement after receiving a telegram informing her that Emma had suffered an accident. Her hand had been crushed in a door and, although she recovered, she suffered badly with her nerves for months afterwards.[11]

Perhaps that illness was all the more worrying for Catherine because William was up and down with depression. By 1872 William was again indisposed, and this time the doctors diagnosed a nervous breakdown brought on by hard work and exhaustion. A long period of rest was recommended and William once again found himself at Smedley's Hydropathic Establishment in Matlock.

1872

*My Dearest, my Darling, my own Love,*
*How mysterious the tie that binds us together!*
*How wonderful the union! How lost and lonesome I*
*am without you. Life loses half, nay, all its charm. I am*
*only living and working here to get better to return to*
*you. My last and first thoughts are given to you. Oh,*
*let us cherish and keep stronger with a living glow the*

*holy flame of love as kindled in our hearts for each
other. I am oppressed with the thought and feeling of
my unworthiness of the devotion you manifest for me.
The Lord reward you!*

> *If 'tis love to wish thee near,*
> *To shed for thee the silent tear,*
> *To start at every step and fear,*
> *Yet hope, that it will bring thee near –*
> *If this be loving, then I love.*
> *If 'tis love to wish that I,*
> *Knit by some strange mysterious tie,*
> *Might with thee live or with thee die,*
> *Then dwell with thee eternally –*
> *If this be loving, then I love.*

> *Your own, your husband,*
> *William.*

---

*Willie, or rather Bramwell, as I like to call him now,
has just left me. He is a good lad – a real precious
boy. I manage him a little better than you do, I think.
Perhaps it is because I let him have his own way rather
more. I have no fault worth calling a fault to find with
him. His thoughtfulness for the real interests of the
Mission, his responsibility as to business, his manly
dealing with men and things, are in my estimation
very remarkable. Then he is, I think, really good, open*

*to spiritual influences to any extent. Poor boy! Were
he only stronger I should rejoice in contemplating his
future, and push him on to aim at far greater things.*

*I don't know whether I told you how pleased I
was with dear Katie speaking in the streets on Sunday
morning. It was very nice and effective. Bless her! I am
delighted with all the children more and more. Willie is
the greatest help I have ever had in the office.*

*I heard Ballington give out a hymn and say a few
words at Bethnal Green last night. He did not know
that I was there. I was surprised and gratified in the
extreme. He has an extraordinary voice and will be able
to give out a hymn with more effect than many a man
could produce with a sermon. The little he did say was
spoken with force and feeling. They think very much
of the promise he gives for ability at Bethnal Green.
He will make a mighty man with the Divine blessing.
But it will be a serious matter. I could not touch him in
effective giving out of a hymn in the open-air, and he is
only seventeen. Willie's voice and chest are so weak that I
don't see how he is going to make a preacher.*

A knock came at the door.

"Enter! Ah, Mr Railton, how are you today?"

George Scott Railton: now here was a blessing from God! How
long had he been with them now? Just two years? And already an
indispensable right-hand man, his "lieutenant"!

He had introduced himself to William by means of a letter and
then had travelled to London. He was some twenty years William's

junior, with an already receding hairline, a good growth of thick black beard, and still a hint of his native Scotland in his voice. Educated, with a passion for God.

"I was so impressed by this article you wrote." He had acquired a copy of William's pamphlet "How to Reach the Masses with the Gospel", and soon after reading it had declared his intention of joining the Christian Mission and working under William.

Although already "saved", Railton had a reputation as a somewhat impulsive Methodist preacher, which Catherine, in particular, had felt a little anxious about. But there was no deterring the man and he had even argued with his own brother about joining the Booth movement.

As the two men had become acquainted, George Railton had shared his story of faith. At one point he had been determined to make a life as a missionary overseas and, indeed, had even taken himself off to Morocco, where he'd soon found himself destitute. Yes, George Railton was a man after William's own heart! Except more learned, and much more organized. Just the kind required.

William Booth was gradually gathering around him a group of helpers, assistants, and followers who would later play an important role in the founding of The Salvation Army. George Railton was one of those.

He shared the Booths' enthusiasm for saving souls but was considered a bit of a "radical". He had been brought up as a Methodist and well educated, but was rather temperamental, with an adventuring spirit. He first heard of the Booths while working in Middlesbrough and although it took William a few weeks to decide whether this young man was the sort he wanted in his fold, once appointed as his "assistant" Railton would prove invaluable, particularly in providing some intellectual input to the Christian Mission, which had hitherto been absent.[12]

On his arrival to work for the Christian Mission in London in 1872, Mr Railton moved in "temporarily" with the Booths in Gore Street opposite Victoria Park. A decade later he was still there and had become indispensable to William, being largely responsible for much of the writing and promotion of the new Salvation Army. He had also become something of a surrogate son to Catherine.[13] In Railton, Catherine had an ally as she promoted the role of women in the Christian Mission. He would play a leading role in persuading William Booth to give women equal place in The Salvation Army, and his ideas and enthusiasm certainly gave the new Army organization the impetus it required to grow quickly in the first decades. Railton also accompanied William on his travels and was a helpmate, especially when Catherine was away from home, either preaching or recovering from one of her numerous bouts of ill health.

### 1876 OR 77

*I am in a corner, having had all sorts of interruptions. I have your affectionate letter. I do indeed reciprocate all you say. I love you BETTER, more as a woman would wish in her soul to be loved than I did when at Matlock. I have more sense, more heart, and more religion than I had then, and all I have I lay at your feet and as much on your shrine as ever I did in my life.*

*I have been during our late separation in much uncertainty as to where you were, and Willie opens my letters, and I can't write as freely, and many things have been on my heart and held me down, but when I get free my heart comes bounding off to my first love as much and far more than when it seemed miles between Newington Gate and Russell Street.*

*… I think of you all alone, and when a gleam of sunshine comes into my heart or through my window my soul turns to you at once. If I only thought you would be happy with me it would make me glad beyond description; but, unfortunately, you get so anxious about me when there is really no occasion. I am wonderfully better again. I do MORE work, and do it far more easily, than I did when an Evangelist in these parts 22 years ago.*

1877

*I have your two letters by this morning's post. They perplex me much. I am distressed that you are not more settled and happy… You evidently can't settle where you are without me. Why not?*

*If you want to come home, you must. I don't care what I do or where I go or what happens now, if I can but feel you are happy… I want you ten thousand times to be at home tomorrow and only counsel your staying away for your OWN DEAR SAKE.*

*My life is a drag without you, BUT I want you to get better.*

# CHAPTER

# 15

"Throw a few more coals on the fire, Willi… Bramwell!" urged William.

The three men had been at it for hours and had hardly noticed how the winter chill had crept into the room. Planning a Christmas campaign and appeal for the ever-expanding Christian Mission was no mean task.

Young Bramwell Booth did as his father instructed, and then returned to the desk where the lists of campaign ideas, venues, and participants were being drawn up like a military campaign.

Where should they concentrate their efforts? What sort of response would they receive? Could they rely on any funds coming in?

"Mama, Ballington and Katie, of course, and the others will all be part of it!" William announced. The older children were all now capable evangelists despite their youth. Katie, in particular, was as able a preacher as her namesake, darling Catherine, and exuded enthusiasm and character although still not yet twenty years old.

"William, you do know that you are favouring dear Katie just a little, don't you?" Catherine had warned a couple of years before. "Ballington and Bramwell are good boys and they will also be fine evangelists, but you need to be cautious with your treatment of them!"

William looked across at his eldest son. He really was growing into a fine man. Twenty-one years old and for a couple of years now

William's right-hand man. He and Catherine had been so proud of Willie when he took responsibility for the Food-for-the-Millions programme – when was it ... seven, eight years ago? For a brief moment William Booth felt a pang of remorse as he remembered how hard his young son and Mr Flawn had worked on the food relief programme, and yet they had still understood and submitted when the business was sold four years later. It was just bleeding finances, and the Christian Mission was suffering as a result, so it was the only practical thing to do!

On the other side of the table, Mr Railton looked up from his paper.

"Sir, shall we take a look at the printer's proof for the poster?"

In front of George Railton was the first draft for the proposed handbill to promote the campaign. Mr Booth had dictated much of it, but here they had the first proof of what it might look like on paper. The text looked good, with its introduction "Recruited from amongst the multitudes who are without God and without hope in the world, devoting their leisure time to all sorts of laborious efforts for the salvation of others from unbelief, drunkenness, vice, and crime", followed by the two quotes – from no less than the Archbishop of Canterbury and the Earl of Shaftesbury.

And so to the heading. At the top of the page, the words "The Christian Mission".

Beneath the heading, "Under the Superintendence of the ... "

Next Line: "Rev. William Booth".

And then on the subsequent lines the words "Is A" and "Volunteer Army".

The three men looked at the sheet. William nodded and stroked his beard, mumbling what sounded like "good" under his breath.

"No!" William and George Railton looked up. Bramwell was shaking his head.

"I don't agree with this at all! As I said when you were dictating the letter, Father, I don't like the words 'Volunteer Army'. Yes, we're a band fighting sin and the devil, out there to get people saved against the odds. But I'm no volunteer. I'm a full-timer!"

It wasn't often that Bramwell stood up to William but here he was – so like his father with his thick dark hair, an already developing beard, tall and upright – with his hands on his hips, as if ready to go into battle.

William Booth looked at his firstborn, and then again over Mr Railton's shoulder at the words on the sheet. Then he suddenly leaned forward, grabbed the pen from his secretary's hand, dipped it into the ink and crossed out the word "Volunteer".

In its place he wrote, in capital letters, the single word "SALVATION".

He stood back and the three men looked down at the paper.

"The Christian Mission Under the Superintendence of the Rev. William Booth is a SALVATION ARMY."

The renaming of the Christian Mission as the more distinctive "Salvation Army" was a turning point for the organization that William and Catherine Booth had been toiling in for thirteen years. Early in 1878 publicity was issued with both names attached, but by May of that year the name "Christian Mission" had been finally dropped.

Although the Christian Mission had had some success, the new title almost immediately coincided with tremendous growth of the Booths' organization. When William and Bramwell Booth, along with William's secretary George Scott Railton, produced that first leaflet carrying the name "The Salvation Army", it seemed as if the world caught the vision that had been implanted in the Booths' hearts so many years before.

Late nineteenth-century Britain was a militaristic society, so the embracing of a military-style culture by the new mission organization was not entirely alien and indeed contributed to its popularity.

Throughout the previous hundreds of years, especially during the centuries of world exploration in which European countries such as Portugal, Spain, and England sent out adventurers to map and claim unknown territories, the British Empire had expanded exponentially and often the success of growth and the creation and retention of overseas possessions and dominions depended on military and naval might. In the mid part of the nineteenth century, the British infantry and cavalry had fought major conflicts in the Crimea and India, and they also battled a series of internal uprisings and wars with other nations over disputed territories in places as far afield as Burma, Afghanistan, China, and the Caribbean. By the latter part of the nineteenth century Britain's economic and military domination was beginning to wane and military campaigns were being used to shore up the edifice.[1] About the time William, Bramwell, and George Railton were renaming the Christian Mission, war was again in the air with a potential conflict against Russia and within months of the renaming of the organization the first Boer War against the settlers in South Africa was under way.

William Booth had been using military imagery for quite a while before The Salvation Army was born in name. In accordance with its Methodist heritage, the organization that William and Catherine had founded still held an annual conference for decision making, or, in later years, for announcements on policy decided by the Booths, and at the June 1877 Conference of the Christian Mission William declared to the delegates, "This is our Council of War. We are here to consider practical questions and how we can best deal with them; to receive reinforcements and re-station our army…"[2]

Instead of war against military enemies or to ensure the security of empire, the Booths' war was waged on sin. The name "The Salvation Army" first appeared on a public poster in Plymouth,[3] and soon afterwards Bramwell Booth had it painted across the back of the platform in the Whitechapel Hall, much to the consternation of some of the older members of the Mission who believed that the new name would do the organization no good whatsoever.

Some time before the name change, the Annual Conference of the Christian Mission had decided against the use of the title "Reverend" for their evangelists, but "Mr", "Mrs", and "Miss" were also considered unsatisfactory as that did not have wide appeal to the masses.[4] One of the leading lights of the Mission, a converted chimney sweep called Elijah Cadman, had as early as 1873 referred to himself as a "lieutenant" to William's "General" – short for "General Superintendent of The Christian Mission"[5] – and on another occasion had called himself a "captain" in the "King's Army". This tiny man – just five feet tall – was a giant in personality. His November 1877 campaign in Whitby, a fishing village on the east coast of Yorkshire, called for "200 Men and Women wanted at once to join the Hallelujah Army". Cadman believed the title "captain" would attract the seamen and dockers who he hoped would attend his revival meetings.[6]

Gradually the militaristic terms stuck. Assistant evangelists became "lieutenants". Elders and class leaders became "sergeants" and "sergeant majors". The rapid growth of the organization after 1878 meant that The Salvation Army could not continue to be run entirely from the London headquarters, so districts, or "divisions" and "commands" were created. These areas would be run by more experienced evangelists, who became "majors" and "colonels".

George Scott Railton had been editor of *The Christian Mission Magazine* and from September 1873 was appointed General Secretary of the Mission. As William's second-in-command he was eventually titled "Commissioner". In 1880 he sailed to New York with Captain Emma Westbrook and six other young women who were dubbed the "Hallelujah Lassies". The Salvation Army in the United States of America had already been unofficially started by the Shirley family who had emigrated to Philadelphia, and was growing organically, as The Salvation Army invariably did in those early days. But Railton's arrival in New York in March 1880 marked the official beginning of the work in the USA. Much against his will, the following year Railton was ordered back to London and thereafter spent the rest of his life travelling the world to establish or reinforce the expanding Salvation Army.[7]

In 1881 General William Booth appointed Bramwell as his "Chief of the Staff of The Salvation Army", a title he would hold until his father's death in August 1912, when, under the terms of William's will, he was named as the second General of the Army.[8] Despite their differing temperaments, the relationship between father and son was close as they not only worked but ministered together.

MARCH 1878

*Bramwell started a letter the other day by saying, "I do miss you so much. I hope I don't love you too much." Those words follow me up and down like heavenly music. I seldom hear of anybody loving me. I don't think my people do, and that my family do I have to take very much on trust. So to hear him go out of his reticent course to tell me so comforted me much.*

# CHAPTER

# 16

*... we are mobbed and hunted almost out of the town.*
*At present every hall and room is closed against us.*
*The only promise is an old coach house, 4s per week,*
*and that not certain! Outdoors the Evangelists have*
*to get into houses to escape the mob, and on Sunday*
*they had to close the meetings – could not go on. Police*
*refuse protection. Nevertheless there is a good Society.*
*A lot saved. We must not give up; we will not.*

*(William)*

The crowd was becoming noisy and the new Salvation Army recruit was feeling rather anxious. Elizabeth had heard about the trouble the band of evangelists might encounter when they set out to lead a meeting in the square, but she had had no thought that the reaction would be so extreme.

Captain Cadman – all the girls had laughed at first at his small stature but had soon understood the power of the little man with his strange Midlands accent and desperate love for lost souls – was at the head of the small group.

"Are we all ready? We walk, and we sing, and we pray! We smile and we fend off any flying objects!" he shouted.

Elizabeth took her place in the centre of the small crowd of Salvation Army lasses and lads. She adjusted her big black poke bonnet. When she had left home she had been instructed to bring any clothing that was dark in colour, for although there was not yet an official "uniform" Captain Cadman wanted all his little gang to be identifiable, not just so that others could note the evangelists, but also in order that he might spot his group if there was trouble.

The small group walked through the inquisitive crowd to the market square, where Captain Cadman began to speak. Elizabeth almost lost herself in the moment and forgot she was there as one of the saved. He was so convincing; she almost wished she could be saved anew, just for the thrill of responding to "Fiery Elijah" pleas.

"The Lord is calling you… calling YOU, and YOU, and YOU," the little man said, pointing at individuals in the crowd. "He wants you to turn your back on your sin and your old destructive habits. God wants you to give yourself to Him and to live your lives for Him, in His service! Will YOU give up the drink, you drunkard husbands? Will you cease from wife beating? Will YOU surrender your life of vice in the brothels, all you poor women?"

From the back of the crowd, which was already restless, came a voice.

" 'ere, mate. Don't take all our fun away!"

Elizabeth looked up from under the brim of her bonnet. She didn't see the first missile coming but it hit her full in the face. An egg! She'd been warned about this in Mrs Booth's preparation classes. The main aggressors were the innkeepers and the publicans, who feared for their livelihoods. The police were nowhere to be seen, of course. The authorities didn't want the Army there either!

Captain Cadman was getting down from his wooden box.

"Keep together, and heads down! Let's try to make a run for it!" he yelled above the noise of the mob.

The young man in front of Elizabeth, who had previously introduced himself as James, fell to the ground in front of her, a huge gash on his head – caused by a flying bottle – gushing blood. Captain Cadman picked James up and the group of evangelists began to edge quietly away from the disturbance. He might be small but that converted chimney sweep was certainly strong!

The early opposition to The Salvation Army came from a variety of sources. Publicans, certainly, were unashamedly opposed to this vigorously outspoken Temperance Movement which threatened their profits, and the "mobs" that were rounded up also found great sport in attacking the latest group of evangelists who swept into their towns with their message of salvation from sin.

This wasn't a new phenomenon. There had been attacks on religious groups down the ages, from opposition to John Wesley's preaching to early attacks on the Quakers, the Congregationalists, and the Baptists.[1] Riots and general public disorder were also not unknown in this period. For Britain and Europe the nineteenth century was a time of great social unrest as people fought for new civil and political rights. France had already ditched its monarchy and in Russia the momentum towards social freedoms would ultimately result in the rise of Communism and the 1917 Revolution. Many rebellious citizens wanted the old order to be done away with and a new democracy introduced, and in England the Chartists stood at the forefront of this.

Chartism was a working-class movement born during hard economic times in the late 1830s and 1840s. "Working Men's Associations" sought political reform and adopted a People's Charter, which, among other things, demanded the vote for all men over twenty-one. In the days when owning property and having personal income was a ticket into Parliament, the Chartists wanted the property qualification to be dropped and Members of Parliament to receive a wage. They demanded a secret ballot so that voters might not be intimidated, annual elections for Parliament, and equal-sized constituencies.[2]

Although William Booth had had some political awareness as he grew into adulthood, he had not got involved in the uprisings of his youth. In 1844, when the Chartists invaded Nottingham calling for a "general strike" to bring the country to a halt and force the government to pass the People's Charter, William reportedly hung about at the edges of the crowd, listening in on the radicals.[3] But now it was the mob that attacked William and his Salvation Army troops. Some of the hooligans who rioted at the open-air meetings and attacked the evangelists dubbed themselves "The Skeleton Army". In Whitechapel there was "The Unconverted Salvation Army" and in Salisbury "The Society for the Suppression of Street Parading", while Guildford boasted the "Red (Nose) Army".[4]

But opposition to The Salvation Army came not just from the grass roots of society. Demonstrations against the new religious movement made the newspapers and there were questions in Parliament about whether The Salvation Army had the right to march in public.

Local magistrates often rejected rulings that favoured The Salvation Army.[5] Until the Army's right to parade and preach in the "open air" was finally established, rather than arresting members of the mob who attacked the "Salvationists", as they were becoming known, magistrates often threw the evangelists into prison for public disorder. Although this was distressing, it did not deflate the Salvationists' enthusiasm. Indeed, those thrown into jail often emerged as heroes, having made a sacrifice in the name of Jesus Christ, which The Salvation Army publicized and made a virtue.

Some elements of the wider traditional church were also far from enamoured of the antics of this new movement of fervently evangelistic Christians. Although within a few years The Salvation Army would become tolerated, if not entirely accepted, by many other denominations, at the start it was regarded as radical and disruptive. But that hardly worried the Booths.

1880

*The more I see of fashionable religion the more I despise it; indeed, how can fashionable religion ever be any other than despicable? I was thinking the other day what a reproduction of the same classes of character this age presents as were in Jerusalem when Jesus lived and died. The Pharisees of that day wanted a Christ Oh, yes! But he must be a reigning Christ. And now there are thousands talking about His second coming who will neither see nor receive Him in the person of His humble and persecuted followers. Christ manifested in flesh, vulgar flesh, they cannot receive. No, they are looking for Him in the clouds. What a sensation there would be if He were to come again in a carpenter's coat. How many would recognise Him then, I wonder? I am afraid it would*

be the old story, "Crucify Him!" "Away with Him!"
"Whoever denieth that Jesus is come (not did come)
in the flesh is anti-Christ. Oh, for grace always to see
Him where He is to be seen, for verily flesh and blood
doth not reveal this unto us. Well, bless the Lord, I
keep seeing Him risen again in the forms of drunkards
and ruffians of all descriptions.

I would have given a trifle for you to have been
with me at Poole, and here on Tuesday night. A
glorious band, sweet in spirit and valiant in fight!
Driven close to God and each other by furious
persecution from without. The Lord will give us a
triumphant victory in this place, a priest-ridden,
proud cathedral city, with unfaithful shepherds
enough to lead a whole generation into hell. Oh, for an
earthquake to open their eyes!

… I had a drawing-room meeting here yesterday
morning and I preach to-night in the Assembly Rooms
… I preached in the Town Hall on the Sunday night
on Faith. Lady C … had besought me not to ask
people out; she was sure that in proud Bournemouth
no one would come, and feared it might create
prejudice. I told her I dare not preach without, and
was quite willing to leave consequences with God. The
hall was packed, the power came down and twelve
came forward. Everybody was amazed, and I hear
people are asking in all directions whether I am going
again. One clergyman who was there told a friend that
he got richly blessed. So you see, dear, God still sustains
poor me and gives me the victory over rich and poor.

Catherine was visiting the south coast of England. In the days of their travelling ministry, when William Booth would often preach to what might be considered the "lower classes" Catherine had ministered to the more refined, particularly women. Now The Salvation Army was proving popular not only with the poorest and neediest of society, but also with individuals from the "higher classes".

As The Salvation Army was so radical in its approach to "equality", former drunkards, layabouts, and labourers with working-class political aspirations stood side by side in ministry with former public-school boys. Titled ladies scrubbed the floors of slums alongside former prostitutes and women with no education. In equal measure, men and women led the new Salvation Army mission stations, which were soon renamed "corps", and women "officers" were (if more experienced) even placed in charge of their male junior officers. The militant and even aggressive style of Christianity that The Salvation Army brought with it, which appeared to threaten the status quo, was just what its followers were seeking.

Catherine and William, their children – all except the sickly Marian – and their growing group of senior "officers" toured the new Salvation Army "corps" which sprang up across the country as opportunities for growth were grasped. In 1878, the Christian Mission had thirty "stations" and thirty-six "missioners" across the United Kingdom. The last of the Christian Mission conferences in August 1878 unanimously adopted the new Salvation Army brand and by the end of the year it was estimated that The Salvation Army had eighty-one corps and 127 officers, of whom 101 had been recently converted at its own meetings.[6]

The adoption of uniforms and other military paraphernalia was part of its popularity. It fostered a culture of spiritual "togetherness" and symbolized the aggressive spirit of the new Christian movement. The Christian Mission evangelists had all worn modest frock coats, tall hats, and black ties, while the women donned plain dresses, jackets, and poke bonnets. Not exactly trendy for the times, but distinctive. At the 1878 Conference one of the Christian Mission's leading lights, Elijah Cadman, who had also been among the first to use military terminology in his campaign publicity, had declared that he wanted to wear clothes that would "let everyone know I mean war to the teeth and salvation for the world".[7] Thus the Salvation Army uniform was gradually developed, modelled on Victorian military dress.

*Emma looked across at her mother. Catherine had that determined look in her eyes, and she knew that meant either trouble, or a good deal of work.*

*Even though she was now principal of The Women's Training College and responsible for all the young female "cadets", as the trainee "officers" were becoming known, the naturally shy Emma Booth was still in awe of her parents, and particularly her mother.*

*So what was it that Catherine needed to say to Emma? The young woman adjusted the pince-nez on her nose, tucked a stray hair behind her ear and lifted her face to her mother.*

*"Now, dear, don't think me trivial … but I really think we have to do something about this uniform!"*

*Emma was shocked. No new spiritual instructions. No suggested outline for her next sermon.*

*"I'm not really sure I know what you mean, Mother dear," she replied. It had always been difficult to judge her mother's moods. She was so intense.*

*"I'm just a little concerned that, unless we devise something standard, we may be encouraging people to become a little vain in*

their attire. I was thinking particularly of the bonnet. I saw Miss C the other day and I thought I caught a glimpse of a piece of lace. Now, while that might have been perfectly acceptable in her previous life, and even if this were still the Christian Mission, I just think our Army should, perhaps, be beyond such vanity. What do you think, dear?"

Emma was a little taken aback but dared not say so. They had encouraged the young cadets to arrive at the college with dark dresses and coats and she knew there were some in the Army who were already thinking about standardizing a sort of uniform, but they hadn't thought about headgear.

"I'm concerned that the girls also need something to protect them when they are out in the open air. Do you realize that every time the mobs attack us, we're at risk of serious injury if a missile lands on our heads? No, we need something strong, cheap, and large enough to protect us! I've been thinking about this a great deal. Here look, I've gathered up all the bonnets I could find and I thought we could make a start!"

Emma looked down at the open hamper at her mother's feet, full of black straw bonnets. She recognized a few of her mother's and a couple of her own. There was Katie's favourite – the one she used to wear such a lot before the Army. There was Lucy's little bonnet, the one which had once boasted a red ribbon.

"Hand me my sewing box, dear, and let's get to work!"

The next couple of hours passed quickly. They cut and shaped, sewed and pinned. They laughed as Emma could hardly remember laughing with her mother before. The first model, which Catherine favoured, was to Emma's mind quite ugly. Should she say so?

"What do you think? Be truthful, Emma!" Catherine turned to her daughter, the hideous contraption on her head.

"Oh, Mama, I cannot have my girls made to look like workhouse inmates!" Although vanity was not to be encouraged, she just knew her cadets would be horrified if they had to walk down the road with such a plain, crude affair on their heads.

"I suppose so!" Catherine removed the bonnet from her greying curls.

The designers worked on and eventually there emerged a poke bonnet, plain and sturdy, on which they could agree. It was still rather "old-fashioned" and Emma feared that some of the girls, even though dedicated to the Army cause, might still object just a little. But Catherine was determined.

"If they have complaints, I'll just come and explain to them how important it is for us all to wear neat and plain bonnets that keep us safe and make us stand out as… Salvationists!"

"The Hallelujah Bonnet" made its first appearance in public when the twenty-five female cadets from The Salvation Army training school marched, with Emma Booth and her assistant Captain Rose Clapham, from Hackney to the People's Hall in Whitechapel. It was 16 June 1880 and The Salvation Army was gathering to celebrate the silver wedding anniversary of its founders, General William and Mrs Catherine Booth.

Emma and Catherine's original bonnet design had been handed to Cadet Annie E. Lockwood, who had trained as a milliner. She was one of the ten young women who had entered the training school in May 1880, and, helped by another cadet, she trimmed the bonnets using plain black silk and black strings. By September of that year the "regulation bonnet" was on sale for six shillings.[8]

But the design of headgear wasn't Catherine Booth's only creative input into the new Salvation Army. Just a few days after the new Salvation Army name was formally adopted, the Booths started a two-month campaign across the Midlands and the north of England, including a short but memorable stay in Coventry. Here it was recorded that five thousand people marched, they were denounced as "red hot Salvationists" by the local newspaper, and six "Coventry lasses" were added to the officer list[9] while Mrs Booth formally presented the first "Salvation Army flag" to the new "corps" in the town. The idea of "colours", or flags, which armies have traditionally marched behind and rallied around, was an enticing concept. That first Salvation Army flag was crimson red, with a navy blue border, symbolizing holiness, and a yellow sun in the middle, which was later replaced by a star, signifying the fiery baptism of the Holy Ghost.

Gradually these new "Salvationists" adopted not just military ranks but also military vocabulary to describe their religious practices. The Army "revival services" were first called "sieges", places of worship were dubbed "corps, citadels, and outposts". Even death was translated as being "Promoted to Glory".[10]

Although many in society thought the new organization ridiculous for its pretensions, the military metaphors appealed to thousands of others much more than traditional church. The Salvation Army was independent, appealed to women, to whom it gave equality, and was strictly based on the idea of simple "salvation", holiness theology, and revival. Moreover, at the head of the organization were the Booths. They were in charge. This was no democracy. They had both long since decided that was not for them, and they took no orders from others. Theirs was an autocratic leadership, which appealed to their followers, who wanted to be led and needed guidance.

Within a few years of The Salvation Army taking its new name, the authorities and the churches could no longer ignore it. There was no escaping its appeal, not just in Great Britain but also abroad. The Army had spread quickly to the United States of America, Canada, France, Australia, Sweden, Switzerland, and even India. "General" Booth was now an international leader of a growing evangelistic organization which, wherever it established itself, did not just preach the gospel but increasingly set about working among the people, assisting the vulnerable.

William Booth collapsed onto the chair behind the huge oak desk in his office at 101 Queen Victoria Street and put his head in his hands.

"O God," his heart cried out. "Give me the answer. Show me what you want!"

His Bible was at his right hand and he opened it. Many times before the Lord had given him a verse, and he prayed for that inspiration today. But, no matter how many times he opened the pages, no appropriate lines came to him.

William moved to the door, picking up his thick double-breasted coat and his tall hat. He would take a cab home and there discuss the matter further with dear Catherine. She would bring some clarity to the situation, just as she always did.

He glanced in the small mirror to ensure that his hat was straight. An old man looked back. Greying to white beard now where once it was dark. His untidy hair streaked with grey. Fifty-two years old this year but feeling much, much older. How he wished he could bound around as he used to. How he yearned for the energy he once had.

"Goodnight General!" Captain M, sitting at the large reception desk, stood to attention as William walked through the lobby. As he stepped into the waiting cab, William looked back at the imposing building, now The Salvation Army's international headquarters, here on the banks of the River Thames, just south of St Paul's Cathedral.

How excited they had all been the year before when they had moved into this impressive building. William and Catherine had been concerned that it was overly ostentatious, but they had been persuaded. A new headquarters was required and this was an excellently situated building, in the heart of the City. Perfectly placed for high-level meetings.

It had been a good base for the recent discussions with the bishops who had come calling.

William could still recall his surprise when Bramwell had informed him that the Church of England wished to enter into negotiations in advance of a potential merger.

"But is that what we really want, William? Have we not struggled to create an identity separate from the denominations? Is a union what God wants for our Army?" As usual, Catherine had brought some reality to the situation

Now the negotiations were concluded, and a final decision had to be made. Ultimately, he and Catherine knew, it was theirs to make.

By 1882 the Church of England was seriously considering a union with The Salvation Army. A committee was established and respectful negotiations continued until early the following year. But there were questions to be addressed on both sides before any union could be considered.

First, given that the quickly growing Salvation Army was stronger in some parts of the country than the Anglican Church, what would William's place be in the new merged organization? What would the future hold for Salvation Army officers? It soon became clear that the female officers could not expect to become Anglican ministers or priests. Indeed, it would be more than a century before the Church of England would ordain women priests. Third, there was contention over the "sacraments" – the taking of bread and wine – and the matter of baptism.

Although in the days of the Christian Mission the Lord's Supper, or the Eucharist, was administered and people were baptized, increasingly Catherine Booth's heart and mind were focused more on "practical holiness". George Scott Railton, although raised with the sacraments, like his mentors the Booths, wanted the new Army to be free of ceremonial.

William Booth didn't want to be out of step with fellow Christians but, under the influence of his wife and his second-in-command, he weighed the matter up. He observed the Quakers, the Society of Friends, who appeared to be able to live and sustain a spiritual Christian life without "sacramental aids". He noted that views on and practices of sacraments were divisive in the different Christian denominations. There were arguments about the rights and wrongs of adult baptism, full or partial immersion, and infant baptism.

Differing theology of and views on the bread and wine, the Lord's Supper, he argued sadly, also led to division among churches. In addition, William was aware that many of his converts were reformed drunkards and alcoholics. What kind of wine could be used in a Salvation Army Eucharist that would not tempt them back to their old ways? There was also the question of whether anyone would tolerate receiving Communion from a woman. Regardless of the perceived equality between men and women in the new Salvation Army, this was a step too far even for the General.

So he was persuaded of the argument that the sacraments were "not necessary for a real experience of God's Grace" and that the freedom bought for mankind by the death and resurrection of Jesus Christ also included freedom from ritual. Although not everyone was happy with the decision to exclude the sacraments from Salvation Army worship, they fell in line with their Founder.[11]

By early 1883, even as the negotiations with the Anglican Church were proceeding, the matter of the sacraments was decided, and the proposal to link the Church of England with the vibrant, exciting, popular Salvation Army eventually came to nothing. For some bishops, who were still very unhappy about The Salvation Army's evangelistic tactics – open-air services, emotional pleas for altar calls, and other behaviour considered rather outrageous – this must have come as something of a relief.[12] Although some on both sides regretted the decision, it set the course for an independent Salvation Army, which continued to grow, with its strange mix of personnel.

There was the upper-class, public-school-educated Frederick Tucker, who was captivated by the Booths' message and ministry. He would eventually marry Emma Booth and return to his birthplace of India, where his forebears and he had been part of the Raj, the British establishment, and where he would oversee the growth of The Salvation Army in the subcontinent.[13]

There were the Elijah Cadmans of the young Army, the illiterate, rough and ready former drunkards who became stalwarts and saints. Forced up chimneys as a sweep from the age of six – seven years before a law was passed which prohibited this exploitation of young boys – by the time he was seventeen, Cadman claimed he could "fight like a devil and drink like a fish". Aged twenty-one he had turned up to listen, and heckle, a street preacher in the town of Rugby, was converted to Christianity, and became a Methodist lay preacher.

In 1876, after coming into contact with the Christian Mission, the former chimney sweep sold his home, and his chimney-sweeping business, uprooted his wife and children to London and took up his first appointment with the Mission in Hackney, where he preached at night and visited the slums by day. This little man who came from nothing would eventually travel the world, campaigning on behalf of The Salvation Army in South Africa, the United States of America, Canada, the West Indies, Australia, New Zealand, India, Scandinavia, Germany, and beyond. It was he who took charge of The Salvation Army's City Colony, a shelter for the homeless in London which gave board and lodging to the poor and destitute in exchange for a day's work, the development of which was so much part of William Booth's later vision for mission and social outreach combined with ministry and evangelism.

# CHAPTER

# 17

The child was pretty, bright, and fresh-looking. Around thirteen and a half. She quietly entered the room where her mother, already half cut – perhaps the result of last night's drinking with Father or maybe the consequence of a pint or two of ale this very morning – was talking with a strange woman.

"This is Lily! Pretty, ain't she?" her mother's voice was whining and begging.

"She will do very nicely," the other woman said.

"Now, my lovely, you're to go with this lady and she's to bring you to a house where you'll be working as a maid. Now, don't blub. It's about time you went out to work."

"But… "

"No buts… that's the way it is! Your dad and me, we had to go to work when we were young, and so do you!" Her mother fell back on the crude chair in the bare little room which served as living and sleeping quarters for the whole family in the poor and rundown building in this overcrowded, infested part of the city.

"Have you got your things, dearie?" The stern-looking woman turned to Lily. Her voice was softer than expected, and rather kind. The terrified child pointed to the corner of the room, to what looked like a bundle of rags.

"Well, never mind. First thing we'll do is we'll get you some nice new things. Alright?"

Lily nodded. It was no use protesting, she knew that. If Ma and Pa had decided that she was to go with this nicely dressed woman, then go she must. She feared the stick from her father, who was out at the alehouse already despite the early hour of the day, and her mother's hand, which she liberally used on Lily and her brothers and sisters.

The lady took Lily by the hand and they walked down the stairs to the street. She would be pleased to leave this house, what with all the comings and goings in some of the rooms. She'd often been scared here, with strange men wandering around.

As she left the building, Lily could hear the sound of her mother's drawling inebriated voice rattling down the wooden steps.

"Bye 'bye, my Liza Lily. Be a good girl!"

What Lily, or Eliza Armstrong, to give her real name, did not know when she walked from that building was that she was at the centre of a conspiracy that would blow open the child sex trafficking trade across Britain. The woman who had collected Lily from her parents' hovel of a dwelling in a brothel house in Lisson Grove in West London was Rebecca Jarrett, a reformed prostitute and brothel keeper.

Rebecca hadn't long been out of the trade and was staying in Winchester as assistant to Josephine Butler, a devout Christian, vehement feminist, and passionate campaigner for the welfare of prostitutes.[1] Mrs Butler had been contacted by W. T. Stead, the editor of the *Pall Mall Gazette* newspaper, who was writing a series of articles on the sex trade and felt that maybe Mrs Jarrett could help.

Encouraged by Bramwell Booth and his mother, Catherine, what Stead actually wanted was someone who would help him not just to expose the evil trade, especially the buying and selling of young girls into prostitution, but to prove without doubt to the world that it happened. Child prostitution was not only common but accepted in Victorian London, with girls as young as nine or ten being "bought" from their parents and sold to brothels not just across Britain but also in Europe.[2] It was a trade that many knew about but to which most turned a blind eye.

Josephine Butler and others like her, including Catherine Booth, were incensed by the hypocrisy and evil they saw around them. She was particularly offended by something called the Contagious Diseases Act, which was passed first by the United Kingdom Parliament in 1864 and later updated. The Act was a response to the growing contagion of venereal disease and had resulted from a government investigation two years earlier into the prevalence of sexually transmitted diseases such as syphilis and gonorrhoea within the armed forces.[3]

Campaigners for the rights of women were furious when, instead of taking the opportunity to address the morality of the time which accepted prostitution as a norm, the legislation instead criminalized those offering sexual services. The act allowed police to arrest prostitutes in some ports and army towns, subject them to compulsory checks for venereal disease, and, if found to be infected, permitted their locking-up in an isolation centre, or "Lock Hospital", until they were "cured". The original act meant women could be imprisoned for up to three months, a period gradually extended to one year by the time the Act was updated in 1869. Most offensive to the campaigners was the fact that the prostitutes' clientele were not subjected to similar examinations.

Bramwell looked at his mother. She was so pale. She had been very unwell recently, more than usual, but still her eyes shone brightly with her passion for the lost.

He remembered her reaction when he'd come home just a few months ago and reported that the officer opening up the Queen Victoria Street headquarters building that cold February morning had found a young girl sleeping on the steps. Like many, the child had come to London seeking employment in service, but had found herself in a brothel and the newest "girl" to be enjoyed by the many male customers. She'd managed to escape and find her way to The Salvation Army, who she trusted would help.

Mother had been incandescent with righteous rage.

"How long ago was it I preached at the Midnight Movement for Fallen Women? Twenty years ago! How long has dear Mrs Butler been campaigning against those odious Contagious Diseases Acts? How long until those men in high places understand that while we judge and punish the girls and let their abusers go free, we are falling in with the Devil, as a society and as individual members of it?

"Willie. I need you to go away and pray about it. But do it quickly! I don't have the energy, although I will be writing to Mrs Butler again. And I think I might write to the Queen about it all. And the Home Secretary. What do you think?"

"I'll give it some thought and prayer, Mama. Now... you rest... please."

The person to whom Bramwell Booth turned was an old friend of the General.

William Thomas Stead was a long-time admirer of the Booths, having first met William when he was successfully ministering in Gateshead and Stead was the editor of the

*Northern Echo*. By 1885 Stead was a renowned campaigning journalist and editor of the *Pall Mall Gazette* in London.

Bramwell, his mother, and his wife, Florence, whom he had married just two years earlier, were already fired up for a campaign not against prostitutes, whom they saw as the victims, but against the sex trade itself. They wanted to expose the hypocrisy of the law and reveal to the world the evil that was the child sex trade.

Bramwell Booth must have been aware of Stead's reputation for rather scandalous journalism, but if something were to be done, it would have to be sensational. Bramwell was, after all, his father's son, and William Booth had never shied away from any publicity, however outrageous, that might help the cause.

William knew the value of media. He made increasing use of photography and later of film-making when it was in its infancy, and had undoubtedly coached his children on the value of a good headline. If this eldest son, whom he was grooming to take over the Army when he was no more, was to follow in his father's footsteps, he needed to be sure of how to keep The Salvation Army's profile in the public domain.

Initially, Stead was unconvinced that there was a story to be told. He was disinclined to believe Bramwell's claim that there were several thousand child prostitutes operating in the East End of London alone and also refused to believe that girls of not yet thirteen were being exported to France and the continent to meet the demands of the sex trade there. A few enquiries, however, confirmed not just this information but a good deal more. Stead was hooked.[4] He devised the scheme to "buy" a child for prostitution, proving that it could be done. The story would be written up as part of a series of articles in the *Pall Mall Gazette*, which Stead called "The Maiden Tribute of Modern Babylon".

Rebecca Jarrett was recruited, despite her misgivings. As a relatively new Christian and convert to The Salvation Army she may have not wanted to go back to her "old life", albeit temporarily and for a good purpose, but she agreed. A procuress of children for the sex trade, a woman called Nancy Broughton, whom Rebecca had known in her previous life, arranged the meeting with the alcoholic mother of Eliza Armstrong and a price was agreed. Eliza would be acquired for five (old British) shillings (5/-).

The first three shillings were received by the parent when Eliza was handed over to Rebecca. In line with the usual protocol, the balance would be received once it was proved that the child was a virgin. A "midwife" usually performed that task, and these women were canny in their investigations. The girls under scrutiny were usually unaware that they were destined for the brothel, so any examination had to be made carefully. These "midwives" were often called upon to perform backstreet abortions and some also did a trade in "reversing" lost virginity. Undefiled girls were highly regarded and could command a higher fee, so often young girls who had been forced to have sex were later submitted to an operation during which their intimate insides were sewn back together again so that they could be reoffered as "virgins". All this in the days before decent medical care. It was a dirty business in every sense.

Eliza Armstrong, also known as "Lily", was taken by Rebecca Jarrett to the chosen brothel, where she was locked in a room and drugged, as was often the case when a child was first put to the sex trade, unless the client preferred their young girls to feel pain, which many did. A man then entered the room and he was, of course, W. T. Stead. He spent the night watching over the sleeping girl, who eventually awoke and screamed on finding a strange man looking at her from across the room. The brothel keeper was convinced that the hysterical child had been used for the purpose for which she was intended, and Stead left.

"The Maiden Tribute of Modern Babylon" was published in the *Pall Mall Gazette* in July 1885, once Eliza, accompanied by Rebecca and still a virgin, had travelled to Paris, where she was taken into the care of The Salvation Army.

The series of articles outraged polite society, including Queen Victoria. Everyone was scandalized by the mentioning, in public, of such private matters. But they eventually led to a public petition in favour of raising the age of consent from thirteen to eighteen. Nearly four hundred thousand names were collected, largely as a result of the work of The Salvation Army in gathering support and signatures. This petition was delivered to the House of Commons on 30 July 1885 in a great show of publicity by General Booth, the huge petition being paraded through the streets before its arrival at Parliament. The Criminal Law Amendment Act was passed on 14 August 1885, although the age of consent was then raised only to sixteen.

Despite the success of the campaign, W. T. Stead, Rebecca Jarrett, Bramwell Booth, and others involved in the Armstrong "abduction" found themselves on trial. Technically, Stead had broken the law because he had procured Eliza without her father's knowledge.[5] The others were complicit in the affair.

For William Booth a public trial was not necessarily a bad thing. He wasn't over-keen on Stead's approach to journalism but had been aggrieved that the Maiden Tribute articles, while mentioning others involved in the scheme, such as his son Bramwell, made no reference to the role of The Salvation Army. While some believed that the notoriety of the trial would damage the Army, William Booth thought the high-profile court case, featuring the Army's second-in-command – the Chief of the Staff

– would only benefit their cause. Although he wished to distance himself from Stead, he also became determined that the matter should not rest with the end of the trial but that he could use this publicity to further his Army.

Family members including Bramwell's wife and some of his siblings attended court for the Maiden Tribute proceedings, along with senior Salvation Army staff such as George Scott Railton. Catherine, meanwhile, was away on evangelistic campaign in the north-west of England.

ROOKWOOD ROAD, STAMFORD HILL, LONDON, N.
SUNDAY SEPT. 13, '85.

*My Dearest Love,*

*We have had an anxious day, altho' I should not be anxious myself, but that it is Bramwell who I fear will worry about things. Still I believe that if they are committed tomorrow, which we all expect, he will feel much better. Rebecca [Jarrett] is all right they say, and has consented to some evidence coming out which blacks her.*

*The cross-examination on Saturday showed up Mrs Broughton as a very low, bad woman. But Ranger and all think they are certain to commit whether the matter ever comes to a real trial or not, very doubtful in the estimation of Russell and others. They think that the Government has felt so bespattered with these Revelations that they have felt compelled to discredit them before the world, consequently they have fallen upon this case. Perhaps they may never push the thing* to the extremity of a trial; if they do, nothing very much can possibly come of a conviction if any Jury can be got together that will say "Guilty."

My opinion is that anyway the Army cannot suffer very much. We shall have after the trial, whichever way it may go, a splendid text for an appeal to the Country. If they convict, we can show up the injustice of the thing – if they acquit, we can show the infamy and groundlessness of the prosecution.

If B goes to prison, they will make a martyr of him, and this alone will make him a heap of new friends and bind the Army and him more closely together and make thousands burn to go to prison too. Only one thing can hurt us, our own fears and worries; in other words, OUR OWN UNBELIEF.

Have faith in God, Lucy has written across her breast. Oh, let us have it written across our hearts, and act it out.

Now, my darling, I do hope God will guide you to-morrow night … You should not say anything that links Bramwell with STEAD in ANYTHING – any day some more unwise things may come out yet …

You must be careful – there's some sort of a threat to bring an action for libel and damages against all concerned for asserting that Mrs Armstrong sold her child. Now there are a lot of scoundrels who would find money for anything to get at our throats, so we must be careful. I hate this litigation. The time it consumes is awful. I can't make out why it should be so. But it goes to the heart direct.

*We must at once get up some sort of Counter-demonstration in the shape of a big influential defence Committee.*

*You will see the card Railton has got out – I enclose a rough proof – … he thinks it will attract attention and associate us with the prayers every time people read them at Church. It can't do any harm. We shall send them to the Queen, Cabinet ministers, Bishops, etc., etc. Our People will buy them … An effort is to be made to get some down to Bradford.*

*My darling, if I could always be assured of your welfare and that you don't worry or care, I should be comparatively reckless about the other things. Let us cast our care on Him who cares for us – all our care – our care for those who are dearest and nearest and weakest in our circle.*

*All seem well here. Florrie has done well today. I do think she helps Bramwell much. I am sure she will prove a great power for good and a helper of our joy and usefulness beyond what some have feared.*

*My heart's love to Herbert. His telegram cheered the Chief. Could you get a simple vote of sympathy with the Chief of Staff and Stead in this prosecution on Monday night and wire it in time for War Cry on Tuesday morning? Indeed, there must be a Press telegram if you had a good go.*

*Keep within the law, and we will have counsel's advice as to how far we can go when the Committal has taken place.*

*Good-night. Jesus Christ is a Brother born of adversity. We suffer in the Name for His sake and through His Spirit in us. Let us bear it like the saints; be strong; "we'll be Heroes." Now is the time. God bless and keep my beloved.*

*Your affectionate husband, W.B.*

*P.S. Since writing the above I have had a talk with Railton about expressions of sympathy with the Chief in meetings, and about explanations of the matter altogether; and he argues with a good deal of force that anything like votes of sympathy of Soldiers or anybody else with Superior Officers is unwise and prejudicial to discipline. He thinks that explanations are beneath us; but would advocate the pushing forward of our Rescue Work, the showing up of what we are doing in this direction, bringing out the case, and then remarking that this is the sort of thing for which they are attacking our Chief of the Staff. There is something in all this … I am sure the best answer we can make to the whole affair is to go on with our own work, keep our heads up, and keep on with the song of victory.*

*The lasses went past here this morning from Tottenham, singing "Victory." They had had a quiet meeting, sold 200 War Crys, and had a collection of 15s in the open air.*

*W.B.*

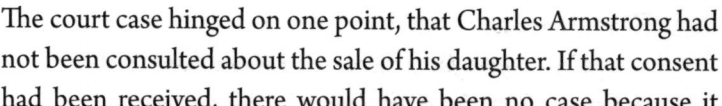

The court case hinged on one point, that Charles Armstrong had not been consulted about the sale of his daughter. If that consent had been received, there would have been no case because it was legal to "sell" a child as long as both parents were consulted and agreed. Mrs Armstrong, of course, raged that she had truly believed that her daughter was going into "service" as a maid. The charge against Stead and the others was therefore one of "feloniously and by force and fraud (the defendants) had led away and detained one Eliza Armstrong, a child under fourteen, with the intent to deprive her parents of possession". Conviction would lead to prosecution for assault.[6] Two trials were held – one for abduction and the second for assault.

William Booth remained intent on distancing himself from Stead even during the trial. He was appalled when the editor apologised to the readers of the *Pall Mall Gazette* for the methods he employed to raise the issue of the child sex trade.

Catherine Booth, however, was determined to petition everyone and anyone – from the Queen herself and down – in the cause of the defendants and the Criminal Law Amendment Act.

ROOKWOOD, STAMFORD HILL,
MONDAY NOV. 9, '85.

*My dearest Love,*

*I have yours proposing Meeting at Exeter Hall, but I must say I am heartily sick of the whole affair. The enclosed is Stead's account of things, which appears in to-night's Pall Mall Gazette. It is such a throwing up of the sponge and leaving us all in the lurch that I cannot go any further on in the agitation. To soap anybody down in that fashion is to me disgusting. I understand all the way through that the Attorney-General was hard upon our people, and* on Sat. all said that the Judge was quite a partisan. And here is Stead, abandons poor Rebecca, and said that the verdict is just, etc., etc., etc., according to the evidence, etc.

... We shall see what is done to-morrow. Stead won't be put in prison, in my opinion, but will drop back into his old role of journalist, and leave us smeared with the tar of this affair to fight it out with blackguards and brothel-keepers all over the world.

I am sure the S.A. is the thing, and our lines are all right. We shall see tremendous things. We are deciding for our International Council in June next, and shall have Soldiers from all parts of the world and 2000 Officers. This will wipe out the very memory of Eliza Armstrong.

Bramwell is not quite out of the wood yet. We will wire you to-morrow how things go.

*(William)*

ROOKWOOD ROAD,
MONDAY NOV. 9, '85

My dearest Love,

I have yours this morning. I like the telegram to Her Majesty. They will have wired you the Queen's reply, which I think is very good. Of course the torpid people will say you should have waited until the trial was concluded. Altho' I have not heard any say so yet. I don't think so!... You will have seen something of the papers this morning, I suppose. The Daily News is bitterness itself, only a sentence or two against Bramwell; but of course we are implicated in its sweeping, scathing sarcasm. The Standard I hear is bad, and I fully expect they will all be alike. I have not a hope from any newspaper in the land except the religious ones, and only partially from them. However, this is just what we expected, and although I feel it at the moment, our turn will come by-and-by.

We are not doing any meetings until after the trial. God must help us, and He will! It is no use anticipating evils. I shall not allow myself to do so. The matter will for the season drop out of sight in consequence of the election strife, and it is quite possible the verdict may be reversed on appeal, the thing will work round… Do be restful and get some strength. We have a lot of fighting yet before we go to rest, I hope.

101 Queen Victoria Street,
Tuesday Nov. 10, 1885.

My darling,

… You will have got our wire with reference to the trial this morning. So far as we are concerned now the trial is at an end. I understand that the Judge remarked this morning that Mr Bramwell Booth was justified in believing that Mrs Armstrong sold her

*child. Why didn't he say so on Saturday? Perhaps he
has had some new light.*

*The trial of Stead and Jarrett … for the indecent
assault is now going on. Bramwell is in court – of
course wanting to be as near Stead as he can when the
sentence is pronounced. But I don't believe that Stead
will go to prison; and I don't think that very much
will be done to Rebecca. If there is, I think we can get a
remission of the sentence. We will try, but beyond that
I don't see any way clear of fighting on those lines. I am
sure our work has materially suffered by our attention
being taken from it to give the other; we may have
been paid back to a certain extent, and in the long run
much good may be done, but I thoroughly believe in
"Salvation" being a panacea for the world's sins and
sorrows, and that while there are other medicines that
look in the same direction, the largest amount of good
can be accomplished, with the least expenditure of
time and money, by simply getting the people's souls
saved and keeping them saved …*

*I hope you won't strongly object to it, but I
propose that we are content with the Thanksgiving
Meetings throughout the country on Monday next…
I have been writing a column for the [War] Cry this
morning, and have made a very decent flourish.
Of course, with what the Judge said this morning,
we come out of the thing with flying colours. And if
(as I fully expect) some further evidence will be got
in vindication of Rebecca the tables will be turned
altogether yet.*

*Mrs Butler is fast at Winchester with bronchitis, working on a pamphlet on Rebecca Jarrett. When the thing is quite over, the probability is that Stead will kick out again, and renew the fight. Anyhow, we can lend a hand, along with our other duties, to a good cause… You rest – there's a darling. They will take care of Stead – of course it will make him.*

*Just got the sentences we have wired you:*

*Stead 3 months*

*Jarrett 6 months (not hard labour)*

*Jacques 1 month*

*Mourez 6 months' hard labour.*

ROCKWOOD ROAD,
WEDNESDAY NOV. 11, '85.

*My dearest Love,*

*… After mature deliberation on the subject, I have come back to my impression formed before I heard the sentence, that we ought not to involve the Army in any great struggle on the subject.*

*To begin with, Stead has innumerable friends who worship him, and who will agitate the country, and do so far better without us mixed up in it, than with us. Indeed, it is a far greater relief to them, I have no doubt, for us to be out of it, so that they can ask for a favour to Stead, or justice, if you like to call it, without having to ask for us at the same time. We shall therefore* embarrass them by mixing ourselves up with it, so that on his account it will be better for us to remain separate.

Again, there are things in the thing that are very discreditable to us, that is in the way the thing was done. The jury have absolved us from blame, and all the Judge could rake up to say was, "that we ought to have given up the child," which had we known what he knows now we would have done. If we could help Stead, we ought to do so, and we will help him by petitioning or holding meetings on our own lines.

Then as to Jarrett, the sentence is not a heavy one; she has no hard labour, her disease will get her all manner of attention; it is possible that she will be treated as a first-class misdemeanant, and on the whole it may really be better for her to be in than out.

Then again, she has behaved badly in some respects, perhaps we could not expect anything else from her; still when we remember what she was, and the notice that has been taken of her, she was under a very great obligation to us. It may do her soul good; she says it will, and that she will come out and spend the rest of her days working for God…

I know what can be said with regard to a great deal of this, and will talk it over with you. You say there is nothing to be done. Well, the independent party will have a meeting in Exeter Hall and try and get a Bishop in the chair; but they won't want us there, and we can have our meetings, send up our petitions; and with regard to Jarrett, I think we may use some private influence. A letter from you to the

*Home Secretary, for instance, might have weight; but
I am hardly inclined to our troubling the Queen on the
matter. I shall see you to-morrow.*

*(William)*

When Bramwell Booth was acquitted on all charges, William and
Catherine saw this as a complete vindication of the role of The
Salvation Army in the Eliza Armstrong/Maiden Tribute matter.[7]
Although he continued to distance the Army from Stead – no
senior representative attended a rally on the day of Stead's release
from prison – just five years later Stead helped William to write his
landmark work on poverty, *In Darkest England and The Way Out*,
and a year later General Booth referred to the newspaperman as
"one of the greatest men of our time".[8] The two men were destined
to die in the same year. General Booth of old age on 20 August
1912 and W. T. Stead on 15 April – he was one of the more than
1,500 people who died on board the RMS *Titanic*, which sank
when she hit an iceberg in the North Atlantic Ocean during her
maiden voyage from Southampton on the south coast of England
to New York.

Stead had not suffered unduly in prison; indeed, the Home
Secretary gave him the status of "first-class prisoner" so he
avoided many of the trials of normal inmates. In the months
following the case, Catherine quietly petitioned among others
the Home Secretary on behalf of the defendants who were
serving sentences.

And what of Eliza? She was returned to her parents,
put through school, and finally did enter service as a maid in a
private household.

# CHAPTER

## 18

*In every direction people speak in the highest terms of your books and ask most affectionately after you. Mr G … , my host, said last night that he came back from England thinking forty times as much of the Army as when he left … and that among other things with which his visit had delighted him had been the delight and profit with which he heard Mrs Booth; that you were the most eloquent speaker he had ever listened to; that to see you "shake your little fist" and hear you speak at Exeter Hall was worth going 16 000 miles.*

*A Wesleyan Minister, the Chairman of the Toronto District, has just been in to see me, and has been telling me how he has read your books with profit, that they are the primitive Methodism of John Wesley and John Fletcher.*

*An old man from the interior of the City grasped my hand in the carriage yesterday and bade me tell you*

*what a blessing your books had been to him and that*
*he read them first himself and then lent them to his*
*neighbours. Continually these testimonies are coming up.*
*    … I had letters from Bramwell and a short*
*note from Railton. Railton was kind, Bramwell was*
*OFFICIAL, I suppose he had not time for more. But I*
*have been away from you all for 15 days, and I certainly*
*longed for a few special words.*

Catherine picked up her Bible. She took comfort from the verses, as she had done so many times before. But William was so far off – all that way in Canada – and she missed him dreadfully. Although they were often apart she yearned for him more now, especially as the children were all grown.

The past few years had been so frantic. Who could have judged how successful The Salvation Army would become, so quickly? Just as she had always known he would, her William had proved the critics wrong, and together with their troops they were changing the world.

She reflected on the past year, and the campaign to free young girls from the "white slave trade". It had been immensely stressful for all, especially the ordeal of the trial. She thanked God for dear Florence and her support not just for Bramwell but also for her mother-in-law. How blessed Catherine felt to have such a thoughtful, spiritual woman married to her eldest son.

"Just the sort of girl he needs!" William had announced after Bramwell had confided that he was thinking of asking Miss Soper to be his bride. Of course, she had already, in the short time since she had been "saved" and joined the Army, been invaluable despite her young age.

Catherine remembered the day they had bidden farewell to Katie, whom William had assigned to "open fire" in France, with Florence as her lieutenant. How young they had both looked, Katie barely twenty-two and Miss Soper not yet twenty years of age, as they stood on the platform at St James' Hall, Regent Street for the "farewell meeting". Catherine remembered praying over them and being filled with the Spirit of God as she did so.

Catherine looked at the framed image of her eldest daughter on her bureau, smart in her uniform. She had always been a clever girl, probably far more so than the boys. That The Salvation Army would attract similarly clever and even ambitious girls to the ranks, Catherine had never been in doubt. After all, what would a young woman like Florence Soper have become had she not found God and The Salvation Army? She had once confided to her mother-in-law that she had a secret ambition to become a doctor – her father, after all, was a physician – but that might have proved difficult, given her gender. Catherine was aware that the London School of Medicine for Women was now training women doctors, but it was certainly not yet common to see women in the professions.

No: Florence, now the next-generation Mrs Booth, was just where God needed her. Catherine's heart rose as she thanked God for the blessings of family, all safe and secure in the Lord's work.

But that didn't stop her missing darling William. She picked up another of his letters, and reread his dear words, penned way across the ocean in Canada. If she could not be with him in body, she could certainly share with him in spirit.

HALIFAX, SATURDAY 9 OCTOBER 1886

*Before starting on anything else, and I have plenty*
*before me, I must scribble a few lines to my beloved.*

*My thoughts have been with you through the night. When I awake I can safely say my heart comes over to you, and I embrace you in my arms and clasp you to my heart and bless you with my lips and pray God to keep you from all harm and bring me safely to meet you again on earth. The time is flying. The third week has passed since I gave you that hurried farewell, for truly there was no time for a deliberate farewell kiss or time thoughtfully to say, "Goodbye."*

*That was a remarkable day. How dark things looked at the beginning and how different at the end. So has it not been with us, my darling, all the way through life. Go back to the very outset of our acquaintance. Had we not all manner of difficulties to cloud our first acquaintance and to dampen our earliest joys? Did not the first prospects and controversies concerning all that was dearest to us outside each other becloud our first acquaintance and threaten our path with thorns and difficulty – and yet has not God cleared the way? Has He not led us onwards? And oh what a position is this!*

*The most popular Methodist minister in St. Johns, New Brunswick, greeted me on Friday night on leaving for Halifax in the most respectful and affectionate manner, saying that next to John Wesley he hailed me benefactor of the world. He had relapsed from his simplicity, given himself up to popularity-hunting, lecturing, etc. He has come to our Army Meetings, gone out for a new and full surrender and got a clean heart, brought his people, and is now a leader in the Christian world of that City and neighbourhood.*

> *... The reception was immense. The Mayor and the City Marshal (the latter a Catholic, one third of the population is Catholic) met me at the station. The Mayor rode with me in my carriage. We had torch lights and red lights and crowds and music and volleys and a wind up on the parade, where an electric light had been fixed over where my carriage halted. Here I addressed for a short time the assembled multitude. There was a little hubbub at the start, but the police soon settled that, and all was still and quiet as a church, while I showed them that only righteousness could exalt their City or themselves personally. I only regret I did not go on longer.*

In the 1880s, The Salvation Army spread like wildfire across Great Britain and then the world. By the turn of the decade it was active in Scotland, the Isle of Man, and the Channel Islands. William Booth travelled extensively, sharing God's message of salvation and the Booths' particular style of evangelism, worship, and service. To the overseas contingents were quickly added the USA, Ireland, Australia, France, Canada, India, Switzerland, Sweden, Sri Lanka, South Africa, New Zealand, and Pakistan, then part of India.

Catherine, whose continuing delicate health would not permit extensive overseas travel, remained at home but still travelled, ministered, and helped to oversee an organization that was not just expanding its evangelistic outreach but also beginning to formalize its work with the poor and needy.

After Captain Florence Soper married The Salvation Army's Chief of Staff, Bramwell Booth, on 12 October 1882 at

Clapton Congress Hall in East London, before a congregation of 6,000 Salvationists, she became part of the Booth clan and central to its development. In 1884 this refined and rather delicate-looking young woman was instrumental in setting up the first shelter for vulnerable women – in Hanbury Street, Whitechapel. Working with Mrs Elizabeth Cotterill, who as part of the Whitechapel Corps congregation had first "rescued" girls from the street and accommodated them in her own home, they established what was to be the first formal expression of Salvation Army "social work".

Across the world this outreach and mission was developing as The Salvation Army grew. In Melbourne, Australia, the Army initiated work with prisoners in 1883. News about the expanding ministry of The Salvation Army was carried in its new publication the *War Cry*, which was first published in December 1879, the same year that the uniform was formally introduced. Music was also becoming a focal point of Salvation Army worship and outreach, the first Salvation Army corps band having been constituted in Consett in County Durham in north-east England.

The Booth children were taking on more responsibility and creating their own families. There was not just Bramwell and Florence. Second son Ballington had married Maud Charlesworth in September 1886. She was already a seasoned Salvation Army campaigner, having replaced Florence in France to work alongside Katie Booth. Catherine Junior had been dubbed "la Maréchale" (the Field Marshal) in France but she had suffered persecution both there and in Switzerland. She married one of her co-workers in those territories, Colonel Arthur Clibborn, in February 1887.

A year later, quiet Emma, who was especially close to her father, married the former Indian civil servant Frederick Tucker.

He had already taken The Salvation Army to the land of his birth and had married in bare feet and Indian dress before returning to India with his Booth bride.[1]

The Booth family was increasingly international. Third son Herbert married a Dutch Salvationist, Cornelie Ida Ernestine Schoch, in September 1890. Youngest child Lucy married a Swedish officer, Emanuel Daniel Hellberg, in October 1894.

Marian remained an invalid living at home, and Evelyn, who was later known as Evangeline, also never married but spent her life in the ranks of the organization her parents had created, eventually becoming the fourth General and first woman leader of the movement. The wider Booth household also included two adopted boys – George, who took the name Booth, and Henry Andrews, who would become a pioneer of The Salvation Army's medical work across the world.[2]

Wherever they went, the Booths drew attention. They were adored, sometimes to the point of idolatry, by the growing international ranks of Salvationists, and thanks to William Booth's interest in and insistence on good publicity, their presence during any visits, at home or abroad, never went entirely unnoticed.

CANADA, OCTOBER 1886

*Ballington made a tremendous impression here;*
*the press men speak of this when they interview me,*
*and the people themselves mention his name with*
*enthusiasm. He must come again next year, if spared,*
*with Maudie. God bless them; tell them of my love for*
*them when you write.*

*(William)*

The train was slow and rocked rather a lot. William had so wished to be able to write during this rather long and tiresome journey, but it was proving impossible. He leaned his head back against the padded headrest. It wasn't an entirely uncomfortable journey. Certainly these American trains were a good deal better than the rickety wooden contraptions he had endured in the early days of his ministry. How those carriages had swung around.

William Booth flicked back the little curtain – these trains really were so warm and comfortable it was astonishing – and looked out at the expanse of the world outside. In these weeks in Canada and now in the United States of America he had been overwhelmed by the sheer vastness of the place. It was his first time on the American continent and his travels had once again brought home the needs of the world.

How curious these Americans seemed to him. Some of them appeared so stand-offish.

William thought back to the previous night. How awfully stiff the meeting had been. He smiled when he remembered the seven ministers sitting in a row on the platform, looking – as he'd written to Catherine just that morning – "solemn as death"; how she would laugh at that description!

But it had been no joke for him. He had turned up to find a crowd, but there was no topic announced for his sermon. He had struggled to preach effectively at first and then just decided to be simple and straight. He loved it when this happened, when the Holy Spirit took over and worked out the plan. Before long, the atmosphere had lifted in the hall. He had found himself speaking freely and finishing in a tornado! "God wants to pardon!" he remembered almost shouting. "God wants to cleanse and sanctify!" How solemn those ministers had appeared but at the end, to a man, they had shaken his hand heartily and thanked him for his words. All that staring, as if they were little impressed, but really they had been touched deeply by his words.

William looked up at his companions. Maudie was dozing quietly in the corner opposite, while Ballington was attempting to look through his papers. William was so grateful for their presence and for Ballington's ability to organize. William determined, once and for all, that the couple should return soon to the United States and take charge of this exciting appointment where there was, he believed, so much potential.

William closed his eyes, just for a moment, and thought about what he would say in Boston. It was an important appointment, with the Evangelical Alliance. He'd already been told that upwards of 300 ministers might attend to learn more about the work of the Army. What an opportunity! A short snooze would not go amiss before they arrived.

### LONDON, FRIDAY 29 OCTOBER 1886

*It is over five weeks since you left us… I got home from my last tour and saw your clothes hanging up, I felt awful. I thought what it must be when the occupant is gone forever – at least for time! I long for you daily.*

*(Catherine)*

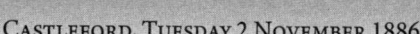

### CASTLEFORD, TUESDAY 2 NOVEMBER 1886

*I have had a grand time here – they are a dear lot of soldiers… I have written a letter to The Times about some slanderous attacks on us.*

*… Some of our halls here are getting quite chappelly … This packing takes up so much time, so I write you generally in a hurry … I think of you continually and wish, oh, so much! But wishing is fruitless work. I must save up all till you return … If I am able, after a fortnight at home, another tour will be the best for the Army.*

(Catherine)

USA, probably October or November 1886

*Love me as in the days of old. Why not? I am sure my heart feels the same as when I wrote you from Lincolnshire or came rushing up the Brixton Road to hold you in my arms and embrace you with my young love.*

*… Send me love-letters and particulars about yourself. Tell me how you are; how you get up and go about, and what you do and what time you retire, and whether you read in bed when you feel sad. Tell me about yourself. To know what you wear and eat and how you go out, indeed, anything about yourself, your dear self, will be interesting to me.*

*… You must go on thinking about me; I reckon on this.*

*I came here, Washington, Saturday night. It is, as you know, the Capital City of the States. The seat of Government, a great centre of learning, wealth, fashion and influence. We have only a young Corps here, twelve months old. Still they gave me a good reception on Saturday night, and we marched through the principal parts of the City. A crowded meeting followed, at which I spoke with only little liberty; could not get away. How mysterious these hard times are. I was sorry afterwards, as I learned that influential people were there. You cannot judge your audiences in this country from appearances. For instance, you cannot tell which are ministers from their dress. Yesterday afternoon there sat opposite me three of the leading ministers of the City, two of them D.D.'s, and but for their close attention and a certain refinement of feature I should not have supposed them to be ministers. Indeed, in the Old Country I should have said it was not so. They dress just as ordinary business men and often very shabby and slouchy.*

*However, I have since Saturday had good times and wonderful afternoon meetings. On Sunday we had the penitent-form full after each meeting. Last night the Hall was crowded and they had to go away... I spoke an hour and a half with unabated interest to the audience. The shaking hands afterwards was immense.*

*I like the "South" so far better than the North. They told me I should, and the farther South I go the warmer-hearted they say the people are. Anyway, I like these*

*Washington people. Oh what a splendid City this is and is going to be. I have no doubt but they will make it the finest City in the world.*

USA, PROBABLY NOVEMBER OR EARLY DECEMBER 1886

*I am well this morning. The weather has been charming but is a little cooler this morning. But yesterday I could only wear the same things I wore in the summer in England. It is so far all a hoax about the cold. They say there is seldom snow till the middle of December on any account.*

*I have taken such an extra delight in fresh air and fresh water that I could, if I had time, bath with pleasure two or three times a day. I surprise all my hosts by my pertinacious cold-water operations in the morning. They are all for hot water and hot rooms, etc., etc.*

*I don't sleep quite as much perhaps. The climate stimulates me I think… Altogether I am really well. Never better, and altho' working hard am looking, I think, quite as well as for months.*

USA, EARLY DECEMBER 1886

*You must not be anxious about me on the water. I have not a fear. You cannot judge the weather at sea from what it will be on shore. So do not lie awake one hour on my account if you hear the wind blow. God will take care of me.*

*Goodbye … take a little care of yourself so as to be able to sit at the table and welcome me when I return. I long for your smile and voice and to lay my head on your bosom once more. I am just the same, your husband, lover and friend, as in the earliest days. My heart can know no change.*

# CHAPTER

## 19

"Mrs Booth is here, sir; shall I bring her in?"

Sir James Paget looked up from his desk and nodded. No matter how many years he was in practice, this remained the worst part of the job.

The small woman entered the room.

"Good day, Mrs Booth. Please, take a chair."

Catherine Booth slipped onto the chair on the other side of the large heavy oak desk on which the consultant had her paperwork spread out in front of him. She sat carefully, smoothed her dark skirts with her delicate hands, and slid off her gloves.

"Has no one accompanied you today, Mrs Booth? One of your daughters? Your husband?"

"No, sir. I have come alone. I thought it best. The General… Mr Booth, that is… is preparing for a trip and leaves shortly. He wanted to come but… there is so much to do."

Catherine Booth spoke softly, and precisely. There was no hint of emotion in her voice, although her face was as white as snow, framed by her greying hair under her dark poke bonnet.

"Well, Mrs Booth. I have my conclusions."

Sir James looked at the woman across the desk. She smiled a wry little smile.

"And, Sir James? Is it what we thought it was?"

"I'm afraid so."

"And... ?"

"Well, as we feared, the disease is quite advanced already."

"My mother died of it. Did I tell you that?"

"Yes, Mrs Booth."

"And... " she swallowed deeply... "Is there anything... ? I mean, what... time... "

Sir James Paget looked at Catherine Booth. His heart ached for her.

"Well, as I said before. In this stage it could be eighteen months, maybe two years. But there is really... nothing much... we can do."

Catherine Booth cleared her throat and then smiled, sadly but sweetly.

"God is good, Mr Paget. He knows what He is about. But there is one thing perhaps you can do for me."

"Anything, Mrs Booth."

"Might you be so kind as to ask your secretary to perhaps call me a cab? I do need to get home. William... Mr Booth... will be anxious."

It was February 1888. Catherine had been ill for a while. Sometime during the previous year she had found a lump in her breast and her family doctor had warned that it was, more than likely, cancerous.[1] Eventually she was persuaded to make an appointment with the eminent Harley Street consultant, surgeon, and pathologist Sir James Paget, who confirmed that Catherine had incurable cancer. She had been in agony for some while, but the news that she was dying left William, in particular, inconsolable.

On her return home after that appointment with the doctor, William was waiting and ran out into the street to meet her and help her into the house, where she broke the news just received from Sir James.[2] William later recalled the emotional meeting.

> *She tried to smile upon me, through her tears; but drawing me into the room, she unfolded to me gradually the result of her interview. I sat down speechless. She rose from her seat and came and knelt beside me, saying, "Do you know what was my first thought? That I should not be there to nurse you, at your last hour."*
>
> *I was stunned. I felt as if the whole world was coming to a standstill. She talked like a heroine, like an angel, to me. She talked as she had never talked before. I could say nothing. I could only kneel with her and try to pray.*[3]

William was due to leave for a series of meetings in Holland that night and Catherine insisted he went, although he left early to return to London where, he recalled, "life became a burden, almost too heavy to be borne, until God in a very definite manner comforted my heart." The 3 March 1888 edition of the Salvation Army newspaper, the *War Cry*, delivered the news that The Army Mother, as Catherine was beginning to be known, was seriously ill.

Daughter Emma's wedding to Frederick Tucker was brought forward to April in order that Mama could be present. Catherine's last public engagement was on 21 June 1888, when she delivered an address at the City Temple, a free church in Holborn in London.

She managed to attend William's sixtieth birthday celebrations in The Salvation Army's Clapton Congress Hall in

East London on 10 April 1889 and, although she missed the dinner, where a reported 2,000 people sat down to eat, Catherine did address the gathering and reflected, with humour, on their early days together:

> *As my dear husband was speaking, I thought of his*
> *beloved mother, whom I loved as much as my own,*
> *and admired more than almost any woman I ever*
> *knew. When he was speaking of her, and making you*
> *laugh over his likening himself to her in his meekness*
> *and self-depreciation, I said to my friend there: "It is*
> *quite true, though you would not think it," for no one*
> *knows the bolstering-up, and almost dragging-up, I*
> *was going to say, that sometimes I had to do for him*
> *in those early days. You would think now that he had*
> *always been the bold and self-sufficient – as some*
> *people think – man he is, but I can assure you he went*
> *forth ofttimes with so great trembling and fear for*
> *himself that he would ever have gone if I had not been*
> *behind him.*[4]

Catherine was still the only person who could be completely honest with and about William Booth, who even his most loyal supporters, friends, and colleagues recognized to be an autocratic leader and, particularly as he grew older, less patient and kind with those around him.[5] For William, his wife's rapid decline after her diagnosis was unbearable, as he anticipated the loss of the one with whom he had shared his life for nigh on forty years.

The family, who had moved from their home in Rookwood Road in Stamford Hill in the borough of Hackney, where they had lived for a few years, to Hadley Wood, a more leafy suburb further north, which was thought to be more conducive to Catherine's good health, were now on the move again.

Soon after his birthday party in 1889, the family relocated to Clacton-on-Sea on the Essex coast, in order that she could have her dying wish – to be "Promoted to Glory" near the ocean. Family and Salvation Army life continued. William spent as much time as he could in Clacton, virtually moving his office to Essex.

During her long final illness, when Catherine Booth could do little more than occasionally attend private meetings and functions and then not even that, her main focus became her family, her friends, The Salvation Army, and her writing. She penned letters and notes to individuals and articles for Salvation Army publications. Even if she could not physically work, she was determined that her spiritual warfare would continue. Among the letters and articles were those to comrades at home and overseas, which were designed to reassure and encourage:

> *Regard no opposition, persecution or misrepresentation. Millions upon millions wait for us to bring to them the light of life.*

> *Although not able to be at the front of the battle in person, my heart is there, and the greatest pain I suffer arises from my realisation of the vast opportunities of the hour, and of the desperate pressure to which many of my comrades are subject, while I am deprived of the ability to help them, as in days gone by.*[6]

A number of times the family were called to Catherine's bedside, but she persistently clung to life. 1889 turned into 1890 and in September of that year she was still with them, insisting, despite her son's protestations, that Herbert marry his Miss Schoch, as planned. Although she could not attend the wedding, a chair and her portrait were set in the place where the groom's mother should have sat.

Although heartbroken, William continued with his work. Even while his wife was dying, he was writing a book that would become central to The Salvation Army, its ministry and its witness in the future. Catherine encouraged him, and indeed continued to give constant advice as her husband wrote *In Darkest England and The Way Out*, described as a "social manifesto".

This 140,000-word tome explored ideas that had been gradually gestating in his and Catherine's hearts, minds, and ministry (if in fact they had not been there from the outset), including providing shelter, food, and training for the poor. Early on, even in the days of the Christian Mission, soup kitchens and food distribution had been included in the Booths' outreach to the disadvantaged. Work among prisoners and with homeless and vulnerable men and women had already commenced and Salvation Army refuges were emerging. William's book developed these ideas further and also explored the concept of helping those without hope to learn new trades, primarily in agriculture, and then assisting them to emigrate to better lives in the New World.

Aided in its writing by William's old friend, the newspaperman W. T. Stead, *In Darkest England and The Way Out* compared what was considered to be "civilized" England with "Darkest Africa", a continent then viewed as backward and poverty-stricken. William Booth suggested that many of the inhabitants of London and England, despite the "Industrial Revolution", were not much better off when it came to quality of life than those in the underdeveloped world. The book drew on recent research by another Booth, the philanthropist and social researcher Charles Booth, who was documenting working-class life near the end of the nineteenth century. William's book also expounded the concept of "The Submerged Tenth" – the proportion of the population that he claimed were living on the border of or in poverty, and which the *Darkest England* schemes would be there to save: three million and more men, women, and children who needed "rescuing".[7]

William Booth's vision to help the poor out of the distress they found themselves in was by no means unique – Christians had been practising "good deeds" throughout history and attempts to rehabilitate the poor were common in Victorian England. But the book, which was published just two weeks after Catherine's death, was destined to become a bestseller and formed the foundation of The Salvation Army's modern social-welfare approach to faith and salvation. It would capture the imagination of the masses, much to the discontent of those in society who wished the poor to remain, largely, in their place.

As in the early days of The Salvation Army, when William and Catherine battled with those who believed their new Christian movement to be outrageous, the language of the book and its programme were viewed as radical. It advocated the abolition of poverty and vice by, among other things, a link between the Christian gospel and a strong work ethic, and promoted the establishment of communities for homeless people, where they could be trained for appropriate employment. Out of this vision came the Farm Colony at Hadleigh in Essex, which did just that, preparing people for a future often as emigrants to a new life abroad. The book also proposed homes for fallen women and released prisoners, schemes for legal assistance for the poor, banks and clinics, industrial schools, and so much more.

William Booth proposed that if the state failed to meet its social obligations it should be the task of each Christian to step into the breach – a snipe at the government if ever there was one.

For some, this might have sounded radical. For William and Catherine Booth there was no confusion. They were not turning their backs on their spiritual convictions. Far from it! All the projects and programmes and outreach outlined in *In Darkest England and The Way Out* had just one aim – to ensure that people became Christians.[8] What good was it to have "saved" people if they continued to be in desperate circumstances and unable to fulfil their new potential as children of God? What hope had they of responding to the gospel if they were drunk, hungry, homeless, abused, and without hope?

William's book was being finished as Catherine was dying, and in the introduction he paid tribute to the wife so recently departed:

> *To one who has been for nearly forty years indissolubly associated with me in every undertaking I owe much of the inspiration which has found expression in this book. It is probably difficult for me to fully estimate the extent to which the splendid benevolence and unbounded sympathy of her character has pressed me forward in the life-long service of man, to which we have devoted both ourselves and our children. It will be an ever green and precious memory to me that amid the ceaseless suffering of a dreadful malady my dying wife found relief in considering and developing the suggestions for the moral and social and spiritual blessing of the people which are here set forth, and I do thank God she was taken from me only when the book*

*was practically complete and the last chapters had*
*been sent to the press.*

For Catherine there was now not much more time. One of her
final messages for her beloved Salvation Army came in a letter
to Salvationists from her bed for the 1890 annual Self Denial
campaign and appeal.

*My Dear Children and Friends,*

*I have loved you so much, and in God's strength have*
*helped you a little. Now, at His call, I am going away*
*from you.*

*The War must go on. Self-Denial will prove your*
*love to Christ. All must do something.*

*I send you my blessing. Fight on, and God will*
*be with you. Victory comes at last. I will meet you in*
*Heaven.*

*Catherine Booth.*[9]

This was published on 4 October 1890. Three days before,
Catherine had suffered a massive haemorrhage. The family
gathered for the final time around her bed in Crossley House in
Clacton-on-Sea for a four-day vigil, during which they all prayed
and sang. On the day of the publication of her final letter, at 3.30
in the afternoon, Catherine Booth, aged sixty-one, was finally
Promoted to Glory.

*My darling One,*

*I never thought of you wanting a line or you should have had a better one, but you will accept this, just to assure you of my fullest and most satisfying assurance of your unalterable and eternal love to me. I have never doubted the possession of your heart from the day you first declared it mine. We were wed for ever, and though I go first you will soon follow and we shall find our all again in that eternal day, Amen, Amen.*

*Goodbye, darling, till then. I shall be the first to greet you on that eternal shore with all our children and thousands of spiritual children from all lands.*

*Yours as ever, Catherine.*

# CHAPTER

# 20

## EPILOGUE

The large doors creaked slowly open.

Staff Captain Carr, who had nursed Catherine in those final months, raised the flag just in front of the coffin and started slowly to walk into the great void that was the Olympia arena.

William walked, alone, head held high but his obvious pain etched on his ageing features, teeth firmly gritted. He could sense the family behind him but he had chosen to walk by himself, as close to Catherine as possible. He could sense the sadness and shock of those who had gathered to pay respect and homage to Catherine – 36,000 silent mourners. Although her death had been a long time in the coming, the reality of losing the Army Mother had still had a deep impact on all those who had loved her, on all those whose lives she had touched.

Behind the family, William knew the flags of the nations where their Salvation Army was already flourishing were now making their appearance. Then there were the banners of the corps. George Railton had done a good job, organizing the events of the past ten days since Catherine's death.

*Ten days. Ten days since she drew her last breath. Ten days since that terrible, yet strangely wonderful, day when his beloved had finally and triumphantly entered Glory, for there she surely was. There would be no black armbands for his Catherine, but white. White armbands and white ribbons atop the flagpoles.*

*The procession had almost reached its destination at the front of the hall.*

When Catherine Booth was "Promoted to Glory", the description that The Salvation Army uses for the death of a Christian, it was not just a family loss. Tens of thousands of Salvationists across the world also mourned the passing of a woman who had been so instrumental in the creation of this new and vibrant Christian movement.

By now The Salvation Army, although still a rather peculiar notion for many who did not understand it, was gaining credibility, and Catherine's passing was notable. The *Methodist Recorder* of 9 October 1890 paid tribute to her as "the greatest Methodist woman of this generation" and, as when William eventually died, there were also other newspaper tributes.

William's right-hand man, Commissioner George Railton, was given command of the arrangements, although the family and William were obviously involved. This was not just to be a funeral for a beloved wife and mother but also a spectacle to show what the Army had become and was becoming. Had William and Catherine spoken about this during her long illness? Possibly, because they discussed most things, especially when it came to the promotion of their Army and the gospel of Jesus. Would she have objected to her funeral becoming a means of promotion for the Army? Not at all! The development of The Salvation Army had latterly been all-consuming for them both, and there is no doubt Catherine would have approved.

Catherine was placed in a simple coffin – oak with a glass cover, draped in the Salvation Army flag she had helped to design so many years before – which also bore a brass plate bearing her name, dates, and the inscription "More than Conqueror". Her body first lay in state at The Salvation Army's Clapton Congress Hall, where it is estimated 50,000 mourners from all walks of life processed past the coffin over a five-day period. After the funeral service at Olympia on 13 October 1890 she was taken to The Salvation Army's International Headquarters in Queen Victoria Street, very near St Paul's Cathedral, where she continued to lie in state until the following morning. Three thousand Salvation Army officers made up the funeral procession on 14 October. Catherine's coffin was placed on an open hearse and William followed in an open landau, standing occasionally to bow solemnly to the crowds as his wife's funeral procession made its way through the City of London into the East End and then onto Abney Park.

The Salvation Army had lost its Mother, but so had her family. While she was still with them, the Booths had existed if not entirely in harmony then at least not in open warfare. When she went, the family lost something of its focus.

After Catherine's death, William took to the road again, returning to his first love of evangelism. For the next twenty and more years, before his own death on 20 August 1912, he travelled the world spreading the Good News of Jesus Christ and The Salvation Army. There were tours of South Africa, Australia, New Zealand, and India. As the twentieth century dawned, General William Booth, now no longer a pariah in society, was greeted like a world statesman everywhere he went. He met the kings of Norway and Sweden and the emperor of Japan. In 1905 he visited the Holy Land and preached at the Garden Tomb. He frequently visited the United States of America, where he was received by

President Theodore Roosevelt and lead the Senate in prayer. Even without Catherine at his side, William was determined to continue along the spiritual path they believed God had set them on sixty years before.

Always keen to use modern inventions, and at a time when motor cars were extremely rare and even viewed with suspicion, General Booth's motorcade toured the United Kingdom seven times. Now the poor lad from Nottingham received the freedom of the city of his birth. The man who had avoided academic study received an honorary degree from Oxford University, and on 24 June 1904 he was invited to Buckingham Palace to meet King Edward VII, and the King asked William for his autograph.

The young lad who had been so determined not to be one of the "commonalty" might have been tempted to be somewhat pleased with himself. But his note to the King showed that, down the years and despite the controversies that had surrounded him, his wife, their personalities, and their Salvation Army, he had kept one aim in mind. For the King of England, he wrote: "Some men's ambition is art. Some men's ambition is fame. Some men's ambition is gold. My ambition is the souls of men."

While William continued to travel the world even as he struggled with blindness and increasing frailty, it was down to the Booths' eldest son, Bramwell, to run The Salvation Army. William had already willed that Bramwell should replace him as General on his death, but it wasn't necessarily a decision with which everyone in the family was happy. While the Booth children had grown up with and become used to Catherine and William's autocratic authority and control – which had extended even to William's insistence that his sons-in-law change their surnames by deed poll to include the Booth name – they did not manage to tolerate Bramwell's high-handed approach.[1]

Eventually, relationships soured. Ballington Booth was already in open disagreement with his elder brother, The Salvation Army's Chief of the Staff. He and Maud had played a tremendous part in organizing and structuring The Salvation Army in the United States, and at the end of 1895, when the decision was made to reassign them and remove them from their beloved USA with little by way of negotiation, they left The Salvation Army. They went on to form their own organization to reach out to the marginalized and poor of America – "God's American Volunteers", which was soon renamed "Volunteers of America". Many American supporters of The Salvation Army, including soldiers and officers, left with them and Ballington would become "General" of his own organization,[2] but the worldwide Salvation Army and the family was left stunned, shocked, and saddened.

The beloved Katie, who had been so fêted by her parents from such a young age and had achieved so much for the infant Salvation Army, was also destined to separate from the family. After marrying Arthur Clibborn, she continued to work for the Army until the birth of her tenth child. Increasingly unhappy with the restrictions now embedded in The Salvation Army's restrictive and militaristic culture and government, the Booth-Clibborns resigned in January 1902. Arthur had become involved with John A. Dowie, the controversial leader of a sect, and, although Katie disapproved, she went with her husband. They joined the Pentecostal church a few years later and continued as travelling evangelists in Europe, Australia, and the USA. Katie would have no further contact with her father, her siblings or the rest of her family who remained in the Army.

Herbert and Cornelie Booth would also leave the ranks. Herbert, who William believed had great leadership ability and should be General after Bramwell, opposed the control that was being asserted over the international Salvation Army. He felt that authority should be "decentralized", and here he locked horns not only with his father, but also with his eldest brother. Most importantly, he and Cornelie wanted to be able to determine their own future and not leave their destinies in the hands of the autocratic General and his Chief of the Staff. Less than a month after Katie and Arthur resigned, Herbert and his wife did the same, leaving to continue an independent ministry where they were at the time, in Australia, and then in Canada and the USA. The very character traits that Catherine and William Booth had passed to and encouraged in their children – independence and outspokenness, courage and a deep sense of the calling of God on their lives – eventually resulted in family division.

When William Booth was Promoted to Glory, Ballington and Herbert were not allowed to participate. Katie had visited her father on his deathbed but was prohibited from revealing who she was to her blind, almost unconscious, parent. The other member of the family missing from his funeral was Emma. In 1903 she had been killed in a train crash in the USA, where she and her husband, Frederick Booth-Tucker, were commanders, a loss which had left her old father devastated.

By 1912, The Salvation Army was a thriving international Christian movement with extensive and ever-growing missionary outreach and social services. It was already operating in fifty-eight nations, and boasted nearly 16,000 officers and cadets and many hundreds of thousands of "soldiers".

When "the old warrior laid down his sword", as William's death at the age of eighty-three was described in August of that year, the world stopped to pay tribute. He too would lie in state at Clapton Congress Hall and 65,000 people would file past his coffin. Thirty-five thousand people would attend William

Booth's funeral, also at London's Olympia, and 5,000 uniformed Salvationists would march behind the cortège to the burial in Abney Park in Stoke Newington in the borough of Hackney, where the Booths had lived and ministered for so many years and where Catherine had already lain for more than two decades. Among the many wreaths there were a dozen from world heads of state and one from the King and Queen of England.[3]

The Booth family breakdown would have repercussions for The Salvation Army as it progressed into the twentieth century and beyond the lives of its founders. It did not, however, prevent the Army from becoming a force to be reckoned with on a global scale. And in October 1890, although the seeds of discontent may already have been there, the family stood united in their grief around the grave of the matriarch, Catherine.

At the graveside in Abney Park Cemetery there were hymns and words from two sons-in-law, Frederick Booth-Tucker and Arthur Booth-Clibborn, as well as from daughter Katie. Bramwell Booth and George Railton committed Catherine's body to the grave and William, in one final act of love, kissed his wife's coffin.

Then, with all the passion that had filled his early letters to his Catherine in the first years when they were so in love, William Booth poured out his anguish at his loss, and had the last word on his darling Kate:

> *If you had a tree that had grown up in your garden,*
> *under your window, which for forty years had been*
> *your shadow from the burning sun, whose flowers had*
> *been the adornment and beauty of your life, whose*
> *fruit had been almost the stay of your existence, and*
> *the gardener had come along and swung his glittering*
> *axe and cut it down before your eyes, I think you*

would feel as though you had a blank – it might not
be a big one – but a little blank in your life!

If you had had a servant who, for all this long
time, had served you without fee or reward, who
had administered, for very love, to your health and
comfort, and who had suddenly passed away, you
would miss that servant!

If you had had a counsellor who, in hours –
continually occurring – of perplexity and amazement,
had ever advised you, and seldom advised wrong;
whose advice you had followed and seldom had
reason to regret it; and the counsellor, while you are in
the same intricate mazes of your existence, had passed
away, you would miss that counsellor!

If you had had a friend who had understood your
very nature, the rise and fall of your feelings, the bent
of your thoughts, and the purposes of your existence; a
friend whose communion had ever been pleasant – the
most pleasant of all other friends – to whom you had
ever turned with satisfaction, and your friend had been
taken away, you would feel some sorrow at the loss!

If you had had a mother for your children, who
had cradled and nursed and trained them for the
service of the living God, in which you most delighted
– a mother, indeed, who had never ceased to bear
their sorrows on her heart, and who had been ever
willing to pour forth that heart's blood in order to
nourish them, and that darling mother had been
taken from your side, you would feel it a sorrow!

If you had had a wife, a sweet love of a wife,
who for forty years had never given you real cause for

grief; a wife who had stood with you side by side in the battle's front, who had been a comrade to you, ever willing to interpose herself between you and the enemy, and ever the strongest when the battle was fiercest, and your beloved one had fallen before your eyes, I am sure there would be some excuse for your sorrow!

Well, my comrades, you can roll all these qualities into one personality, and what would be lost in each I have lost all in one …

My heart had also been full of gratitude because God lent me for so long a season such a treasure. I have been thinking, if I had to point out her three great qualities to you here, they would be: First she was <u>good</u>. She was washed in the Blood of the Lamb. To the last moment her cry was, "A sinner saved by grace." She was a thorough hater of shams, hypocrisies and make-believes.

Second, she was <u>love</u>. Her whole soul was full of tender, deep compassion. I was thinking this morning that she suffered more in her lifetime through her compassion for poor dumb animals than some doctors of divinity suffer for the wide, wide world of sinning sorrowing mortals! Oh, how she loved, how she compassioned, how she pitied the suffering poor! How she longed to put her arms round the sorrowful and help them!

Lastly, she was a <u>warrior</u>. She liked the fight. She was no one who said to others, "Go!" but "Here, let <u>me</u> go!" and when there was the necessity she cried, "I <u>will</u> go." I never knew her flinch until her poor body compelled her to lie aside.[4]

# Notes

## Chapter 1

1. George Scott Railton, *The Authoritative Life of General William Booth, Founder of The Salvation Army*, George H. Doran Company, 1912, ch. 4.

2. The Salvation Army Literary Department IHQ, *They Said It – William and Catherine Booth*, London: Sxalvationist Publishing and Supplies, 1978 © The Salvation Army, ch. 3, p. 14 (CB during the early 1880s).

3. Mildred Duff, *Catherine Booth – a sketch*, originally published 1890. Project Gutenberg http://www.gutenberg.org/cache/epub/7125/pg7125.txt

4. Cyril Barnes, *Words of William Booth*, London: Salvationist Publishing and Supplies 1975 © The Salvation Army, Section 3 (p. 5).

## Chapter 2

1. Roger J. Green, *The Life & Ministry of William Booth, Founder of The Salvation Army*, Nashville: Abingdon Press 2005, ch. 3, p. 44.

2. Roy Hattersley, *Blood & Fire, William and Catherine Booth and Their Salvation Army*, London: Little, Brown and Company (UK) 1999, ch. 2, p. 43.

3. Green, *The Life & Ministry of William Booth, Founder of The Salvation Army*, ch. 3, p. 38.

4. *BOOTH PAPERS. Vols. I–IV. Correspondence of William and Catherine Booth; 1852–1861.* Four volumes. Mss 64806, held in The British Library.

5. http://en.wikipedia.org/wiki/Tuberculosis

## Chapter 3

1. Roy Hattersley, *Blood & Fire, William and Catherine Booth and Their Salvation Army*, ch. 2, p. 51.

2. Hattersley, *Blood & Fire, William and Catherine Booth and Their Salvation Army*, ch. 2, p. 50.

3. Roger J. Green, *The Life & Ministry of William Booth, Founder of The Salvation Army*, ch. 4, p. 56.

4. Harold Begbie, *The Life of William Booth, Founder and First General of The Salvation Army, Vol. 1*, Macmillan Company 1920, ch. 11

5. As above.

6. Abraham Booth, *The Reign of Grace*, first published 1768 – accessed through http://grace-ebooks.com – excerpts from ch. 3.

7. Hattersley, *Blood & Fire, William and Catherine Booth and Their Salvation Army*, ch. 3, p. 54.

## Chapter 4

1. Roy Hattersley, *Blood & Fire, William and Catherine Booth and Their Salvation Army*, ch. 3, p. 55.

2. Roger J. Green, *The Life & Ministry of William Booth, Founder of The Salvation Army*, ch. 4, p. 60.

3. Harold Begbie, *The Life of William Booth, Founder and First General of The Salvation Army, Volume 1*, ch. 12.

## Chapter 5

1. David Malcolm Bennett, *The Letters of William and Catherine Booth* – reproduced with permission and edited by David Malcolm Bennett ©2003 The Salvation Army (The letters): © 2003 & 2011 David Malcolm Bennett (Introductory material and footnotes). Published by Camp Hill Publications (Brisbane, Australia), footnote p. 44.

2. Harold Begbie, *The Life of William Booth, Founder and First General of The Salvation Army, Vol. 1*, ch. 8.

3. George Scott Railton, *The Authoritative Life of General William Booth, Founder of The Salvation Army*, ch. 2.

4. Leah Price, *The History of Shorthand* (London Review of Books) www.lrb.co.uk/v30/n23/leah-price/diary

5. http://en.wikipedia.org/wiki/Christmas#Reformation_into_the_19th_century

## Chapter 6

1. Roger J. Green, *The Life & Ministry of William Booth, Founder of The Salvation Army*, ch. 4, p. 61

2. Derek Elvin, *Catherine Booth 1829–1890*, France, The Salvation Army Éditions du Signe, 2010, p. 3.

3. Frederick Booth-Tucker, *The Life of Catherine Booth, the Mother of The Salvation Army, Vol. I*, International Headquarters of The Salvation Army, 1892, ch. 2.

4. Green, *The Life & Ministry of William Booth, Founder of The Salvation Army*, ch. 3, p. 41.

5. William Booth, *In Darkest England and The Way Out*, London: International Headquarters of The Salvation Army 1890, Part 1, ch. 2.

6. Green, *The Life & Ministry of William Booth, Founder of The Salvation Army*, ch. 4, p. 62.

7. http://www.methodist-central-hall.org.uk/history/
METHODISTNEWCONNEXION.pdf

8. Green, *The Life & Ministry of William Booth, Founder of The Salvation Army*, ch. 4, p. 66.

9. As above.

10. As above.

11. As above.

## Chapter 7

1. http://booty.org.uk/booty.weather/climate/1850_1899.htm

2. The Victorianist: John Snow and the 1854 London Cholera Outbreak
http:/thevictorianist.blogspot.co.uk/2010/11/john-snow-and-1854-
london-cholera.html

3. Lauren Corona, 19th Century Victorian Wedding Traditions
www.ehow.co.uk/info_7954601_19th-century-victorian-wedding-
traditions.html

4. Roy Hattersley, *Blood & Fire, William and Catherine Booth and Their Salvation Army*, ch. 3, p. 73.

5. Queen Victoria's wedding dress: the one that started it all http://
thedreamstress.com/2011/04/queen-victorias-wedding-dress-the-one-
that-started

6. Hattersley, *Blood & Fire, William and Catherine Booth and Their Salvation Army*, ch. 3, p. 73.

7. The Salvation Army Literary Department IHQ, *They Said It – William and Catherine Booth*, London: Salvationist Publishing and Supplies 1978 ©
The Salvation Army – ch. 3, p. 16, Catherine Booth during the early 1880s.

## Chapter 8

1. Roy Hattersley, *Blood & Fire, William and Catherine Booth and Their Salvation Army*, ch. 4, p. 88.

2. Hattersley, *Blood & Fire, William and Catherine Booth and Their Salvation Army,* ch. 3, p. 67.

3. Roger J. Green, *The Life & Ministry of William Booth, Founder of The Salvation Army,* ch. 4, p. 69.

4. Green, *The Life & Ministry of William Booth, Founder of The Salvation Army,* ch. 4, p. 70.

5. Catherine Booth, *Practical Religion,* London: first published as a collection in 1878, revised edition The Salvation Army Salvation Books © The Salvation Army 2008 ch. 1 The Training of Children – an address to parents.

6. As above.

7. http://en.wikipedia.org/wiki/Hydrotherapy

8. Hattersley, *Blood & Fire, William and Catherine Booth and Their Salvation Army,* ch. 10, p. 198.

9. Green, *The Life & Ministry of William Booth, Founder of The Salvation Army,* ch. 4, p. 61.

10. Harold Begbie, *The Life of William Booth, Founder and First General of The Salvation Army, Vol. 1,* ch. 18.

11. http://en.wikipedia.org/wiki/Homeopathy

12. *Chester Chronicle,* 14 Feb. 1857: Roy Hattersley, *Blood & Fire, William and Catherine Booth and Their Salvation Army,* ch. 4, p. 91.

13. Green, *The Life & Ministry of William Booth, Founder of The Salvation Army,* ch. 1, p. 14.

14. David Malcolm Bennett, *The Letters of William and Catherine Booth* – reproduced with permission and edited by David Malcolm Bennett, ©2003 The Salvation Army (The letters): © 2003 & 2011 David Malcolm Bennett (Introductory material and footnotes). Published by Camp Hill Publications (Brisbane, Australia), p. 317.

## Chapter 9

1. Roger J. Green, *The Life & Ministry of William Booth, Founder of The Salvation Army*, ch.5 p76

2. Green, *The Life & Ministry of William Booth, Founder of The Salvation Army*, ch. 5, p. 77.

3. Harold Begbie, *The Life of William Booth, Founder and First General of The Salvation Army, Vol. 1*, ch. 18.

4. Green, *The Life & Ministry of William Booth, Founder of The Salvation Army*, ch. 5, p. 78.

5. Begbie, *The Life of William Booth, Founder and First General of The Salvation Army, Vol. 1*, ch. 18.

6. Green, *The Life & Ministry of William Booth, Founder of The Salvation Army*, ch. 5, p. 79.

7. Begbie, *The Life of William Booth, Founder and First General of The Salvation Army, Vol. 1*, ch. 18.

8. Roy Hattersley, *Blood & Fire, William and Catherine Booth and Their Salvation Army*, ch. 5, p. 100.

9. Green, *The Life & Ministry of William Booth, Founder of The Salvation Army*, ch. 5, p. 79.

## Chapter 10

1. Roger J. Green, *The Life & Ministry of William Booth, Founder of The Salvation Army*, ch. 5, p. 80.

2. Letter from Catherine Booth to Rev David Thomas held in the British Library, MSS 64806.

3. Asbury University – Wesleyan-Holiness Theology
http://www.asbury.edu/about-us/cornerstone-project/holiness-initiatives/wesleyan-holiness-theology

4. Roy Hattersley, *Blood & Fire, William and Catherine Booth and Their Salvation Army*, ch. 5, p. 106.

5. Catherine Mumford Booth, *Female Ministry; or, Woman's Right to Preach the Gospel*, first published by the author 1859 © The Salvation Army. Version used included introduction and editing by Dennis Bratcher Copyright © by Dennis Bratcher and CRI/Voice, Institute.

6. W. T Stead, "Mrs Booth of The Salvation Army", pp. 158–99 from Roger J. Green, *The Life & Ministry of William Booth, Founder of The Salvation Army*, ch. 5, p. 82.

## Chapter 11

1. Roy Hattersley, *Blood & Fire, William and Catherine Booth and Their Salvation Army* , ch. 6, p. 126 / Roger J. Green, *The Life & Ministry of William Booth, Founder of The Salvation Army*, ch. 5, p. 87.

2–6. David Malcolm Bennett, *The Reminiscences of Catherine Booth*, edited by David Malcolm Bennett © 2005 The Salvation Army (The Reminiscences); © 2005 & 2011 David Malcolm Bennett (Introductory material and footnotes). Published by Camp Hill Publications (Brisbane, Australia).

## Chapter 12

1. Frederick Booth-Tucker, *The Life of Catherine Booth, The Mother of The Salvation Army, Vol. II*, London: International Headquarters of The Salvation Army 1893, ch. 49, p. 91.

2. Booth-Tucker, *The Life of Catherine Booth, The Mother of The Salvation Army, Vol. II,* ch. 49, p. 93.

3. Catherine Booth, *Practical Religion*, ch.1 – The training of children.

4. Roy Hattersley, *Blood & Fire, William and Catherine Booth and Their Salvation Army*, ch. 9, p. 171.

5. Booth-Tucker, *The Life of Catherine Booth, The Mother of The Salvation Army, Vol. II,* ch. 73, p. 376.

6. Booth-Tucker, *The Life of Catherine Booth, The Mother of The Salvation Army, Vol. II,* ch. 49, p. 97.


## Chapter 13

1. Roger J. Green, *The Life & Ministry of William Booth, Founder of The Salvation Army,* ch. 6, p. 100.

2. Frederick Booth-Tucker, *The Life of Catherine Booth, The Mother of The Salvation Army, Vol. II,* ch. 51, p. 109.

3. The University of North Carolina at Pembroke / London in the 19th century http://www.uncp.edu/home/rwb/london_19c.html

4. East End of London http://en.wikipedia.org/wiki/East_End_of_London

5. Glenn K. Horridge, *The Salvation Army: Origins and Early Days, 1865–1900,* Goldalming, Surrey: Ammonite Books, 1993, pp. 10–11.

6. Green,*The Life & Ministry of William Booth, Founder of The Salvation Army,* ch. 7, p. 108.

7. Roy Hattersley, *Blood & Fire, William and Catherine Booth and Their Salvation Army,* ch. 8, p. 154.

8. Green, *The Life & Ministry of William Booth, Founder of The Salvation Army,* ch. 7, p. 108.


## Chapter 14

1. Roger J. Green, *The Life & Ministry of William Booth, Founder of The Salvation Army,* ch. 7, p. 111.

2. Harold Begbie, *The Life of William Booth, Founder and First General of The Salvation Army, Vol. 1,* ch. 21 – A Lady Lodger's Account of the Booths' Home Life.

3. Roy Hattersley, *Blood & Fire, William and Catherine Booth and Their Salvation Army*, ch. 9, p. 174.

4. Begbie, *The Life of William Booth, Founder and First General of The Salvation Army, Vol. 1*, ch. 21.

5. Green, *The Life & Ministry of William Booth, Founder of The Salvation Army*, ch. 7, p. 110–111.

6. Robert Sandall, *The History of The Salvation Army, Vol. I, 1865–1878*, ch. 10, p. 109.

7. Green, *The Life & Ministry of William Booth, Founder of The Salvation Army*, ch. 7, p. 113.

8. Begbie, *The Life of William Booth, Founder and First General of The Salvation Army, Vol. 1*, ch. 24.

9. Green, *The Life & Ministry of William Booth, Founder of The Salvation Army*, ch. 7, p. 112.

10. Frederick Booth-Tucker, *The Life of Catherine Booth, The Mother of The Salvation Army, Vol. II*, ch. 64, p. 259.

11. Booth-Tucker, *The Life of Catherine Booth, The Mother of The Salvation Army, Vol. II*, ch. 62, p. 235.

12. Hattersley, *Blood & Fire, William and Catherine Booth and Their Salvation Army*, ch. 10, p. 199.

13. R.G. Moyles (editor), *I knew William Booth, An Album of Remembrances*, Virginia: The Salvation Army Crest Books 2007 © The Salvation Army, p. 17. George Scott Railton, Feb. 22 1896.

## Chapter 15

1. http://en.wikipedia.org/wiki/British_Army_during_the_Victorian_Era

2. Roger J. Green, *The Life & Ministry of William Booth, Founder of The Salvation Army*, ch. 8, p. 126, quoting from *The Christian Mission Magazine*, July 1877, p. 177.

3. Frederick Booth-Tucker, *The Life of Catherine Booth, the Mother of The Salvation Army, Vol. II*, ch. 75, p. 403.

4. Booth-Tucker, *The Life of Catherine Booth, the Mother of The Salvation Army, Vol. II*, ch. 75, p. 403.

5. Green, *The Life & Ministry of William Booth, Founder of The Salvation Army*, ch. 8, p. 126.

6. Roy Hattersley, *Blood & Fire, William and Catherine Booth and Their Salvation Army*, ch. 12, p. 230.

7. http://en.wikipedia.org/wiki/George_Scott_Railton

8. http://en.wikipedia.org/wiki/Bramwell_Booth

## Chapter 16

1. Roger J. Green, *The Life & Ministry of William Booth, Founder of The Salvation Army*, ch. 8, p. 133.

2. http://en.wikipedia.org/wiki/Chartism

3. Harold Begbie, *The Life of William Booth, Founder and First General of The Salvation Army, Vol. 1*, ch. 1

4. Glenn K. Horridge, *The Salvation Army: Origins and Early Days, 1865–1900*, p. 92.

5. Green, *The Life & Ministry of William Booth, Founder of The Salvation Army*, ch. 8, p. 135.

6. The Victorian Web http://www.victorianweb.org/religion/sa1.html

7. http://en.wikipedia.org/wiki/Elijah_Cadman

8. http://www.sawiki.net/index.php/The_Bonnet

9. Robert Sandall, *The History of The Salvation Army, Vol. II, 1878–1886*, London: Thomas Nelson and Sons Ltd © The Salvation Army 1950, ch. 1, p. 3.

10. http://www.victorianweb.org/religion/sa1.html

11. *The Sacraments – The Salvationist's Viewpoint* © The Salvation Army 1960 (short pamphlet issued "by authority of The General").

12. Green, *The Life & Ministry of William Booth, Founder of The Salvation Army,* ch. 9, p. 143.

13. Harry Williams, *Booth-Tucker, William Booth's First Gentleman,* Hodder and Stoughton, 1980 ©The Salvation Army.

## Chapter 17

1. http://en.wikipedia.org/wiki/Josephine_Butler

2. Roy Hattersley, *Blood & Fire, William and Catherine Booth and Their Salvation Army,* ch. 16, p. 307.

3. http://en.wikipedia.org/wiki/Contagious_Diseases_Acts

4. Hattersley, *Blood & Fire, William and Catherine Booth and Their Salvation Army,* ch. 16, p. 310.

5. Roger J. Green, *The Life & Ministry of William Booth, Founder of The Salvation Army,* ch. 9, p. 155.

6. As above.

7. Hattersley, *Blood & Fire, William and Catherine Booth and Their Salvation Army,* ch. 16, p. 323.

8. As above.

## Chapter 18

1. Frederick Booth-Tucker, *The Life of Catherine Booth, The Mother of The Salvation Army, Vol. II,* ch. 10, p. 160.

2. Roger J. Green, *The Life & Ministry of William Booth, Founder of The Salvation Army,* ch. 9, p. 139.

## Chapter 19

1. Roy Hattersley, *Blood & Fire, William and Catherine Booth and Their Salvation Army*, ch. 17, p. 329.

2. Roger J. Green, *The Life & Ministry of William Booth, Founder of The Salvation Army*, ch. 10, p. 164.

3. George Scott Railton, *The Authoritative Life of General William Booth, Founder of The Salvation Army*, ch. 19.

4. Arch R. Wiggins, *The History of The Salvation Army, Vol. IV, 1886–1904*, London: Thomas Nelson and Sons Ltd © The Salvation Army 1964, Section VIII, ch. 2, p. 298.

5. Railton, *The Authoritative Life of General William Booth, Founder of The Salvation Army*, ch. 8.

6. Railton, *The Authoritative Life of General William Booth, Founder of The Salvation Army*, ch. 19.

7. William Booth, *In Darkest England and The Way Out*, London: International Headquarters of The Salvation Army 1890, Part 1, ch. 2.

8. http://en.wikipedia.org/wiki/William_Booth

9. Railton, *The Authoritative Life of General William Booth, Founder of The Salvation Army*, ch. 9.

## Chapter 20

1. Roger J. Green, *The Life & Ministry of William Booth, Founder of The Salvation Army*, ch. 11, p. 184.

2. http://en.wikipedia.org/wiki/Ballington_Booth

3. Roy Hattersley, *Blood & Fire, William and Catherine Booth and Their Salvation Army*, ch. 22, p. 435.

4. The Salvation Army Literary Department IHQ, *They Said It – William and Catherine Booth*, p. 12, William Booth, at Catherine Booth's funeral, 14 Oct 1890.

# BIBLIOGRAPHY

Original source material: *The Letters of William and Catherine Booth* –
originals held in the British Library are part of the Booth family papers,
presented by Miss Catherine Bramwell-Booth, OBE, OF, granddaughter
of William and Catherine Booth, 22 June 1987.

BOOTH PAPERS Vols I–IV. Correspondence of William and Catherine
Booth, 1852–1861. Four volumes. MS 64799–64802.

BOOTH PAPERS Vols V–VIII. Including Letters and papers of Catherine
Booth, the letters chiefly addressed to her parents, John and Sarah
Mumford, [1847]–[late 1870s?] Four volumes. MS 64803–64806.

David Malcolm Bennett, *The Letters of William and Catherine Booth* –
reproduced with permission and edited by David Malcolm Bennett
©2003 The Salvation Army (The letters): © 2003 & 2011 David
Malcolm Bennett (Introductory material and footnotes). Published by
Camp Hill Publications (Brisbane, Australia).

David Malcolm Bennett, *The Diary of Catherine (Mumford) Booth*, edited
by David Malcolm Bennett © 2005 The Salvation Army (The Diary);
© 2005 & 2011 David Malcolm Bennett (Introductory material and
footnotes). Published by Camp Hill Publications (Brisbane, Australia).

David Malcolm Bennett, *The Reminiscences of Catherine Booth*, edited
by David Malcolm Bennett © 2005 The Salvation Army (The
Reminiscences); © 2005 & 2011 David Malcolm Bennett (Introductory
material and footnotes). Published by Camp Hill Publications
(Brisbane, Australia).

Cyril Barnes, *Booth's England*, Egon Publishers Ltd, Baldock Herts., 2000.

Cyril Barnes, *God's Army*, Lion Publishing, 1978 © The Salvation Army.

Cyril Barnes, *Words of William Booth*, London: Salvationist Publishing and Supplies, 1975 © The Salvation Army.

Harold Begbie, *The Life of William Booth, Founder and First General of The Salvation Army Volumes 1 and 2*, Macmillan Company, 1920.

Abraham Booth, *The Reign of Grace*, first published 1768 – accessed through http://grace-ebooks.com

Bramwell Booth, *Echoes and Memories*, Hodder and Stoughton, © The Salvation Army 1925, reprinted 1977.

Catherine Booth, *Popular Christianity – A Series of Addresses by Catherine Booth*, First published 1887. SA Historical & Philatelic Association 2011 (ebook).

Catherine Booth, *Godliness: being reports of a series of addresses delivered at James's Hall, 1881*, October 2004 EBook #6669 The Project Gutenberg – reproduced by a community of volunteers from images made available by the Canadian Institute for Historical Reproductions (Kindle edition).

Catherine Booth, *Practical Religion*, London: first published as a collection in 1878, revised edition The Salvation Army Salvation Books © The Salvation Army 2008.

Catherine Mumford Booth, *Female Ministry; or, Woman's Right to Preach the Gospel*, first published by the author 1859 © The Salvation Army. Version used included introduction and editing by Dennis Bratcher Copyright © by Dennis Bratcher and CRI/Voice, Institute.

Florence Bramwell Booth, *The Army Uniform*, Salvationist Publishing and Supplies (pamphlet no date) © The Salvation Army.

William Booth, *In Darkest England and The Way Out*, London: International Headquarters of The Salvation Army 1890.

William Booth, *Letters to Salvationists on Love, Marriage and Home*, London: The Salvation Army Book Department 1902.

William Booth, *Salvation Soldiery, A Series of Addresses on the Requirements of Jesus Christ's Service* London: © The Salvation Army 1890

Frederick Booth-Tucker, *The Life of Catherine Booth, The Mother of The Salvation Army Vols I & II*, London: International Headquarters of The Salvation Army 1893.

Frederick Booth-Tucker, *William Booth The General of The Salvation Army*, First published 1898. SA Historical & Philatelic Association, 2011 (ebook).

Minnie Lindsay Carpenter, *William Booth, Founder of The Salvation Army*, London: The Epworth Press (Edgar C. Barton).

Richard Collier, *The General Next to God, The Story of William Booth and The Salvation Army*, Collins, 1965.

Andrew Davies, *The People's Guide to London (Central and West End)*, Journeyman Press Ltd, 1984.

Mildred Duff, *Catherine Booth – a sketch*, originally published 1890. Project Gutenberg http://www.gutenberg.org/ebooks/7125

Derek Elvin, *Catherine Booth 1829–1890*, France The Salvation Army Éditions du Signe, 2010.

Jenty Fairbanks, *Booth's Boots – Social Service Beginnings in The Salvation Army*, London: © The General of The Salvation Army 1983.

Christine Garwood, *Mid-Victorian Britain 1850–1889*, Oxford: Shire Living Histories, 2011.

Robert Gray, *A History of London,* London: Hutchinson & Co., 1978.

Roger J. Green, *The Life & Ministry of William Booth, Founder of The Salvation Army*, Nashville: Abingdon Press, 2005.

Stephen Grinsted, *A Short History of The Salvation Army*, London: edited by Major Stephen Grinsted with the assistance of Salvation Army International Heritage Staff and The Salvation Army Schools and Colleges Unit UK, The Salvation Army Shield Books, 2012.

Geoffrey Hanks, *God's Special Army, The Story of William Booth*, Oxford: The Religious Education Press, a division of Pergamon Press "Faith in Action" Series © Geoffrey Hanks, 1980.

Roy Hattersley, *Blood & Fire, William and Catherine Booth and Their Salvation Army*, London: Little, Brown and Company (UK), 1999.

Glenn K. Horridge, *The Salvation Army: Origins and Early Days, 1865–1900*, Goldalming, Surrey: Ammonite Books, 1993.

Lee Jackson, *Daily Life in Victorian London; An Extraordinary Anthology*, Victorian London Ebooks 2011.

Avril Lansdell, *Fashion à la Carte 1860–1900*, Shire Publications Ltd 1985

William Metcalf, *The Salvationist and the Sacraments*, The Salvation Army Challenge Books 1965 © The Salvation Army.

R.G. Moyles (editor), *I knew William Booth, An Album of Remembrances*, Virginia: The Salvation Army Crest Books 2007 © The Salvation Army.

The Salvation Army Literary Department IHQ, *They Said It – William and Catherine Booth*, London: Salvationist Publishing and Supplies 1978 © The Salvation Army.

George Scott Railton, *The Authoritative Life of General William Booth, Founder of The Salvation Army*, George H. Doran Company, 1912.

Robert Sandall, *The History of The Salvation Army Vol. 1, 1865–1878*, London: Thomas Nelson and Sons Ltd © The Salvation Army 1947

Robert Sandall, *The History of The Salvation Army Vol. II, 1878–1886*, London: Thomas Nelson and Sons Ltd © The Salvation Army 1950.

Robert Sandall, *The History of The Salvation Army Vol. III, 1883–1953: Social Reform and Welfare Work*, London: Thomas Nelson and Sons Ltd © The Salvation Army 1955.

W.T. Stead, "The Maiden Tribute of Modern Babylon", *Pall Mall Gazette*, 6 July, 1885.

Charles Terrot, *Shout Aloud Salvation*, London: Collins, 1952.

Bernard Watson, *Soldier Saint – George Scott Railton, William Booth's First Lieutenant*, Hodder and Stoughton © The Salvation Army 1970.

Arch R. Wiggins, *The History of The Salvation Army Vol. V, 1904–1914*, London: Thomas Nelson and Sons Ltd © The Salvation Army 1968.

Harry Williams, *Booth-Tucker, William Booth's First Gentleman*, Hodder and Stoughton, 1980 © The Salvation Army.

Jim Winter, *Travel with… William Booth, Founder and First General of The Salvation Army*, Day One Publications 2003.

*Orders and Regulations for Soldiers of The Salvation Army by the Founder, revised by direction of the General 1950*, © The Salvation Army International Headquarters.

*The Sacraments – The Salvationist's Viewpoint*, © The Salvation Army 1960 (short pamphlet issued "by authority of The General").

*The Salvation Army, Its Origins and Development*, London: Salvationist Publishing and Supplies Ltd © The Salvation Army, first published 1928, revised edition 1973.

## Films/Video/Sound sources

*Our People – The Remarkable Story of William and Catherine Booth and The Salvation Army*, Radiant Films production in association with Carpenter Media. Produced by Corey Baudinette and Peter Farthing © The Salvation Army Australia Eastern Territory, 2008.

*William Booth, a Passion for the Poor*, produced by The Salvation Army Video Production Unit UK © The Salvation Army 2012.

www.sermonindex.net

## Other Salvation Army Sources

www.salvationarmy.org/ihq

www.salvationarmy.org.uk

www.salvationarmy.org.uk/uki/heritage

www.salvos.org.au

## Other internet sources

Leah Price, The History of Shorthand (London Review of Books) –
www.lrb.co.uk/v30/n23/leah-price/diary

http://en.wikipedia.org/wiki/Christmas#Reformation_into_the_19th_
century

http://booty.org.uk/booty.weather/climate/1850_1899.htm

The Victorianist: John Snow and the 1854 London Cholera Outbreak –
http:/thevictorianist.blogspot.co.uk/2010/11/john-snow-and-1854-
london-cholera.html

Lauren Corona, "19th Century Victorian Wedding Traditions" –
www.ehow.co.uk/info_7954601_19th-century-victorian-wedding-
traditions.html

Queen Victoria's wedding dress: the one that started it all –
http://thedreamstress.com/2011/04/queen-victorias-wedding-dress-
the-one-that-started

http://en.wikipedia.org/wiki/Hydrotherapy

http://en.wikipedia.org/wiki/Homeopathy

Asbury University – Wesleyan-Holiness Theology –
http://www.asbury.edu/about-us/cornerstone-project/holiness-
initiatives/wesleyan-holiness-theology

The University of North Carolina at Pembroke/London in the 19th
century – http://www.uncp.edu/home/rwb/london_19c.html

http://www.methodist-central-hall.org.uk/history/
METHODISTNEWCONNEXION.pdf

East End of London – http://en.wikipedia.org/wiki/East_End_of_
London

http://en.wikipedia.org/wiki/British_Army_during_the_Victorian_Era

http://en.wikipedia.org/wiki/George_Scott_Railton

http://en.wikipedia.org/wiki/Bramwell_Booth

http://en.wikipedia.org/wiki/Chartism

The Victorian Web – http://www.victorianweb.org/religion/sa1.html

http://en.wikipedia.org/wiki/Elijah_Cadman

http://www.sawiki.net/index.php/The_Bonnet

http://en.wikipedia.org/wiki/Josephine_Butler

http://en.wikipedia.org/wiki/Contagious_Diseases_Acts

http://en.wikipedia.org/wiki/William_Booth

http://en.wikipedia.org/wiki/Ballington_Booth